HOLIDAY SKITS

BY TOM BOAL

Gospel Light

D1413852

YOU MAY MAKE COPIES OF THE SKITS IN THIS BOOK IF:

■ you (or someone in your organization) are the original purchaser;

■ you are using the copies you make for a noncommercial purpose (such as teaching or promoting a ministry) within your church or organization;

■ you follow the instructions provided in this book.

HOWEVER, IT IS ILLEGAL FOR YOU TO MAKE COPIES IF:

■ you are using the material to promote, advertise or sell a product or service other than for ministry fund-raising;

■ you are using the material in or on a product for sale;

■ you or your organization are not the original purchaser of this book.

By following these guidelines you help us keep our products affordable.

Thank you,
Gospel Light

All Scripture quotations, unless otherwise indicated, are taken from the *Holy Bible, New International Version®. NIV®.* Copyright © 1973, 1978, 1984 by International Bible Society. Used by permission of Zondervan Publishing House. All rights reserved.

ABOUT THE AUTHOR

Tom Boal lives in Leduc, Alberta, with his wife, Marilyn, and their children, Christian and Kelly. Tom writes skits as a diversion from his profession of accounting.

EDITORIAL STAFF

Publisher, William T. Greig ❑ **Senior Consulting Publisher,** Dr. Elmer L. Towns ❑ **Publisher, Research, Planning and Development,** Billie Baptiste ❑ **Senior Editor,** Lynnette Pennings, M.A. ❑ **Senior Consulting Editors,** Dr. Gary S. Greig, Wesley Haystead, M.S.Ed. ❑ **Editor, Theological and Biblical Issues,** Bayard Taylor, M.Div. ❑ **Editor,** Mary Gross ❑ **Associate Editor,** Linda Mattia ❑ **Contributing Editors,** Norman Cruikshank, Sheryl Haystead, LouAnn Oklobzija ❑ **Illustrator,** Curtis Dawson ❑ **Designer,** Carolyn Thomas

Gospel Light

©1995 Gospel Light, Ventura, CA 93006. All rights reserved. Printed in U.S.A.

CONTENTS

ADVENT AND CHRISTMAS 9

LENT AND EASTER 69

HOLIDAY ASSORTMENT 159

CLIP ART 213

ABOUT THIS BOOK

Holiday Skits **is a collection of skits for all ages**—some funny, some serious—that explore holiday themes in a variety of ways. Some skits are taken directly from Scripture, some explore biblical characters and events with a contemporary twist, and some skits are simply fun with a serious message.

And these skits are designed for ease of use with a group of any size or skill level!

Holiday Skits **is all about versatility, too!** The skits vary in length from a few minutes to the better part of an hour. Some skits are pantomimed while narrators do most of the speaking, while others are dramatic readings. Basic stage settings are listed, along with ideas for making simple sets more elaborate. Most of the skits can use players of every age (from first grade through adult), with any skill level (from none to expert)! And many of the skits contain "extra" nonspeaking parts. These parts can be added to or subtracted from the skits to suit your needs.

Imagine a script that suits the ages and number of your players without rewriting, has a greater variety of skit types and lengths to choose from, and has flexibility that will allow you to produce a skit simply or with the most elaborate pageantry! All in all, *Holiday Skits* can lighten the load of the director who already has too much to do when holidays roll around!

THE VALUE OF DRAMA

Drama is a valuable tool for involving audiences in a presented message. But beyond the understanding an audience may gain through dramatic presentation, there are values for the players, too. As they involve themselves in acting out roles, valuable learning takes place beyond line memorization. The process of learning that each person experiences can make Bible stories come alive and Bible truth relevant—regardless of whether the skit is played out in a classroom or before thousands of people. The learning process has innate value for each player regardless of the quality of the final performance.

In addition, acting out a situation can help the players to think about the application of Bible truth to a real-life circumstance. Role-play provides the opportunity to briefly step into another person's shoes, gaining a better understanding of that character's attitudes and feelings. This is especially valuable for children, since it takes the Bible out of the realm of words and literally puts it into action!

Using This Book

COPIES OF THE SKITS

The purchase of this book includes the right to make copies of the skits for those who will be involved in putting on the skits. (When you make copies, be sure to include scripts for the stage manager and prop person. And don't forget to make a few extras. Scripts have a habit of disappearing at the oddest times!)

SKIT FEATURES

Each skit contains the following features to help you prepare:

■ players' list (with suggested ages for each role);

■ suggested props and sets;

■ director's tips;

■ a pronunciation guide for hard-to-pronounce names.

ABOUT AGE SUGGESTIONS

The skits in this book were designed with a wide variety of ages in mind. Although any of these skits could be produced effectively by a group of adults or teens, the simple lines and easier parts are included with the purpose of making younger players a part of the action. Many of the skits also have nonspeaking parts that may be played by players of any age. In addition, there is often a device for bringing the entire cast back on stage at the end of the skit, which is especially effective if you are using these skits with children (their parents will all wants to take photos!). Certainly, some younger players can handle more difficult roles than the suggestions listed. But remember that to keep this an enjoyable experience for the players as well as the audience, it is best to not overburden a younger player just because he or she has a great capacity to memorize.

There are also some parts that are best left to teens or adults. These include playing the part of Jesus, demons and some characters that may require more mature understanding. All of these parts are listed with a "Grade 5 or older" suggested age.

GETTING READY

After you've chosen and reproduced copies of the skit for the participants, here are some tips for preparing for your role as the producer (and perhaps director, too):

READ THE SKIT ALOUD

Make note of vocabulary or pronunciation help you will need to give your players at the first read-through. The skits are written so that parts designated for younger players have the shortest and easiest lines. If you have younger children who are excellent readers or older children who have difficulty reading, you may want to adjust the parts offered to them accordingly.

ADAPT THE SCRIPT TO YOUR GROUP

Depending on your situation, you may want to reduce or increase the number of characters, adapt the set and prop suggestions to your stage, drop or add a scene, etc. Many of these skits contain "extra" nonspeaking parts that can be played by players of any age. Use as few or as many parts as you need. If your group has few or no available players in one suggested age group, cast some teens or adults in your production. They don't have to take the lead roles; the variety of ages will add even more interest in the skit!

DECIDE WHAT PARTS TO OFFER TO WHOM

Will this skit be part of an in-class reader's theater or a multi-age performance for parents? Will it be part of an outreach event put on by the entire church? a skit to amuse and inspire church members? Use the director's tips to give you a better feel for special parts.

COLLECT PROPS AND SET MATERIALS

If you are staging the skit as a larger production, invite (or beg!) a trustworthy individual to be your stage manager. He or she can collect props (and costumes, if needed) or can assign this job to another trustworthy person. In addition, the stage manager arranges for the lighting crew, the moving of sets onstage and offstage by the stagehands, and the sound system. This leaves you free to direct, give cues and focus on the skit and the players.

PRACTICAL TIPS FOR PRODUCTION

One of the nicest things about skits is their flexibility. They can be informal and spontaneous, but they can also be primped and polished into full-scale productions—it all depends on how you want to do it. Here are the basics to go on:

DELIVERY

Good acting is a plus, but it's not essential in order to have a positive experience. What *is* essential is that the lines are understood by the player and heard by the audience. Create a climate during rehearsals that makes players comfortable in talking about their roles. Then, help players learn to speak slowly and clearly—with their mouths directed at the audience. It may help to have players take deep breaths and think *slow motion* before they deliver lines.

MEMORIZATION VERSUS READING

It is not necessary for players to memorize the script. Reading can work just as well. Provide highlighter pens for players to mark their parts. Give out copies of the script ahead of time for them to become familiar with their lines. (If you do hand out scripts ahead of time, bring extra copies on performance day. Someone will undoubtedly forget a copy.)

PRACTICE

Practice will be most important for younger players, players who have difficulty reading, and players for whom English is a second language. Practicing is often more effective in small groups, putting all the parts together in a dress rehearsal.

PROPS

Props are suggested, but in a pinch any real prop can be replaced by an imaginary one.

DIFFICULTY

If any part of a skit proves too difficult for you to stage, turn the script for that scene into a short narrative.

SENSE OF HUMOR

Above all, keep a sense of humor. Experienced producers will tell you that virtually any production will follow the Three-Glitch Rule: At least three things will go wrong. Those things will probably make the skit even more memorable. The more relaxed and lighthearted you remain, the better your players will be!

USING SKITS WITH POOR READERS

Your group may include players with poor reading skills, learning disabilities or those for whom English is a second language. Don't lose heart! With a little planning and some tender loving care, you can help these players gain badly needed confidence and self-esteem—*and* produce terrific skits!

The following list of ideas can be adapted for use in any setting. Choose the techniques that best suit your group and resources.

FOR INFORMAL PRESENTATIONS AND READ-THROUGHS:

■ Highlight each character's lines on separate copies of the script. Add pronunciation pointers as needed.

■ Have the entire group read through the skit in pairs or small groups before rehearsing in a large group.

■ Give everyone in the group a script to follow as selected readers read aloud. Receiving information through more than one sense makes the drama more accessible. This technique also assists students who are better visual than auditory learners. It can also ease performers' nerves a bit by providing something other than the readers on which to focus.

■ Use lots of visual aids and props.

■ Use a "jump-in" technique that gives readers control over how much they want to read: When a volunteer has read as much as he or she wants, another volunteer jumps in and continues reading. Or let each reader choose a helper to consult whenever necessary.

FOR MORE FORMAL PRESENTATIONS AND PERFORMANCES:

■ Assign a "drama coach" to each reader to provide one-on-one help in interpreting and learning lines. The coach may be another student or an adult.

■ The director may want to read aloud all character parts before they're assigned and discuss the tone of the skit, pronunciation and meaning of difficult words, and make suggestions for changes and word substitutions.

■ Players can practice by making cassette recordings of their parts, replaying them over and over. To provide extra help, the director may want to record each character part on a separate cassette to distribute to each player. Record each part twice, the first time speaking slowly and distinctly with no dramatic flair, the second time with dramatic flair so students hear how the lines should be delivered. This will be a great help to auditory learners.

■ Write out each sentence on separate index cards—this makes the job look smaller, and each line is an accomplishment.

■ Hand out the script well in advance of the performance date. Call and have the student read his or her part to you over the phone to practice.

■ Give permission to improvise! Students who understand the sense of a speech or whose verbal skills are better than their reading and memorization skills, may communicate better and more freely if they paraphrase.

ADVENT AND CHRISTMAS

(ADVENT ONE)
THE PROPHET SPEAKS

(APPROXIMATE TIME FOR EACH SKIT: 10 MINUTES WITH CAROL)

SYNOPSIS
Anna, Simeon and visitors to the Temple talk of the coming Messiah.

STAGE SETTING: THE TEMPLE AT JERUSALEM
- Chair for Anna, Center Stage
- Candles on stands, wall hangings to suggest the Temple
- Optional—sign on stand lettered "The Temple at Jerusalem"

THE PLAYERS
SHEPHERD ONE (Grade 1 or older)

SHEPHERD TWO (Grade 3 or older)

TEMPLE VISITOR ONE (Grade 5 or older)

TEMPLE VISITOR TWO (Grade 1 or older)

TEMPLE VISITOR THREE (Grade 3 or older)

ANNA (Grade 5 or older)

SIMEON (SIM-ee-un) (Grade 5 or older)

STAGEHANDS (All ages)

NONSPEAKING SHEPHERDS AND VISITORS (all ages)

SUGGESTED PROPS
- Canes for Anna and Simeon
- Shepherd's crooks for Shepherds
- Bible-times clothing

DIRECTOR'S TIPS
1. Cast some older players in nonspeaking parts to help lead younger players around the stage.

2. Stagehands can also have other parts.

3. Anna and Simeon are very old. Their movements should be slow and unsteady and their voices should waver a bit. However, do not sacrifice clarity of speech for technique.

4. Suggested Christmas carol: "Come, Thou Long-Expected Jesus." Another similar carol may be substituted.

(ADVENT ONE)

THE PROPHET SPEAKS

(VISITORS and SHEPHERDS are milling about the Temple. Occasionally, two people bump into each other. Sometimes they are polite ["Excuse me"; "Don't mention it."]. Other times, they are rude ["Why don't you watch where you're going?"; "Oh yeah? Same to you, Buddy!"]. Into this seeming chaos, ANNA enters, Stage Right, leaning heavily on cane. She walks to front of stage and looks around her, looks up, etc.)

ANNA *(puzzled, to audience)*: Something's happening. *(Looks around stage and spots empty chair.)* Oh, good. A place to rest. *(Slowly moves across the stage, through the milling crowd. Just as she reaches the chair, SHEPHERD TWO quickly sits down before she can. Voices die down as people notice the rude behavior of the shepherd.)* Excuse me, sir. But I'm very tired. May I please sit down?

SHEPHERD TWO: Sure. Anywhere on the floor. But the chair's mine.

ANNA: But if I were to sit on the floor, I might not be able to get up again.

SHEPHERD TWO: *(Slowly stretches, then slouches in chair.)* That's not my problem.

(SHEPHERD ONE comes over to chair and kicks foot of SHEPHERD TWO.)

SHEPHERD ONE: Come on. Get up. Let the old lady sit down.

SHEPHERD TWO *(annoyed)***:** Why? I've been working hard all week! I'm tired, too! I've got a right to this chair, same as anyone else!

(SHEPHERD ONE tries unsuccessfully to pull SHEPHERD TWO from chair. TEMPLE visitors begin to gather around.)

TEMPLE VISITOR TWO: *(To TEMPLE VISITOR THREE.)* Have you ever seen such a rude man?

TEMPLE VISITOR THREE: No. And I just got back from Rome!

TEMPLE VISITOR ONE: Somebody should do something.

SHEPHERD ONE: If some of you help me, we could move him. *(Reaches for SHEPHERD TWO.)*

ANNA: No, please. I'll stand. We should not have unkindness in the house of the Lord.

(SHEPHERD TWO senses he might be thrown out of the chair and reluctantly rises. He motions ANNA to chair.)

SHEPHERD TWO: You win. It's all yours.

ANNA: *(To SHEPHERD TWO.)* Thank you, sir. *(To OTHERS.)* Thank you, everyone.

TEMPLE VISITOR THREE: You're welcome.

TEMPLE VISITOR TWO: I think he got off easy.

TEMPLE VISITOR ONE: He shouldn't be here. Let's throw him out.

SHEPHERD ONE: Good idea!

ANNA *(interrupting)*: No! No! This is the house of the Lord. All should be welcome here. There should be no ill will among visitors in the Lord's Temple.

SHEPHERD TWO: *(To ANNA.)* I don't need old ladies to fight my battles. *(To other SHEPHERDS and VISITORS.)* Come on! I'll whip all of you!

ANNA: No! This must not be!

(SHEPHERD TWO steps toward crowd, fists raised, Stage Left. Crowd backs off and begins to mill about. SIMEON enters, Stage Right, sees ANNA and moves to her.)

SIMEON: Anna!

ANNA *(looking up)*: Simeon! What a pleasant surprise.

TEMPLE VISITOR THREE: Anna?

TEMPLE VISITOR ONE: The prophetess.

TEMPLE VISITOR TWO: Hey, everybody! This is Anna! The prophetess.

(VISITORS and SHEPHERDS murmur "Anna" and "The prophetess.")

SHEPHERD ONE: *(Tugs at sleeve of SHEPHERD TWO.)* It's Anna.

SHEPHERD TWO: *(Still angry, pulls away.)* I don't care WHO she is. Leave me alone!

(VISITORS and SHEPHERDS except for SHEPHERD TWO gather and sit around ANNA and SIMEON.)

TEMPLE VISITOR ONE: Have you a word from the Lord, Anna?

ANNA *(hesitantly)*: Well...

TEMPLE VISITOR THREE: Is there a special prophecy for us?

ANNA: Well...

TEMPLE VISITOR TWO: What does the Lord say, Anna?

SHEPHERD ONE: Let her speak. Give her a chance.

SHEPHERD TWO: *(Sarcastically, to audience.)* Sure, she stole my chair. She might as well have the FLOOR.

SIMEON: Tell us, Anna. What has the Lord shown you?

ANNA: Well...I don't know. Something's happening, but I don't know what.

TEMPLE VISITOR TWO: Is it something good?

ANNA: I don't know. In my vision, I see peace and joy. But I also see innocent blood shed. It's so confusing!

SIMEON: I, too, have had a vision.

ANNA: Tell me. Perhaps it will make my vision clear.

SIMEON: I was told in the vision that I would see the Messiah before I died.

ANNA *(thoughtfully)*: Messiah?

SIMEON: Perhaps our visions go together.

ANNA: Messiah. It could be.

TEMPLE VISITOR ONE: *(Shouts to the crowd.)* Did you hear that, everyone! Anna says the Messiah is coming.

TEMPLE VISITOR TWO: *(Shouts.)* Messiah is coming!

TEMPLE VISITOR THREE: *(Shouts.)* He'll overthrow the Romans! We'll be free again!

(Crowd begins to chant, "Messiah! Messiah! Messiah!" SHEPHERD ONE runs over to SHEPHERD TWO.)

SHEPHERD ONE: Anna says the Messiah is coming.

SHEPHERD TWO: Yeah, yeah. I heard. For years now, lots of people have been saying Messiah is coming. But I still see Roman soldiers all over Jerusalem.

SHEPHERD ONE: But Anna says...

SHEPHERD TWO: So an old lady says it. Big deal! I'll believe it when I see it.

(SHEPHERDS and VISITORS except for SHEPHERD ONE and TWO exit, Stage Right, chanting, "Messiah! Messiah! Messiah!")

SHEPHERD TWO: Fools! They'll listen to anyone about anything.

SHEPHERD ONE: But Anna says...

SHEPHERD TWO: You're just as bad as the rest. If a choir of angels tells me, then I'll believe. But not until then! *(Exits, Stage Right.)*

(SHEPHERD ONE follows SHEPHERD TWO saying, "But Anna says....")

SIMEON: Can it be, Anna? Could Messiah be coming? *(Helps ANNA rise from chair.)*

ANNA: It could be. But why do I see innocent blood? I don't understand.

SIMEON: Well, the Lord has spoken to me. He said I will see Messiah. I will come to the Temple every day. When the time is right, I shall see Him. Messiah! *(Crosses to Stage Right with ANNA. Just before they exit, ANNA turns to audience.)*

ANNA: *(Shakes head, bewildered.)* Something's happening! *(Exits with SIMEON, Stage Right.)*

(Audience sings carol.)

(ADVENT TWO)
WILL THE PRIEST LISTEN?

(APPROXIMATE TIME: 10 MINUTES WITH CAROL)

SYNOPSIS

Caiaphas and his scribes try to get information about what's happening.

STAGE SETTING: CAIAPHAS'S OFFICE

■ Table and chair for Caiaphas, Center Stage

■ Table and chair for Scribe One, Stage Left

■ Table and chair for Scribe Two, Stage Right

■ Filing cabinets, storage boxes, etc. to make stage look like an office

THE PLAYERS

SCRIBE ONE (Grade 3 or older)

CAIAPHAS (KAY-eh-fehs) (Grade 5 or older)

OFFSTAGE VOICES (All ages)

SCRIBE TWO (Grade 1 or older)

STAGEHANDS (All ages)

NONSPEAKING SCRIBES (All ages)

SUGGESTED PROPS

■ Bible-times clothing

■ Tables and chairs for Caiaphas and Scribes

■ Office furnishings, books and papers for Caiaphas's office

■ Optional: Sign on stand lettered "Caiaphas's Office"

DIRECTOR'S TIPS

1. Cast some older players in nonspeaking parts to help lead younger players around the stage.

2. Stagehands can also have other parts.

3. Caiaphas is in charge. He is sure of himself and gives sharp orders.

4. The Scribes are harried, rushed and trying to accomplish too much for Caiaphas.

5. Suggested Christmas carol: "Oh, Come, Oh, Come Emmanuel." Another song of similar theme may be substituted.

(ADVENT TWO)

WILL THE PRIEST LISTEN?

(CAIAPHAS is seated at table, writing. SCRIBES scurry about, gathering papers, consulting books. They occasionally take a paper to SCRIBE ONE or SCRIBE TWO. OFFSTAGE VOICES shout, "Messiah! Messiah! Messiah!")

CAIAPHAS: *(Scowls at paper.)* Something's happening.

SCRIBE TWO *(looking up from paper)*: Sir?

SCRIBE ONE *(looking up from his paper)*: Did you say something?

CAIAPHAS *(shouting)*: Somebody shut that window!

(All SCRIBES freeze, afraid to move. SCRIBE TWO rises and crosses to edge of stage, mimes shutting window. OFFSTAGE VOICES quiet down. SCRIBE TWO returns to desk and sits.)

CAIAPHAS: That's better. Now I can hear myself think.

SCRIBE ONE: *(To audience.)* Better you hear yourself thinking than we have to hear you speaking.

CAIAPHAS: *(Suspiciously, to SCRIBE ONE.)* Did you say something?

SCRIBE ONE: *(To CAIAPHAS, nervously.)* I said, "It's murder thinking with all that shrieking."

CAIAPHAS: Where's that latest report on the number of Roman soldiers in Judea?

SCRIBE TWO: I have it right here, Sir. *(Searches on desk.)* It's right here...somewhere!

CAIAPHAS: *(To other SCRIBES.)* Well, don't just stand there. Help him look!

(SCRIBES hurry to desk and search through papers. One finds and hands it to SCRIBE TWO.)

SCRIBE TWO *(holding up paper)*: Here it is, Sir.

CAIAPHAS *(sarcastically)*: Well I can't read it from there, can I?

SCRIBE ONE: *(To audience.)* I thought his eagle eye saw all.

CAIAPHAS: *(To SCRIBE ONE.)* WHAT did you say?

SCRIBE ONE: *(To CAIAPHAS, nervously.)* I said, "It looks like an early fall." *(Holds up book.)* I was consulting the almanac.

CAIAPHAS: Oh. *(Looks at SCRIBES.)* Well, why are you standing around? Get back to WORK!

(SCRIBES continue searching through books and papers, sometimes taking papers to SCRIBE ONE or SCRIBE TWO. CAIAPHAS, SCRIBE ONE and SCRIBE TWO continue reading papers at their tables.)

CAIAPHAS: It's too hot in here. Open the window!

(SCRIBE TWO goes to edge of Stage Left and mimes opening window. OFFSTAGE VOICES shout, "Messiah! Messiah! Messiah!")

CAIAPHAS *(shouting)*: Shut that window!

SCRIBE TWO: Yes, Sir. *(Mimes shutting window. OFFSTAGE VOICES are quiet. Returns to table.)*

CAIAPHAS: What's the matter with those people, anyway? Why are they shouting?

SCRIBE TWO: They say Messiah is coming.

CAIAPHAS: I KNOW what they're saying. They've been shouting all week. "Messiah! Messiah! Messiah!" All that shouting will be the death of me.

SCRIBE ONE: *(To audience, sarcastically.)* Too much to hope for!

CAIAPHAS: What was that?

SCRIBE ONE: *(To CAIAPHAS, nervously.)* I said, "Terrible uproar," Sir.

CAIAPHAS: *(To SCRIBE ONE.)* What are you reading?

SCRIBE ONE: *(Holds up a book.)* The Scriptures, Sir.

CAIAPHAS: Why are you wasting your time reading Scripture? Don't you realize that something IMPORTANT is happening?

SCRIBE TWO: I don't waste MY time that way.

SCRIBE ONE: I thought they might give me some insight into the coming of Messiah.

CAIAPHAS: I don't care about the coming of Messiah! I care about the coming of Roman troops. Look at this chart. *(Lays out chart on table and shows to SCRIBE ONE and SCRIBE TWO. All study chart.)*

CAIAPHAS *(pointing)*: Look at all this movement. Something's happening.

SCRIBE TWO: Why are you worried about Roman soldiers?

CAIAPHAS: Because if they're moving around, it means some kind of change. Change is dangerous. If I do the wrong thing, I could lose my position of power.

SCRIBE ONE: But the Romans wouldn't stop you from being a priest.

CAIAPHAS: But I could lose my political power. I may never get to be High Priest.

SCRIBE TWO: Oh. I see.

CAIAPHAS: So, this means burning the midnight candle. *(Points to SCRIBE TWO.)* You!

SCRIBE TWO: Yes, Sir.

CAIAPHAS: I want you to take home all the Roman troop reports for the last year. Graph everything to see if this is something special or if it might be part of a normal pattern. I want that graph on my desk first thing in the morning.

SCRIBE TWO: But that will take me all night!

CAIAPHAS: Do I look worried? *(Speaks to SCRIBE TWO as he motions to other SCRIBES.)* Take some of these flunkies with you. They can help you.

SCRIBE TWO: Yes, Sir. *(Begins to gather up papers from his table.)*

CAIAPHAS: *(To SCRIBE ONE.)* And you!

SCRIBE ONE: *(Snaps to attention.)* Yes, Sir.

CAIAPHAS: Leave the reading of Scripture to the rabbis. Do something worthwhile with your time!

SCRIBE ONE: Yes, Sir. Such as?

CAIAPHAS: Check out all the past history we have of Augustus and Herod. I want a detailed report showing how they use troops and what kinds of decisions they make. I need to know what's going on!

SCRIBE ONE: *(To audience.)* There goes my night.

CAIAPHAS: What did you say?

SCRIBE ONE: I said, "Here I go! Right!" Yes, Sir! I'll get this done for you. *(Gathers an armload of papers from his table.)*

CAIAPHAS: Have you got everything you need?

SCRIBE TWO: *(Arms full of papers.)* Everything I need.

SCRIBE ONE: *(Arms full of papers.)* More than I want.

CAIAPHAS: Then go! And have those reports for me first thing tomorrow.

SCRIBE ONE: Good night, Sir.

SCRIBE TWO: Good night, Sir. *(SCRIBES ONE and TWO exit, Stage Right.)* *(CAIAPHAS sits in his chair, thinking, then rises and moves to exit, Stage Right. Just before exiting, he turns to look at audience.)*

CAIAPHAS *(thoughtfully, shaking finger)*: Something's happening. *(Exits, Stage Right.)*

(Audience sings carol.)

(ADVENT THREE)

DEVIL'S DILEMMA

(APPROXIMATE TIME: 10 MINUTES WITH CAROL)

SYNOPSIS

Satan and his demons do a bad job of trying to predict Messiah's arrival.

STAGE SETTING: SATAN'S OFFICE

■ Table and chair for Satan, Center Stage
■ Flames cut from red, orange and yellow paper, attached to walls
■ Office equipment to suggest an office
■ Optional: sign on stand lettered "Satan's Office"

THE PLAYERS

DEMON GOFER (Grade 3 or older)

MALEFICENT—A DEMON (me-LIH-fe-sent) (Grade 5 or older)

SATAN (Grade 5 or older)

NONSEQUITUR—A DEMON (non-SEK-wih-tur) (Grade 5 or older)

STAGEHANDS (All ages)

NONSPEAKING DEMONS (All ages)

SUGGESTED PROPS

■ Business suits for Demons
■ Books, maps, charts, etc. for Demons
■ Towel

DIRECTOR'S TIPS

1. Satan is controlled but on the brink of hysteria. However, he is not a buffoon and should not be played as one.
2. The Demons scurry about nervously. Occasionally, there may be collisions. Warn the players not to hurt each other. What may look like a collision to the audience should be a practiced move by the players.
3. Suggested ages may vary, based on your players' abilities. Because of the nature of this skit, however, older players are recommended.
4. Stagehands can also have other parts.
5. Suggested Christmas carol: "O Little Town of Bethlehem." Another carol of similar theme may be sung.

(ADVENT THREE)
DEVIL'S DILEMMA

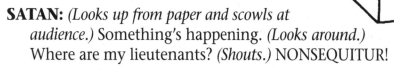

(SATAN is seated at table, reading reports. DEMONS, all dressed in business suits, are scurrying about. When they bump into each other, they snarl, "Watch where you're going!" "Oh, yeah? You watch where you're going." "Get out of my way!" etc. Whenever SATAN speaks, DEMONS stop what they are doing and move as quietly as they can. Each has incurred SATAN's wrath before.)

SATAN: *(Looks up from paper and scowls at audience.)* Something's happening. *(Looks around.)* Where are my lieutenants? *(Shouts.)* NONSEQUITUR!

(NONSEQUITUR enters, Stage Right, wiping his hands on a towel.)

NONSEQUITUR: You called, Most Evil Satan.

SATAN: Where have you been?

NONSEQUITUR: Just washing up. After all, cleanliness is next to... *(Stops and covers his mouth.)*

SATAN: Cleanliness is next to WHAT?

NONSEQUITUR *(nervously)***:** Next to impossible around here. Soot is everywhere.

SATAN *(sarcastically)***:** Well, if you're quite CLEAN enough, I've got something to discuss with you.

NONSEQUITUR: I'm listening.

SATAN: Something's happening in Judea. Have you got everything under control there?

NONSEQUITUR: *(Smiles confidently.)* Absolutely. I've got politicians making promises. I've got priests worrying about politics instead of Scripture. I've got people seeing saviors when there aren't any.

SATAN: So all this "Messiah! Messiah! Messiah!" I keep hearing is your work.

NONSEQUITUR: *(Looks down.)* Well, not exactly.

SATAN *(viciously)***:** Then whose work IS it?

NONSEQUITUR *(very nervously)***:** Well, it's really difficult to tell. I got them going about a hundred years ago and the thing has just snowballed.

SATAN *(sneering)***:** Well, we all know snowballs don't have much of a chance around HERE. *(Laughs, then turns vicious again. Stands.)* I don't like things happening when I'm not CONTROLLING them. Go to Judea and make sure this is just another false alarm. If you've messed up, you can be REPLACED.

NONSEQUITUR (*backing away*): Don't worry. I'll see to it, right away.

SATAN: I'm not the one who has to worry, am I? YOU are. (*Points at exit and shouts.*) GO!

NONSEQUITUR: I'm gone. (*Hurriedly exits, Stage Right.*)

(*SATAN goes back to reading papers. Looks up and scowls. Calls to DEMON GOFER, who is working in the crowd of DEMONS.*)

SATAN: (*Points.*) You! Come here!

(*DEMON GOFER Approaches SATAN timidly.*)

DEMON GOFER: Yes, Sir. You bellowed?

SATAN: I need to look something up. HE'S... (*Looks up and points straight up.*) ...up to something. I can feel it. Bring me the Scriptures.

DEMON GOFER (*whining*)**:** Please, Sir. Not that.

SATAN (*shouting*)**:** What? Are you refusing?

DEMON GOFER (*whining*)**:** But that book HURTS me. It always feels like a sword cutting me.

SATAN: I'm not ASKING you to bring it. I'm TELLING you. Now DO IT!

DEMON GOFER: (*Defeated.*) Yes, Sir. (*Goes to back of stage, picks up book. Brings to SATAN, passing it from one hand to the other saying, "Ow! Ow! Ow! Ow!" Places book on SATAN's table.*)

SATAN: Weakling! Now get back to work!

DEMON GOFER: Yes, Sir. (*Goes back to shuffling papers.*)

(*SATAN begins to read and make notes, thumbing through Scriptures. Every time he touches a page, he says, "Ow!"*)

SATAN: Just as I feared. (*Shouts offstage.*) Maleficent!

(*MALEFICENT enters, Stage Right. He appears to be evil tempered. He approaches SATAN, pushing other DEMONS saying, "Get out of my way."*)

MALEFICENT: (*Bows deeply.*) You called, Most Evil Satan?

SATAN: (*Admiringly.*) You're such a snake. Tell me, what do you make of what's happening in the world?

MALEFICENT: (*Smiles confidently.*) Couldn't be better. We have the cruelest possible government running things!

SATAN: Do we? Or does it just SEEM to be under our control?

MALEFICENT: What do you mean?

SATAN: What's happening in Rome right now?

MALEFICENT: A piece of genius on my part. I convinced Caesar that he needed more money. (*Chuckles.*) So he's ordering everyone to be taxed even more!

SATAN: And you find that amusing?

MALEFICENT: I think it's great. It will make everyone in the civilized world miserable.

SATAN: And how is Caesar planning to make sure the whole world is taxed?

MALEFICENT *(excitedly)*: This is the best part! Everyone has to go back to their ancestors' hometowns to be counted. People everywhere are having to leave their homes and travel to uncomfortable places. It's great! Everyone is so MISERABLE!

SATAN: *(SATAN points to page in the Scriptures.)* Read this.

MALEFICENT: *(Reads.)* "But you, Bethlehem...though you are small among the clans of Judah, out of you will come for me one who will be ruler over Israel, whose origins are from of old, from ancient times."[1] *(To SATAN.)* So?

SATAN: This is prophecy. The Messiah is to come from BETHLEHEM.

MALEFICENT: Nothing to worry about! They've been yelling "Messiah" for years.

SATAN: *(Rises in anger.)* You don't get it, do you? Bethlehem WAS small; we could keep track of what was going on. Suddenly, every relative of King David goes there. It's full of people! *(Shouts.)* How will we know which one is the Messiah?

MALEFICENT: Hmm. That is a tough one.

SATAN: You've played right into HIS... *(Looks and points upward.)* ...hands! Go and stop the census AT ONCE!

MALEFICENT: That might be easier said than done. I did a terrific selling job. Took me the better part of a year. And Greed has been working with me. Caesar really wants that extra tax money.

SATAN: I don't care HOW you stop it. *(Shouts.)* But STOP it! GO!

MALEFICENT *(backing away)*: I'll try. But I can't guarantee results. *(He exits, Stage Right.)*

SATAN *(shouting after him)*: I can guarantee punishment for FAILURE! *(SATAN sits, begins to read Scriptures again. Looks up and scowls at audience.)*

SATAN: *(Points to DEMON GOFER.)* You! Come here!

DEMON GOFER: *(Approaches SATAN timidly.)* Yes, Sir. You bellowed?

SATAN: I need to know what's happening in heaven. Take some troops and see what Michael and his warrior angels are doing.

DEMON GOFER *(whining)*: But it's HARD to look into heaven, Sir.

SATAN: Then don't look into heaven. See where the angels are moving on earth. Got that?

DEMON GOFER: Yes, Sir. *(Exits, Stage Right, taking along several other DEMONS.)*

(NONSEQUITUR enters, Stage Right, shoving a few other DEMONS as he passes them.)

NONSEQUITUR: I've checked out the cause of the latest Messiah scare.

SATAN: And?

NONSEQUITUR: *(Laughs.)* It's beautiful. A bunch of visitors to the Temple misunderstood Anna. They're running around looking for the Messiah.

SATAN: *(Claps his hand to his forehead.)* Of course. Anna! Why didn't I THINK of that?

NONSEQUITUR: Think of what?

SATAN: Check out the prophets. *(Points offstage.)* Find Anna. Check out her dreams. NOW!

NONSEQUITUR: I'm on my way. *(Exits, running, Stage Right.)*

SATAN: *(To himself.)* Maybe I'm imagining things. Maybe Messiah isn't coming, yet.

(MALEFICENT, NONSEQUITUR and other DEMONS enter, Stage Right.)

MALEFICENT: Ah, your Evilness. *(Bows low.)* It's just as I feared. There's no stopping Caesar. But it's not MY fault. Greed did his work too well. Caesar really wants that extra tax money.

DEMON GOFER: Happy to report, no angel movement on earth at this time.

NONSEQUITUR: There's something strange about Anna's visions. I can't get into them. HE... *(Looks and points upward.)* ...is guarding her thoughts.

SATAN *(shouting)***:** Get out, all of you! I need to think.

(All DEMONS run to exit, Stage Right.)

SATAN: *(Thinks deeply, then holds up hands. Motions with right hand.)* Hmm. Lots of people are going to Bethlehem. *(Motions with left hand.)* But THIS Messiah craze is just like the past ones. *(Motions with right hand.)* Anna's dreams are being guarded. *(Motions with left hand.)* But Michael and his warriors aren't positioning themselves on earth. *(Rises, thinking. Motions with right hand.)* Messiah is coming? *(Begins to walk toward exit, Stage Right. Rubs chin thoughtfully.)* Maybe not.

(Stops before exiting to turn and scowl at audience. Leans forward, shaking fist.) But I tell you. Something's happening! *(Exits, Stage Right.)*

(Audience sings carol.)

[1]Micah 5:2

(ADVENT FOUR)

HEAVENLY PEACE

(APPROXIMATE TIME: 10 MINUTES WITH CAROL)

SYNOPSIS

Michael, Gabriel and the angels prepare to announce Messiah's arrival.

STAGE SETTING: HEAVEN

■ Tables and chairs for Michael and Gabriel, Center Stage

■ Blue paper, white clouds, etc. to suggest heaven

■ Optional: sign on stand lettered "Heaven"

THE PLAYERS

ANGEL ONE (Grade 1 or older)

ANGEL TWO (Grade 3 or older))

ANGEL THREE (Grade 3 or older)

MICHAEL (Grade 5 or older)

GABRIEL (Grade 5 or older)

STAGEHANDS (All ages)

NONSPEAKING ANGEL CHOIR (All ages)

SUGGESTED PROPS

■ Music for Gabriel

■ Maps for Michael

■ Papers for Angels to bring to Michael and Gabriel

DIRECTOR'S TIPS

1. Heaven is calm, peaceful and cheerful. Movements are serene.

2. Michael and Gabriel are gentle but authoritative.

3. Depending on your players, a younger student may be able to handle a more difficult part than listed here.

4. Cast some older players in nonspeaking parts to help lead younger players around the stage.

5. Stagehands can also have other parts.

6. Suggested Christmas carol: "Angels We Have Heard on High." Another carol of similar theme may be sung.

(Advent Four)
Heavenly Peace

(*MICHAEL and GABRIEL are seated at tables. MICHAEL studies maps and GABRIEL studies sheet music. ANGELS enter at intervals from both sides of stage, carrying papers to tables, picking up other papers and exiting. Everything is done serenely. No one bumps into anyone else. MICHAEL looks at ceiling, then begins to chuckle. The chuckle becomes a full laugh.*)

MICHAEL (*laughing*)**:** Something's happening.

GABRIEL: What's the joke, Michael? Have you got another of those human's maps? The ones with all the rivers and oceans in all the wrong places?

MICHAEL: No, Gabriel. I was just thinking. Satan must be going crazy right now.

GABRIEL: Why?

MICHAEL: Well, we all know something's going on. Something AMAZING.

GABRIEL: Sure. We can feel it. It's in the air.

MICHAEL: Well, if we've noticed, Satan has noticed it, too.

GABRIEL: (*Begins to chuckle.*) I see what you mean!

MICHAEL: Imagine how he must feel right now. He knows something's happening, but he doesn't know what it is. (*Starts to chuckle again with GABRIEL. Soon, both are laughing loudly.*)

(*ANGEL TWO enters, Stage Right, and approaches tables.*)

ANGEL TWO (*clears throat*)**:** Ahem. Excuse me.

(*MICHAEL and GABRIEL wipe eyes, get laughter under control.*)

ANGEL TWO: Is this a private joke or can you share it?

GABRIEL: We were just thinking about poor old Satan.

MICHAEL: Something big is happening. And he doesn't know what it is.

GABRIEL: And he's got to be driving himself and his demons CRAZY trying to figure it out!

MICHAEL: And we sit here in peace, knowing that when the time is right, God will explain His plan to us.

ANGEL TWO: Well, here's the first part of the explanation. Right from the throne. (*Hands paper to GABRIEL and exits, Stage Right.*)

GABRIEL: Well, here we go! (*Reads from paper.*) "Organize choir practice."

MICHAEL: Go ahead; don't mind me. I'll do some battle planning while you rehearse.

GABRIEL (calling offstage): Choir! Come together! It's time for rehearsal.

(ANGEL CHOIR enters smiling, Stage Right, and assembles quietly onstage. GABRIEL leads them in the chorus of "Angels We Have Heard on High." Satisfied, he dismisses the ANGEL CHOIR. ANGEL CHOIR exits, Stage Right.)

GABRIEL: Well, it sounds like we're ready. (Smiles.) Always lovely. But being angels, they all have perfect pitch!

MICHAEL: Your choir is always great. I'm thankful we don't have to put up with human choir members. They NEVER sing on key! (Looks down at maps.) Well, I'd better prepare my angels. (Calls offstage.) Lieutenant!

(ANGEL ONE enters, Stage Left, and salutes.)

ANGEL ONE: You called, Sir?

MICHAEL: Yes. Assemble the soldiers. We have some planning to do.

ANGEL ONE: Yes, Sir. (Salutes and exits, Stage Left.)

GABRIEL: Aren't you jumping the gun just a bit?

MICHAEL: What do you mean?

GABRIEL: We don't know what's happening yet. How can you prepare for it?

MICHAEL: Well, we have SOME idea. You spoke to Mary and told her that she will have a baby. We know the baby will be the Messiah. That was about nine months ago, wasn't it?

GABRIEL: Of course. But Satan doesn't know that. (Looks at MICHAEL. Both begin to chuckle, then roar with laughter. Slowly, they get control of themselves again.)

MICHAEL: Well, the Messiah will come from Bethlehem. Maleficent and Greed have made sure that Mary and Joseph will travel to Bethlehem.

GABRIEL: (Laughs again.) All the time thinking they were doing evil, those two demons have helped to further God's plans! God's sense of humor is super!

MICHAEL: Well, when Satan knows the Messiah is in Bethlehem, he'll storm the town. My soldiers have got to be ready. At least I can study the maps and such.

(SOLDIER ANGELS enter, Stage Left, marching in an orderly fashion to gather around MICHAEL.)

ANGEL ONE: (Salutes.) All present and accounted for, Sir.

MICHAEL: OK, soldiers. (Shows ANGELS the map.)

MICHAEL: (Points.) Here's Bethlehem. Look at the hills around. We expect a lot of trouble soon in this area. So we'll position ourselves here... (Points on map as he speaks.) ...here and here. Any questions?

(ANGELS all murmur, "No, Sir.")

MICHAEL: Good. Dismissed. But remember, we're on battle alert.

(ANGELS exit, Stage Left, in orderly fashion.)

(ANGEL THREE enters, Stage Left.)

ANGEL THREE: (To MICHAEL.) Message for you, Sir. (Hands paper to MICHAEL.)

MICHAEL: (*To GABRIEL.*) Well, this is it. Our marching orders are ready. (*Reads paper. Looks puzzled. Reads it again.*) I don't understand this.

GABRIEL: What's wrong? Aren't you going to defend Bethlehem? Maybe the Lord's planning to use your angels as a diversion.

MICHAEL: I would understand THAT. But listen to THIS. "Assemble soldiers with choir. Practice singing together. Gabriel will lead the combined choir."

GABRIEL: (*Snickers.*) God wants your soldiers to be singers?

MICHAEL: Apparently. (*To ANGEL THREE.*) Did the Lord say why we were to sing?

ANGEL THREE: Yes, Sir. It seems that there's a shepherd who won't believe unless he hears an angel choir.

GABRIEL: Well, we have an angel choir. We'll sing for him.

ANGEL THREE: Yes, Sir. But the Lord says He will give the shepherd the biggest angel choir the universe has ever known.

MICHAEL: All that, just so one person will believe! But that's just like the Lord. He cares for every single one of His creatures. And what a sense of humor! I love it!

GABRIEL: (*Shakes head, chuckling.*) Well, we have our orders. (*To ANGEL THREE.*) Call all the choir and the soldiers.

ANGEL THREE: Yes, Sir. (*Exits, Stage Left.*)

MICHAEL: I guess I'm a singer now, too. Where do you want me?

(*All ANGELS enter, Stage Left and Stage Right, and arrange themselves in an orderly fashion.*)

GABRIEL: I think we'll put you on the end, right there.

(*MICHAEL takes his place and GABRIEL leads the ANGEL CHOIR in the chorus of "Angels We Have Heard on High." Satisfied, he dismisses all the angels. ANGELS exit, Stage Left and Stage Right. MICHAEL and GABRIEL remain onstage.*)

GABRIEL: I think I'll work out a few more arrangements. I'll see you tomorrow.

MICHAEL: If I'm going to sing, I'd better practice a little more tonight. It's been a long time since I was a choir angel! I'll see you later.

(*GABRIEL begins to leave, Stage Right. MICHAEL leaves, Stage Left. Both stop just before exiting, turn to look at audience.*)

GABRIEL and MICHAEL: (*To audience.*) Something's happening. Something BIG is happening! (*Both exit.*)

(*Audience sings carol.*)

(CHRISTMAS)
SOMETHING HAPPENED!

(APPROXIMATE TIME: 25 MINUTES WITH CAROLS)

SYNOPSIS
The story of Jesus' birth is told from the viewpoints of many witnesses, believers and unbelievers.

STAGE SETTING
■ Manger with doll, two chairs, Center Stage
■ Optional—Podiums for dramatic readings placed at Stage Left and Stage Right

THE PLAYERS

ANNA (Grade 3 or older)

SIMEON (SIM-ee-un) (Grade 3 or older)

MARY (Grade 1 or older)

JOSEPH (Grade 3 or older)

GABRIEL (Grade 5 or older)

TEMPLE VISITOR ONE (Grade 5 or older)

TEMPLE VISITOR TWO (Grade 1 or older)

TEMPLE VISITOR THREE (Grade 3 or older)

CAIAPHAS (KAY-eh-fehs) (Grade 5 or older)

SCRIBE ONE (Grade 3 or older)

SCRIBE TWO (Grade 1 or older)

ANGELS (Grade 3 or older)

SATAN (Grade 5 or older)

SHEPHERD ONE (Grade 1 or older)

SHEPHERD TWO (Grade 3 or older)

DEMON ONE (Grade 3 or older)

MICHAEL (Grade 5 or older)

NONSPEAKING SHEPHERDS, VISITORS and DEMONS (All ages)

NONSEQUITUR—A DEMON (non-SE-kwa-tur) (Grade 5 or older)

MALEFICENT—A DEMON (me-LIH-fe-sent) (Grade 3 or older)

SUGGESTED PROPS
■ Bible-times clothing   ■ Business suits for Demons   ■ Angel costumes

DIRECTOR'S TIPS

1. This skit is in the form of a dramatic reading. In a dramatic reading, the action is limited and the script is often read rather than memorized and performed. The action is mainly symbolic.

2. This piece works best as the final skit of the Advent series. However, it may be performed alone as well.

3. If podiums are used for dramatic readings, provide sturdy stools for smaller children to stand on.

4. Mary and Joseph should have chairs to sit on at the manger scene. They should be looking down at the manger during the entire play. Choose players who can sit quietly for these roles.

5. After each reading, those who understand that the baby is Messiah move to the manger area to stand or kneel.

6. The Angels block the path of Demons, Caiaphas and other unbelievers, so evil cannot come near the child. This should not become chaotic. Angels should outnumber Demons two-to-one.

7. Suggested Christmas carols: Scene One, "What Child Is This?"; Scene Two, "O Little Town of Bethlehem"; Scene Three, "Silent Night"; Scene Four, "Go Tell It on the Mountain"; Scene Five, "Joy to the World." Other carols with similar themes may be substituted.

(CHRISTMAS)
SOMETHING HAPPENED!

(Lights are bright on manger scene. MARY and JOSEPH are seated, looking down at the child in the manger. ANGELS enter from both sides of stage to stand in a protective semicircle behind MARY and JOSEPH.)

SCENE ONE: PROPHECY SPEAKS

(ANNA, SIMEON, GABRIEL and TEMPLE VISITORS enter, Stage Left, and move to Stage Left podium. All speeches are directed to the audience.)

ANNA: Something happened!

TEMPLE VISITOR ONE: We waited for the Savior, the one promised in the Scriptures. We thought He would overthrow Rome. Israel would again be a great and mighty nation, ruled by the Son of David!

SIMEON: I knew that I would live to see Messiah. Through the Holy Spirit, God promised me I would live to see the holy One.

TEMPLE VISITOR THREE: We were so excited! Anna had told us the Savior was coming. Messiah would soon be with us!

ANNA: *How would He come?* I wondered. Would He ride into Jerusalem on a mighty white horse? Would He wear bright armor and fight the Roman guards? Would all Israel rise to fight with Him?

TEMPLE VISITOR TWO: I would! Free Israel!

SIMEON: Then one day, the Holy Spirit called me to the Temple. Would this be the day? I saw nothing unusual. Many visitors, there to see the beauty of the Temple, milled about. Then, I saw them—a man and woman bringing a baby toward me.

TEMPLE VISITOR ONE: A baby?

TEMPLE VISITOR TWO: A BABY?

TEMPLE VISITOR THREE: *A BABY?*

ANNA: Of course! A baby! This is what the prophets said would be the sign: For to us a child is born, to us a son is given, and the government will be on his shoulders. And he will be called Wonderful Counselor, Mighty God, Everlasting Father, Prince of Peace.[1]

TEMPLE VISITOR ONE: A baby?

TEMPLE VISITOR TWO: A BABY?

TEMPLE VISITOR THREE: *A BABY?*

SIMEON: (*Looking up to heaven.*) Lord, now let Your servant depart in peace, according to Your Word.

TEMPLE VISITOR ONE: A baby?

TEMPLE VISITOR TWO: A BABY?

TEMPLE VISITOR THREE: A *BABY*?

ANNA: Certainly! The prophets told us, "The Lord himself will give you a sign: The virgin will be with child and will give birth to a son, and will call him Immanuel."[2] "Immanuel" means "God with us."

TEMPLE VISITOR ONE: A baby?

TEMPLE VISITOR TWO: A BABY?

TEMPLE VISITOR THREE: A *BABY*?

SIMEON: (*Looking up.*) Ah, Lord! Thank You! My eyes have seen Your salvation—a light for revelation to the Gentiles, and the glory of Your people Israel![3]

TEMPLE VISITOR ONE: The Messiah CAN'T be a baby! He must be a WARRIOR!

TEMPLE VISITOR TWO (*thoughtfully*)**:** The Messiah COULD be a baby.

TEMPLE VISITOR THREE: The Messiah MUST be a baby!

ANNA: The prophets have spoken.

SIMEON: My eyes have seen.

ANNA: Something happened!

(*ANNA, SIMEON, TEMPLE VISITOR TWO and TEMPLE VISITOR THREE leave podium area and approach manger as ANGELS speak. They kneel to worship the child.*)

ANGELS: Glory to God in the highest, and on earth peace to men on whom his favor rests.[4]

(*TEMPLE VISITOR ONE approaches manger scene but is blocked by the ANGELS. TEMPLE VISITOR ONE turns away to exit, Stage Left.*)

TEMPLE VISITOR ONE: (*Stops just before exiting, turns to audience.*) The Messiah CAN'T be a baby! (*Exits.*)

(*Audience sings carol.*)

SCENE TWO: PRIESTS PONDER

(*CAIAPHAS, SCRIBE ONE and SCRIBE TWO enter, Stage Right, and move to the podium.*)

CAIAPHAS: Something happened!

SCRIBE ONE: I tell you, Caiaphas, I hear it everywhere! "Messiah is coming!" It's shouted from the streets; it's shouted in the Temple. "Messiah is coming!"

SCRIBE TWO: I don't believe it!

CAIAPHAS: SOMETHING happened! The Romans have moved; they're all over the land. Then the decree came down from Caesar. All returned to their ancestors' towns to be counted—and taxed.

SCRIBE ONE: I tell you, Caiaphas, I hear it everywhere! "Messiah is coming!"

SCRIBE TWO: I don't believe it!

CAIAPHAS: No wonder more Roman troops have come. The people are ready to revolt. Another tax increase! We must stop all the rumors or Rome will never trust me with the power I should have!

SCRIBE ONE: I tell you, Caiaphas, I hear it everywhere! "Messiah is coming!"

SCRIBE TWO: I don't believe it!

CAIAPHAS: I must control the people. If I can't, how can I ever gain a position of power? The Romans will only allow leaders to remain in power when they CONTROL the people.

SCRIBE ONE: I tell you, Caiaphas, I hear it everywhere! "Messiah is coming!"

SCRIBE TWO: I don't believe it!

CAIAPHAS: Stop the cries of the people. Messiah will not come in our lifetimes. We must see what is happening!

SCRIBE ONE: I tell you, Caiaphas, I hear it everywhere! "Messiah is coming!"

SCRIBE TWO: I don't believe it!

CAIAPHAS: This nonsense reaches into every household in the land. Even Herod's palace is not free from the cries. He wants to know where the King of the Jews is to be born! I have no time for such unimportant things. So I gave it to an assistant.

SCRIBE ONE: But you, Bethlehem...though you are small among the clans of Judah, out of you will come for me one who will be ruler over Israel, whose origins are...from ancient times.[5]

SCRIBE TWO: I don't believe it!

SCRIBE ONE: I must go to Bethlehem and see for myself. I must see the Messiah. *(Approaches manger scene and kneels to worship.)*

ANGELS: Glory to God in the highest, and on earth peace to men on whom his favor rests.

CAIAPHAS: Something happened! Caesar made a decree. People moved all about Israel. But to believe the MESSIAH was born? In Bethlehem? Only a fool would believe.

SCRIBE TWO: I don't believe it! *(Moves toward exit, Stage Right, following CAIAPHAS. They approach manger scene but are blocked by the ANGELS. They turn to exit, Stage Right. SCRIBE TWO stops just before exiting, speaks to audience.)* I don't believe it!

(Audience sings carol.)

SCENE THREE: SHEPHERDS SEE

(SHEPHERD ONE, SHEPHERD TWO and other SHEPHERDS enter, Stage Left, and approach podium.)

SHEPHERD ONE: Something happened!

SHEPHERD TWO: We were out in the field, watching over our flocks. It was just another night, no different from any other night. We didn't think it would be special.

SHEPHERD ONE: We were wrong.

SHEPHERD TWO: It's always hard to watch sheep at night out in the hills. It's dark, it's cold and there's always danger. But we would give our lives for our sheep. We protect them from anything or anyone who might harm them.

SHEPHERD ONE: And we've had lots of practice. So don't you people try anything.

SHEPHERD TWO: Anyway, we're not the best men in the world. Not the most religious. Not clean and fit to go to the Temple.

SHEPHERD ONE: Not like priests or Pharisees.

SHEPHERD TWO: We're just ordinary people. So what a surprise!

SHEPHERD ONE: The brightest light I ever saw. I was scared to death!

SHEPHERD TWO: But then, we heard a voice.

GABRIEL: Do not be afraid. I bring you good news of great joy that will be for all the people. Today in the town of David a Savior has been born to you; he is Christ the Lord. This will be a sign to you: You will find a baby wrapped in cloths and lying in a manger.[6]

SHEPHERD ONE: It was an ANGEL! And suddenly, there were thousands of angels.

ANGELS: Glory to God in the highest, and on earth peace to men on whom his favor rests.

SHEPHERD TWO: It was the biggest choir I'd ever seen. Almost like God was telling me, just ME, that something special was happening!

SHEPHERD ONE: We wanted to see what was happening, what the angel talked about.

SHEPHERD TWO: So we rushed to Bethlehem. And there, we saw that what the angel had told us was TRUE!

SHEPHERD ONE: He was just a little baby, lying in a manger.

SHEPHERD TWO: But He was special. We knew it.

SHEPHERD ONE: Something happened!

GABRIEL: Do not be afraid. I bring you good news of great joy that will be for all the people. Today in the town of David a Savior has been born to you; he is Christ the Lord. This will be a sign to you: You will find a baby wrapped in cloths and lying in a manger.

(GABRIEL, SHEPHERD ONE, SHEPHERD TWO and other SHEPHERDS approach manger scene and kneel to worship. ANGELS step back to let them pass.)

ANGELS: Glory to God in the highest, and on earth peace to men on whom his favor rests. *(Audience sings carol.)*

SCENE FOUR: DEMONS DESPAIR

(SATAN, MALEFICENT, NONSEQUITUR, DEMON ONE and other DEMONS enter, Stage Right, and move to podium. MICHAEL enters. GABRIEL joins him and they stand a few feet behind DEMONS.)

SATAN: Something happened!

MALEFICENT: Something terrible!

NONSEQUITUR: Something HORRIBLE!

DEMON ONE: The Savior was born.

SATAN: From almost the beginning of time, I've had my way in this world. When He gave a command to these creatures to have no other gods but HIM...

NONSEQUITUR: I told them, "Don't listen. It's not important."

DEMON ONE: And I helped.

SATAN: So they turned from Him. And no matter who else they said they worshiped, they really worshiped ME. I had them in my power. When He told them to make no idols...

NONSEQUITUR: I told them, "Don't listen. It's not important."

MALEFICENT: And I told them, "Your idol is more important and more powerful than your neighbor's."

DEMON ONE: And I helped.

SATAN: So they turned further from Him. But no matter what image they worshiped, they really worshiped ME. When He told them not to steal...

NONSEQUITUR: I told them, "It's not REALLY stealing. It's just helping people share the wealth."

MALEFICENT: I told them, "Hate those who have more than you. Try to get rid of them." Then, I told those with great wealth, "Keep what you have. You earned it. Nobody else deserves it." So the rich became richer, the poor became poorer, and each hated the other.

DEMON ONE: And I helped.

SATAN: Further and further from Him, I drove them. They worshiped their gold. They worshiped their possessions. They worshiped their own power. But no matter what they said they worshiped, they really worshiped ME. *(Pauses.)* Now THIS has happened.

MALEFICENT *(disgusted)***:** He showed them love and mercy.

NONSEQUITUR: He gave them a prophecy to show who the Savior would be.

DEMON ONE *(wailing)***:** And we can't STOP Him.

SATAN: But we'll try. And even if we lose, we'll take everyone we can with us.

(SATAN, MALEFICENT, NONSEQUITUR, DEMON ONE and other DEMONS move to Center Stage, looking behind them and cowering, as GABRIEL and MICHAEL move to the podium.)

MICHAEL: Hear the word of the Lord to the serpent! "I will put enmity between you and the woman, and between your offspring and hers; he will crush your head, and you will strike his heel."[7]

GABRIEL: To Him give all glory. All peoples and nations, worship Him! He is the King forever!

MICHAEL: The people walking in darkness have seen a great light; on those living in the land of the shadow of death a light has dawned.[8]

GABRIEL: Nations will come to His light, and kings to the brightness of His dawning.[9]

(SATAN, NONSEQUITUR, MALEFICENT, DEMON ONE and other DEMONS run toward manger scene, away from MICHAEL and GABRIEL, who remain at podium. ANGELS group themselves to turn DEMONS away and keep those at manger safe. SATAN, NONSEQUITUR, MALEFICENT, DEMON ONE and other DEMONS visibly give up and slink away to exit, Stage Right. DEMON ONE pauses just before exiting. Turns to audience.)

DEMON ONE *(wailing):* Something HAPPENED!

(Audience sings carol.)

SCENE FIVE: HEAVEN REJOICES

MICHAEL: In the beginning was the Word, and the Word was with God, and the Word was God.[10]

GABRIEL: I bring you good news of great joy that will be for all the people. Today in the town of David a Savior has been born to you; He is Christ the Lord.

MICHAEL: Through him all things were made; without him nothing was made that has been made. In him was life, and that life was the light of men. The light shines in the darkness, but the darkness has not understood it.[11]

ANGELS: Glory to God in the highest, and on earth peace to men on whom his favor rests.

MICHAEL: The Word became flesh and made his dwelling among us. We have seen his glory, the glory of the One and Only, who came from the Father, full of grace and truth.[12]

GABRIEL: I bring you good news of great joy that will be for all the people. Today in the town of David a Savior has been born to you; he is Christ the Lord.

MICHAEL: For God so loved the world that he gave his one and only Son, that whoever believes in him shall not perish but have eternal life. For God did not send his Son into the world to condemn the world, but to save the world through through him.[13]

MICHAEL, GABRIEL and ANGELS: Glory to God in the highest, and on earth peace to men on whom his favor rests.

(MICHAEL and GABRIEL join other ANGELS around the manger scene.)

(Audience sings carol.)

[1]Isaiah 9:6
[2]Isaiah 7:14
[3]See Luke 2:29-32.
[4]Luke 2:14
[5]Micah 5:2
[6]Luke 2:10-12
[7]Genesis 3:15
[8]Isaiah 9:2
[9]See Isaiah 60:3.
[10]John 1:1
[11]John 1:3-5
[12]John 1:14
[13]John 3:16,17

WHAT GIFT WILL YOU BRING?

(APPROXIMATE TIME: 15 MINUTES)

SYNOPSIS

Herod gives a tour of his palace, tells about Jesus' coming to the Temple and meets the wise men—and their wives.

STAGE SETTING: HEROD'S THRONE ROOM

■ Herod's throne, Stage Left
■ Writing table, front of Center Stage
■ Optional—Temple backdrop for Temple scene

THE PLAYERS

JOSEPH (Grade 3 or older)   **MARY** (Grade 3 or older)
HEROD (Grade 5 or older)   **CAPTAIN** (Grade 5 or older)
COUNSELOR ONE (Grade 5 or older)   **COUNSELOR TWO** (Grade 5 or older)
ANNA (Grade 5 or older)   **SIMEON** (SIM-ee-un) (Grade 5 or older)
WIFE ONE (Grade 5 or older)   **WIFE TWO** (Grade 5 or older)
WISE MAN (Grade 5 or older)   **STAGEHANDS** (All ages)
NONSPEAKING SOLDIERS, COUNSELORS (All ages)
NONSPEAKING WISE MEN, WIVES and SERVANTS (All ages)

SUGGESTED PROPS

■ Candle, loose papers, pen placed on writing table
■ Box full of scrolls for counselors, set near writing table (a large box creates more comic effect)
■ Herod's sealing ring
■ Spears, swords, shields and helmets for Soldiers
■ Various types of uniforms for Soldiers (e.g., basketball, baseball, hockey, modern army fatigues, etc.)
■ Baby doll to represent baby Jesus in Temple scene
■ Large (toddler-sized) doll to represent Jesus in final scene with Wise Men; optional—toddler-aged child
■ Small bells for camel sounds
■ Jewelry for wives
■ Gifts for Wise Men to present to Jesus
■ Bible-times costumes

DIRECTOR'S TIPS

1. The audience is an integral part of the play. Herod should look at the audience whenever he speaks to it.
2. If more speaking parts are desired, the Captain and the wise man can share their speeches with other Soldiers and Wise Men.
3. Wife One and Wife Two should overact if possible. Their characters should be somewhat loud and obnoxious for comic effect.

WHAT GIFT WILL YOU BRING?

(A candle is lit on the writing table. HEROD enters, seats himself behind table and picks up a sheet of paper to read. He repeatedly glances up at audience members, then ignores them and goes back to paper. He signs and folds paper, then drips a bit of wax on paper and seals with ring. He drips a bit of wax on himself and exclaims, "Ow!" He picks up another paper, and glances at audience again.)

HEROD *(Calling offstage)*: Guards!

(SOLDIERS enter, Stage Right, dressed in various uniforms.)

CAPTAIN: You bellowed, Sire?

HEROD *(noticing uniforms)*: What are you wearing?

CAPTAIN: The army tailors are trying out new uniforms, Sire.

HEROD: Oh. *(Points to audience.)* Anyway, who ARE these people?

CAPTAIN: Well... *(Pointing.)* That's my mother, and there's Pastor *(give name)*, and there's...

HEROD: NO! Not, "What are these people's NAMES?" What are they DOING here?

CAPTAIN: I don't know.

HEROD: Get my counselors!

(SOLDIERS exit, Stage Right, shouting, "Counselors! Counselors! Counselors!" They enter again with COUNSELORS, then move to back of HEROD's table.)

COUNSELOR ONE: You bellowed, Sire?

HEROD *(pointing to audience)*: Who are these people?

COUNSELOR TWO *(pointing)*: Well, that's my mother...

COUNSELOR ONE *(pointing)*: And that's Pastor *(give name)*...

COUNSELORS *(pointing)*: And that's...

HEROD *(tearing hair)*: STOP! What are they DOING here?

COUNSELORS: Oh. *(They dig through box of scrolls muttering "Anthropology, anthropology, anthropology." They find scroll, bring it out and open it while muttering "Visitors, palace. Visitors, palace." They stop to read, then look at each other.)* Aha!

HEROD: What?

COUNSELOR ONE: It is written...

COUNSELOR TWO: To increase royal revenues...

COUNSELOR ONE: ...tours of the palace shall be given...

COUNSELOR TWO: ...and a tour guide appointed.

HEROD: But there's no tour guide!

COUNSELORS: No, Sire.

HEROD: Guards!

SOLDIERS *(stepping forward)*: Sire!

HEROD *(pointing to audience)*: Throw them out.

(SOLDIERS look nervously at each other, then move slowly toward audience. They stop, then return to HEROD.)

CAPTAIN: Sire?

HEROD: What?

CAPTAIN: There's a LOT of them.

HEROD: I don't care. Throw them out.

(SOLDIERS look nervously at each other and move slowly toward audience.)

HEROD: Wait!

(SOLDIERS return quickly and stand behind HEROD.)

HEROD: Counselors, what IS a tour guide?

COUNSELORS: *(They return first scroll and search for another, muttering "Personnel, personnel, personnel." They find scroll and open it, muttering "Guide, tour. Guide, tour. Guide, tour." They stop and look at each other.)* Aha!

COUNSELOR ONE: It is written...

COUNSELOR TWO: The tour guide shall point out items of interest...

COUNSELOR ONE: ...explaining the significance...

COUNSELOR TWO: ...and history of each item.

HEROD: So a tour guide talks a lot?

COUNSELOR ONE: Yes, Sire.

HEROD: Is it a paying position?

COUNSELOR TWO *(consulting scroll)*: The tour guide shall be paid...

COUNSELOR ONE: ...whatever the king shall deem proper.

HEROD: A tour guide gets paid to talk and I decide his salary?

COUNSELOR TWO: Yes, Sire.

HEROD: Then I shall be tour guide! Dismissed, all of you.

(SOLDIERS and COUNSELORS bow and exit, Stage Right.)

HEROD: *(To audience.)* Hi. I'm your tour guide, Herod. *(Stands.)* You're probably wondering about all the wonderful things you see here. This is my throne, where I sit to make important decisions. This is my royal writing table, where I sign important documents. *(Shows ring.)* This is my ring, with which I seal important royal documents. *(Senses he's losing audience interest, so he looks around for something interesting.)* Aha! *(Points to Stage Left.)* Over here is the royal window. Do you know what's outside? *(Waits to build tension.)* The Temple! A famous historical structure.

(STAGEHANDS begin to set up optional Temple background. HEROD ignores them.)

HEROD: I had my palace built right next door. Don't you want to know why? Of course you do. I thought, *Temple, miracles.* If I had a window overlooking the Temple, I might see miracles. But nothing interesting ever happens in Jerusalem. The most exciting thing that's happened in the Temple was last year. *(Moves to throne and sits, rubbing his chin in contemplation.)* Or was it the year before?

(Lights dim on HEROD and rise on Temple area. MARY and JOSEPH enter, Stage Left, carrying a baby. They are looking up and around in awe at the Temple.)

MARY: The Temple of the Lord. It's so beautiful, so majestic. *(Walks around the Temple with JOSEPH while SIMEON enters, Stage Left.)*

SIMEON: *(Looks up.)* Will this be the day, O Lord? I believe this will be the day.

(ANNA enters, Stage Left.)

ANNA: Simeon!

SIMEON: Anna. How are you? Is something important going to happen today?

ANNA: You feel it, too? The presence of God is here.

SIMEON: But is He not always in His Temple?

ANNA: Sometimes I wonder. His people have not been faithful.

SIMEON: True. But He promised I would see the Messiah before I died.

ANNA: He keeps His promises. He is with those who love Him.

SIMEON: Such as you, Anna. He speaks to you still.

ANNA: Such is the love of God. *(Smiles, shaking head.)* We give Him nothing, but He remains with us.

SIMEON: But how long, Anna? How long before God reclaims His kingdom?

ANNA: I believe it will be soon. He is here. His presence is with us now.

(As MARY and JOSEPH have walked around, looking up in awe, they bump into ANNA and SIMEON.)

MARY: Oh, please forgive us, Aged Mother, Aged Father. We didn't see you.

SIMEON: It is nothing. What brings you to the Temple?

MARY: We have brought this child to the Temple, to present him to God. We have also brought two young pigeons for the sacrifice.

ANNA: *(Shakes finger at SIMEON.)* You see, Simeon—not all have forgotten the Law!

SIMEON: Yes. Some still bring their gifts to God. May we see the child?

MARY: Of course. *(Uncovers baby's face. ANNA and SIMEON gasp in joy.)*

ANNA: Unto us a child is born. Unto us a Son is given. Of course!

SIMEON: *(Gently takes baby from MARY.)* God's goodness is greater than anything! *(Looking upward.)* I have seen Him. I have seen the child!

(MARY and JOSEPH look on in amazement. ANNA and SIMEON continue speaking while holding and looking at the baby.)

ANNA: The government will be on His shoulders.

SIMEON: He will be called Wonderful Counselor...

ANNA: ...Mighty God, Everlasting Father...

ANNA AND SIMEON: ...Prince of Peace.[1]

SIMEON (*looking upward*): Now, Lord, I can depart this life in peace. For I have seen Your salvation.

ANNA (*looking upward*): Thank You, Lord, for you have shown us the answer to the prayers of all Your people—all who have prayed for Israel's redemption.

SIMEON: The salvation for all people. A light to the Gentiles and the glory of Your people Israel.

ANNA: Our joy is complete, for we have seen Your Messiah.

SIMEON (*giving child back to MARY*): Take care of this child! You have truly been blessed among women.

(*Lights dim on Temple scene as ANNA, SIMEON, MARY and JOSEPH exit, Stage Left. STAGEHANDS remove Temple scene as lights are raised on HEROD. He is still rubbing his chin in contemplation. He stops rubbing his chin and turns to face audience.*)

HEROD: And that's the most exciting thing that's happened in Jerusalem since I've been here. Is it any wonder I want to get out? Nothing exciting happens.

(*Loud noises of feet stomping, small bells ringing, voices of WISE MEN and SOLDIERS, etc. are heard offstage.*)

HEROD: Guards!

(*SOLDIERS enter, Stage Right.*)

CAPTAIN: You bellowed, Sire?

HEROD: What's that noise about?

CAPTAIN: I would say about one hundred decibels, Sire.

HEROD: NO! Not "How LOUD is the noise?" Why is it being MADE? Go find out!

(*Noise increases again as SOLDIERS exit, Stage Right. HEROD crosses to table and reads another document. SOLDIERS enter.*)

HEROD: Well? What is it?

CAPTAIN: Some visitors from the East. A whole bunch of them!

HEROD: Probably eastern politicians. I don't need a bunch of easterners telling me what to do. (*Waves.*) Send them away!

CAPTAIN: Very good, Sire. (*Shouts offstage, toward Stage Right.*) OK, you jokers! Pack up your gold and...

HEROD (*shouting*): Wait! Did you say "gold"?

CAPTAIN: Yes, Sire. And frankincense and myrrh.

HEROD (*rubbing hands greedily*): Well, well! That changes everything! Show the eastern gentlemen in.

(*SOLDIERS exit, Stage Right, and return with WISE MEN and entourage. WISE MEN, SERVANTS and WIVES approach HEROD except for WIFE ONE and WIFE TWO who move to stand at the front of Stage Right, whispering.*)

WISE MAN: *(Bowing to HEROD.)* Where is the One who has been born King of the Jews? We have come to worship Him.

HEROD: Of course. You know, those gifts look heavy. *(Pats table.)* Why not put them here on the table? *(Watches as SERVANTS place packages on his table. Catches himself.)* Sorry, you said something? A King?

WISE MAN: We want to find the One who has been born the King of the Jews. We have come to worship Him.

HEROD: King of the Jews? Well, here I am! Go ahead, worship. *(To GUARDS.)* Guards, keep an eye on MY gifts!

WISE MAN: Hmmm... We were expecting someone younger. A child? We saw His star. It shone brightly in the East!

WIFE ONE *(looking up)***:** Again with the star!

HEROD: Counselors!

(COUNSELORS enter, Stage Right.)

COUNSELOR ONE: You bellowed, Sire?

HEROD: Has there been a royal birth I didn't know about?

(COUNSELORS search through scrolls muttering, "Vital records, vital records, vital records." They find scroll, bring it out and open it, muttering "Births, royal. Births, royal. Births, royal." Then they look at each other.)

COUNSELORS: Aha!

HEROD: Well?

COUNSELOR TWO: No. No royal births, Sire.

HEROD: Good! Then the presents are all mine! *(Catching himself.)* I mean...you HAVE come to see ME!

WISE MAN: But I don't understand. The star...

WIFE TWO: The star! How many times do I have to tell you? Don't LOOK at the stars! Do what normal people do. Consult a fortune-teller!

WIFE ONE: And don't FOLLOW stars! Stop at the oasis. Spend a few shekels. Buy a MAP!

WIFE TWO: And if you get lost, ask for DIRECTIONS.

WIVES: *(To audience.)* But does he listen? NOOO!

WISE MAN: *(To WIVES.)* Silence, you two!

HEROD: *(To WISE MEN.)* Well, I'm waiting. Worship me! Shower me with gifts.

WISE MAN: But it CAN'T be you. The star indicates that the King was born recently!

HEROD: *(To WISE MEN.)* Would you excuse us for a minute? *(Points to rear of stage.)* Just wait over there. I need to consult my counselors.
(SERVANTS start to pick up gifts.)
Oh! Don't bother picking up those heavy gifts. Just leave them on the table.
(WISE MEN and entourage move backstage except for WIFE ONE and WIFE TWO. They continue talking, moving along the front of stage.)

WIFE ONE: ...and gifts. Does he ask US?

WIFE TWO: A new King. A baby! What does he bring?

WIFE ONE: Does he bring a rattle?

WIFE TWO: Does he bring blankets? clothing?

WIVES: NOOO!

WIFE ONE: He brings GOLD. Like a King doesn't already have gold?

WIFE TWO: And the others are just as bad.

WIFE ONE: They bring incense. Burn THAT in the nursery! Do you think a baby cares about the smell of incense?

WIFE TWO: And myrrh! That's to BURY people. Why does a baby need myrrh?

WIFE ONE: We TOLD him.

WIFE TWO: Clothing and toys, we told him.

WIVES: *(To audience.)* But does he listen? NOOO! *(Both hurry back to join the rest of the entourage.)*

HEROD: Counselors, these eastern crackpots think some King has been born.

COUNSELORS: Terrible, shocking.

HEROD: But I'm the king and I intend to STAY king.

COUNSELORS: Excellent, excellent.

HEROD: So I need to know if there is another King.

COUNSELORS: Tough, tough.

HEROD *(shouting)***:** SO FIND OUT!

(COUNSELORS mutter together, then look at each other.)

COUNSELORS: Aha! Messiah! *(COUNSELORS search for scroll, muttering "Prophecy, prophecy, prophecy." They find scroll and bring it out. They search through scroll, muttering "Messiah, birth of. Messiah, birth of. Messiah, birth of." They stop and look at each other.)* Aha!

HEROD: Well?

COUNSELOR ONE: Here it is!

COUNSELOR TWO: It says that Bethlehem, in the land of Judah, is not the least.

COUNSELOR ONE *(reading along, pointing)***:** Let's see. "Out of you will come...one who will be ruler over Israel."[2]

HEROD: So, this King was born in Bethlehem. *(Motions WISE MEN forward.)* *(WISE MEN and entourage come forward to their former positions. WIFE ONE and WIFE TWO move to front of Stage Right.)*

WISE MAN: Yes, Your Majesty?

HEROD: When did you say you saw this star?

WIFE ONE *(looking up)***:** AGAIN with the star.

WISE MAN: About two years ago.

HEROD: The records say a King should be born in Bethlehem. Go there and search for this child. When you've found Him, come back and tell me. I want to...uh...worship Him also!

(SERVANTS move to pick up gifts.)

HEROD: *(Gesturing "stop" to SERVANTS.)* Wait! I have an idea. You don't want to carry all those heavy parcels while searching. Why not leave them with me? I'll be sure to take them with me when I go to see this child.

WISE MAN: That's very kind. But we would like to present the gifts ourselves.

(SERVANTS pick up gifts and entourage exits, Stage Right. WIFE ONE and WIFE TWO continue to walk along front of stage, talking.)

WIFE TWO: So now we're going to Bethlehem.

WIFE ONE: But does anyone know where Bethlehem IS?

WIFE TWO: Do we have a MAP?

WIFE ONE: Will he stop and ask for DIRECTIONS?

WIFE TWO: Will he listen to REASON?

WIVES: *(To audience.)* NOOO! *(Both quickly exit, Stage Right.)*

HEROD: Guard!

(SOLDIERS come forward.)

CAPTAIN: Sire!

HEROD: When I give the word, I want you to gather all the soldiers available. My gift for this new King will be the only gift any king has ever given to a usurper of the throne.

CAPTAIN: What gift is that, Sire?

(HEROD is about to speak but suddenly becomes aware of audience.)

HEROD: *(To audience.)* I want this to be a secret. You understand, I'm sure.

(HEROD motions soldiers nearer and begins whispering to them. HEROD and SOLDIERS begin laughing. COUNSELORS start searching through scrolls muttering, "Gifts, gifts, gifts." Find scroll and search through it muttering, "Royal, to usurper. Royal, to usurper. Royal, to usurper." Stop, look at each other, look at audience and draw finger across throat. Lights on palace area slowly fade to black.)

(While palace lights fade, MARY and JOSEPH enter Stage Right to stand with toddler-sized doll or toddler near rear of stage. WISE MEN and entourage enter, Stage Right, present gifts, bow down and worship. Lights on WISE MEN and group rise to full power and hold for a few seconds, then the lights snap to black.)

[1]See Isaiah 9:6.
[2]Micah 5:2

DON'T YOU LOVE CHRISTMAS?

(APPROXIMATE TIME: 45 MINUTES WITH CAROLS)

SYNOPSIS

Reporter Marcy Tan goes back in time to report firsthand on the events surrounding Jesus' birth.

STAGE SETTINGS

SCENE ONE: FOG NEWS OFFICE ("FREQUENTLY ODD GLOBAL" NEWS OFFICE)

■ Table and chair for news desk, Stage Left at front

■ Microphone on table

SCENE TWO: FOG INTERVIEW ("FAIRLY OPEN GEOGRAPHY" INTERVIEW)— SOMEWHERE BETWEEN NAZARETH AND BETHLEHEM

Rock at rear of stage where Mary can rest

SCENE THREE: BETHLEHEM STREET

Building facades for a small-town street, front of stage

SCENE FOUR: FOG PLACE ("FRUGAL OUTDOOR GATHERING" PLACE)—THE STABLE

Manger, rear of stage

SCENE FIVE: JERUSALEM STREET

Building facades for large city street, front of stage

SCENE SIX: FOG CENTER ("FLIMSY, OVERREACTING GOVERNMENT" CENTER)— HEROD'S PALACE

■ Throne in center of stage

■ Wall hangings, etc. to suggest throne room

SCENE SEVEN: FOG NEWS OFFICE ("FREQUENTLY ODD GLOBAL" NEWS OFFICE)

■ Same as Scene One

■ Manger set up at rear of stage

THE PLAYERS

MARY (Grade 3 or older)

YOUNG MARY (Grade 3 or older)

INNKEEPER (Grade 3 or older)

GOFER (Grade 5 or older)

WISE MAN ONE (Grade 5 or older)

WISE MAN THREE (Grade 1 or older)

SOLDIER TWO (Grade 3 or older)

HEROD (Grade 5 or older)

ANGEL (who speaks to Mary and Joseph) (Grade 3 or older)

NONSPEAKING ANGELS, SHEPHERDS and SOLDIERS (all ages)

JOSEPH (Grade 3 or older)

YOUNG JOSEPH (Grade 5 or older)

REPORTER (Grade 5 or older)

MAIN SHEPHERD (Grade 5 or older)

WISE MAN TWO (Grade 3 or older)

SOLDIER ONE (Grade 5 or older)

SOLDIER THREE (Grade 1 or older)

STAGEHANDS (all ages)

SUGGESTED PROPS

- Microphone, other office items for news desk
- Signs with stand, each lettered as follows:
  "Frequently Odd Global News Office" for news office
  "Fairly Open Geography" for road to Bethlehem
  "Bethlehem" and "Jerusalem" signs for towns
  "Frugal Outdoor Gathering Place" for stable
  "Flimsy, Overreacting Government Center" for Herod's palace
- Binoculars
- Notebook, briefcase, papers and pencils for Reporter
- Time machine (one of the following): tricycle, skateboard, pogo stick—anything that the Reporter can use to move forward (ahead in time) or backward (back in time)
- Broom for Young Mary
- Whittling knife and wood for Young Joseph
- Doll to represent baby Jesus
- Foil-wrapped cardboard swords and spears for Soldiers
- Throne for Herod
- Other furnishings for palace room
- Gifts for Wise Men to present to Jesus
- Bible-times costumes, angel costumes, Soldier uniforms
- Watches for Gofer and Reporter

DIRECTOR'S TIPS

1. The Reporter's part is the most difficult. Assign this part three or four weeks before the other parts to give the player ample time to memorize the lines. Take some time before general rehearsals to go over the Reporter's part.

2. The Reporter does not have to be female. If a boy could play the part better, give him an appropriate name (for example, Harvey Paul).

3. The Reporter carries a notebook. Have the Reporter make notes in the notebook to help remember what comes next.

4. Cast some older players in nonspeaking roles to help the younger ones remember their places on stage.

5. Stagehands can also have other parts in the play.

6. Young Mary and Young Joseph can become shepherds for the last scene so they will also be on stage at the end of the play.

7. Appoint someone to lead the carols between scenes. Appropriate Scripture readings could be used instead of the carols.

8. Suggested Christmas carols:
   Scene One—"O Come, All Ye Faithful," "Come, Thou Long-Expected Jesus"
   Scene Two—"O Little Town of Bethlehem"
   Scene Three—"Away in a Manger"
   Scene Four—"As with Gladness Men of Old"
   Scene Five—"Hark, the Herald Angels Sing"
   Scene Six—"Joy to the World"
   Scene Seven—"What Child Is This?"

DON'T YOU LOVE CHRISTMAS?

(Audience sings carol as STAGEHANDS set up news office scene.)

SCENE ONE: THE FOG NEWS OFFICE

("FREQUENTLY ODD GLOBAL" NEWS)

(GOFER is straightening papers, etc. REPORTER enters, Stage Left.)

REPORTER: What a story! What a STORY! WHAT A STORY!

GOFER: A story is a narrative explanation of events involving characters, settings, situations...

REPORTER *(gesturing wildly)*: Not, "What IS a story?" WHAT A STORY! I've been assigned the biggest story of all TIME! I've got so much to do. I have to pack, stop the paper, get someone to pick up the mail and feed the dog. Food. I need to have lunch. No time to go and get any.

GOFER: I'll order pizza. Now, talk! What IS the story?

REPORTER: I'm going to interview people about Christmas.

GOFER: So what? That doesn't sound very exciting to me.

REPORTER: You don't UNDERSTAND. I get to interview Mary, Joseph, the shepherds, everyone who was THERE!

GOFER *(scratching head)*: How are you going to do that? They all died a long time ago.

REPORTER *(grandly)*: I get to use...THE TIME MACHINE! Go get it while I finish packing. *(Throws paper and pencils into a briefcase.)*

GOFER: Right! *(Exits, Stage Left, and returns with time machine.)* Here it is!

REPORTER: Great! I'm off. *(Waves.)* See you in two thousand years! *(Jumps on time machine and travels backwards in a circle around stage to finally exit backwards, Stage Right.)*

GOFER *(waving, while REPORTER travels)*: Have a nice trip!

(Audience sings carol. STAGEHANDS break down Scene One and set up Scene Two.)

SCENE TWO: FOG INTERVIEW

("FAIRLY OPEN GEOGRAPHY")—SOMEWHERE BETWEEN NAZARETH AND BETHLEHEM

(REPORTER enters backward slowly, Stage Right. She travels slowly backward on time machine to Center Stage and dismounts.)

REPORTER: If my calculations are correct, this should be the right time and place. But I'd better hide the time machine. Don't want to raise any difficult questions. *(REPORTER exits, Stage Right, to hide time machine offstage, then returns to Center Stage.)*

REPORTER (raising binoculars, scanning scene)**:** Now, if this is the road between Nazareth and Bethlehem, I SHOULD be able to spot Mary and Joseph. FOG News will be FIRST with this exclusive interview! (Scans with binoculars toward Stage Left while MARY and JOSEPH enter Stage Right. They walk right up to REPORTER.)

JOSEPH: Excuse me. But you're blocking the road and we need to get to Bethlehem before nightfall.

(REPORTER turns with binoculars still up, sees JOSEPH, jumps back.)

REPORTER: Whoa! Giants! (Lowers binoculars.) Oh, right. (Looks at MARY and JOSEPH carefully, then turns to face audience and walks a few steps forward.)

REPORTER: (To audience, counting on fingers.) Hmm. A man, a pregnant woman, going to Bethlehem. (Returns to MARY and JOSEPH. Pulls out notebook and consults a page.) Excuse me, but are you Joseph, son of Jacob, and Mary, daughter of Heli (HE-lie)?

JOSEPH and MARY: Yes. We are.

JOSEPH: How do you know our names?

MARY: We don't know you.

REPORTER: (Holds out hand to shake hands.) Marcy Tan. FOG News. You must have seen me on TV.

(MARY and JOSEPH look at each other and shrug, ignoring the outstretched hand. REPORTER lowers hand since it is being ignored.)

JOSEPH: What is TV?

MARY (touching binoculars)**:** And what is this strange jewelry you wear?

JOSEPH: And what manner of strange clothing do you wear?

REPORTER (indignantly)**:** Hey, fella! Your clothes aren't the best, either!

MARY: We meant no harm. But you look so different from us.

REPORTER: Oh, yeah. I forgot. I'm from a land far away. I wonder, could I ask you a few questions?

JOSEPH: We ARE in a bit of a hurry.

MARY: (To JOSEPH.) I AM a little tired, Joseph. Maybe we could rest awhile and talk with this stranger.

JOSEPH: Very well.

REPORTER: Great! (Takes out pencil and poises it over open notebook.)

REPORTER: Tell me—what do think about Christmas?

JOSEPH (puzzled)**:** Christmas? What is Christmas?

MARY: We don't know anyone by that name. Who are you talking about?

REPORTER: You, of all people, must know. Manger, star, Jesus is born?

MARY (startled)**:** Jesus? That is to be the name of my son.

REPORTER: Right. I keep forgetting. It hasn't HAPPENED yet. This baby you are carrying is...well, special, right?

JOSEPH (suspiciously)**:** How do you know these things?

REPORTER: Sorry. I can't reveal my sources.

JOSEPH: (Sighs.) I'm not surprised that you know. So many strange things have been happening.

REPORTER: Could you tell me about these strange things?

MARY: Of course. But it's a long story. Could we sit down?

REPORTER: Certainly. How about over there?

(MARY, JOSEPH and REPORTER move to the rear of the stage where MARY sits on a rock. They remain there for the next sequence.)

REPORTER: Now, tell me about it.

MARY: It all started about nine months ago...

(YOUNG MARY enters, Stage Left. She sweeps, dusts, etc.)

YOUNG MARY: (To herself.) I can hardly wait. Before the year is out, Joseph and I will be married! (Continues her work.)

(ANGEL enters, Stage Left.)

ANGEL: Hail, Mary. You are specially blessed among women. The Lord is with you.

YOUNG MARY (confused)**:** What? Sir? What do you mean? Who are you? How did you get here?

ANGEL: (Gives a little bow.) I am an angel of the Lord. I have been sent to tell you that you have found great favor. You will have a Son and will call Him Jesus. He shall be great, and His kingdom will never end.

YOUNG MARY: Sir, that's not possible. I am a virgin.

ANGEL: Nothing is impossible with God! The Holy Spirit will come upon you. The power of God Himself will give you a child. Because of this, the baby will be called the "Son of God."

YOUNG MARY: (Bows.) I am God's servant girl. Let all these things be done to me as you have said.

(YOUNG MARY and ANGEL exit, Stage Left. YOUNG JOSEPH enters, Stage Right. He carries a whittling knife and a piece of wood. He punctuates his speech by whittling or pretending to whittle.)

YOUNG JOSEPH: (Shakes head.) What am I going to do? I love Mary, but she's going to have a baby. It's not MINE. (Whittles.) The Law says I can divorce her. What'll I do? (Whittles.) I don't know. But I sure need to think about this. (Yawns.) Maybe a quick power nap will help.

(YOUNG JOSEPH lies down. ANGEL enters, Stage Right.)

ANGEL: Joseph, do not be afraid to take Mary for your wife. Her child does not have a human father but was conceived by the Holy Spirit. When the child is born, call His name Jesus, for He will save His people from their sins.

(ANGEL exits, Stage Right.)

YOUNG JOSEPH: *(Wakes and stretches.)* What a strange dream! I must see Mary and talk to her.

(YOUNG JOSEPH exits, Stage Right. MARY, JOSEPH and REPORTER come forward.)

REPORTER: Amazing! Absolutely amazing!

MARY: We know you find it hard to believe.

JOSEPH: But it happened. Just as we told you. Now, we're on our way to Bethlehem because of the Roman census.

REPORTER: But what about YOUR lives? How do you FEEL about this baby?

MARY and JOSEPH *(puzzled)*: Feel? What do you mean?

REPORTER: YOU believe that He will be the Son of God. But other people won't. They'll call you terrible names. Doesn't that worry you?

MARY: But I've been chosen by God. I'm a little worried, but mostly, I'm excited!

JOSEPH: God has spoken to us both. We know that He is doing something wonderful. If we suffer a few hardships, is that so terrible? This Son we'll raise will save Israel from its sins. That's worth any price on our part.

REPORTER: But...

JOSEPH *(turning to go)*: I'm sorry. We really must go. We have a long way to travel.

REPORTER: But...

JOSEPH: And we must stop to eat soon. Maybe at Jerusalem.

MARY *(rising, to JOSEPH)*: Do you think they'll have any pickles in Jerusalem? *(Walks slowly across stage with JOSEPH toward exit, Stage Left. REPORTER runs to front of stage.)*

REPORTER: *(To audience.)* They're on their way. But with the time machine, I'll get to Jerusalem first! *(Runs offstage, Stage Right to return on time machine, traveling quickly forward across the stage to exit, Stage Left, passing MARY and JOSEPH before they also exit, Stage Left.)*

(Audience sings carol while STAGEHANDS break down Scene Two and set up Scene Three. If stage can be divided front and back by a curtain, they can also set up the manger for Scene Four behind the curtain.)

SCENE THREE: BETHLEHEM STREET

(REPORTER walks onstage, Stage Left. Time machine remains offstage.)

REPORTER: Wow! There are people everywhere. It wasn't easy to hide that time machine. *(Looks around.)* Well, I'd better find a place to spend the night. Here's a nice-looking hotel.

(REPORTER looks toward Stage Right as INNKEEPER enters, Stage Left. INNKEEPER stops behind REPORTER.)

REPORTER: I wonder where the innkeeper is.

INNKEEPER: May I help you?

(REPORTER turns to see INNKEEPER.)

REPORTER: Do you own this place?

INNKEEPER: I do, indeed.

REPORTER: Terrific! I need a room.

INNKEEPER: Sorry. I can't help you.

REPORTER: But I need a room. *(Points to self.)* ME!

INNKEEPER: Are you someone special?

(REPORTER holds out hand to shake hands with INNKEEPER. INNKEEPER ignores the outstretched hand.)

REPORTER: I'm Marcy Tan. FOG News. You MUST have seen me on TV. *(Lowers hand since it is being ignored.)*

INNKEEPER: What's TV?

REPORTER *(shaking head)***:** Forget it. Never mind. I'll find a room somewhere else.

INNKEEPER: Not in Bethlehem! All the rooms are taken.

REPORTER: There must be ONE!

INNKEEPER: Nope. I just gave away the last available space to a couple from Nazareth. And it was only a stable.

REPORTER: *(Slaps forehead.)* Of course! You're the INNKEEPER. *(Takes out notebook, poises pen to write.)* Tell me, what do YOU think about Christmas?

INNKEEPER: What's Christmas?

REPORTER: You know. Christmas. People hustling and bustling, buying presents, that kind of thing.

INNKEEPER: If it's anything like tonight, I hate it. Rush, rush, rush! No time to think. People everywhere. Oh, sure, it's good for business. But it's too busy.

(INNKEEPER looks offstage. Sees someone sleeping in doorway.)

INNKEEPER *(shouting and pointing)***:** You! What do you think you're doing? You can't sleep in the doorway! Get up! Out of there! *(INNKEEPER exits, Stage Right, shaking fist and shouting at person offstage.)*

REPORTER *(calling after INNKEEPER)***:** But wait! Where's the stable? *(To audience.)* How will I find the stable? If Jesus is going to be born tonight, I don't want to miss it. If only there were some shepherds! THEY'D know where the stable is. *(Turns from audience, looking left and right to decide which way to go.)*

(SHEPHERDS enter from audience area and surround REPORTER. SHEPHERDS are talking, gesturing; REPORTER is swept away with them as they exit, Stage Right.)

(Audience sings carol as STAGEHANDS break down Scene Three set and set up Scene Four. If manger has previously been set up behind curtain, STAGEHANDS need only set up sign at front of Stage Right.)

SCENE FOUR: FOG PLACE

("FRUGAL OUTDOOR GATHERING" PLACE)—The Stable

(MARY and JOSEPH are onstage. MARY is placing baby in manger. SHEPHERDS and REPORTER enter, Stage Right.)

REPORTER: *(To SHEPHERD.)* What is this place?

MAIN SHEPHERD: *(Pointing to sign.)* Can't you read? It's the Frugal Outdoor Gathering Place!

REPORTER: Why are we here? This is just a dirty, smelly barn. This assignment wasn't so exciting after all.

MAIN SHEPHERD: We've come to see the Savior. The One the angels told us about!

REPORTER: Oh, this is THE STABLE!

MAIN SHEPHERD: Yes. The Frugal Outdoor Gathering Place. But who are you?

(REPORTER holds out hand to shake hands with SHEPHERD. SHEPHERD ignores the outstretched hand.)

REPORTER: Marcy Tan. FOG News. You must have seen me on TV. *(Lowers hand since it is being ignored.)*

MAIN SHEPHERD: What's TV?

REPORTER: *(Looks upward and sighs.)* Never mind. Now that you're here, what are you going to do?

(SHEPHERDS begin to quietly kneel around the manger, looking at the child. MAIN SHEPHERD remains at the front of the stage to speak with REPORTER.)

MAIN SHEPHERD *(disbelieving)*: What are we going to DO? We're going to CELEBRATE! The Savior has been born!

REPORTER: *(Rubs hands together eagerly.)* You mean a party with lots of food and lots to drink?

MAIN SHEPHERD: No. Can't you read? *(SHEPHERD points to imaginary sign and reads.)* "Animal feeding only."

REPORTER *(disappointed)*: Well, what kind of party is it if there's no food or drinks?

(ANGELS enter, Stage Right and Left, to quietly surround the manger scene.)

MAIN SHEPHERD: It's a party of great joy! Can't you feel the presence of God? Don't you see the angels?

(REPORTER looks everywhere except at the manger.)

REPORTER: No.

MAIN SHEPHERD: I must go and see the Savior. *(Beckoning.)* Come. *(Takes REPORTER by the arm, leads REPORTER to manger. SHEPHERD kneels while REPORTER remains standing to look at the baby. SHEPHERDS worship for a moment.)*

MAIN SHEPHERD: *(Motions to other SHEPHERDS.)* Come! We must tell everyone. We have seen the SAVIOR!

(SHEPHERDS rush off through the audience. On the way, they tell people in the audience that they have seen Jesus.)

REPORTER: *(Walks forward to speak to audience, shaking head.)* Looks like an ordinary baby to me. *(Looks at wristwatch.)* I've got time to make one last time travel—to Jerusalem. Maybe I'll find something exciting THERE, a couple of years from now! *(Exits, Stage Left, and reenters from Stage Left on time machine, traveling forward across stage to exit, Stage Right.)*

(Audience sings carol while STAGEHANDS break down Scene Four and set up Scene Five. If the stage can be divided front and rear, Herod's throne room can be set up behind curtain.)

SCENE FIVE: JERUSALEM STREET

(REPORTER enters, Stage Right, looking up as if looking at tall buildings.)

REPORTER *(looking around)***:** This is more LIKE it. The big city!

(WISE MEN enter, Stage Left. REPORTER, still looking around, bumps into them.)

REPORTER: *(To WISE MEN.)* Hey! Why don't you watch where you're going?

WISE MAN ONE: Where is He? The one born King of the Jews?

REPORTER: Huh?

WISE MAN TWO: We have seen His star. In the East.

REPORTER: Huh?

WISE MAN THREE: *(Bows.)* And we've come to worship Him.

REPORTER: *(Points.)* Aha. I get it. You're the wise men! *(Pulls out notebook and pencil.)*

REPORTER: What do YOU think about Christmas?

WISE MEN: What's Christmas?

REPORTER: You know. The birthday of the King.

WISE MAN ONE: *(To himself.)* The birthday of the KING!

WISE MAN TWO *(gesturing)***:** The greatest day of all TIME!

WISE MAN THREE: *(Bows.)* And we have come to worship Him.

(SOLDIERS enter, Stage Left, while WISE MEN are speaking.)

SOLDIER ONE: *(To WISE MEN.)* King Herod wants to see you.

SOLDIER TWO: Follow us. *(Leads WISE MEN and REPORTER to exit, Stage Right.)*

(Audience sings carol while STAGEHANDS break down Scene Five and set up Scene Six, if not set up before.)

SCENE SIX: FOG CENTER

("FLIMSY, OVERREACTING GOVERNMENT" CENTER)—Herod's Palace

(SOLDIERS, leading WISE MEN and REPORTER, enter, Stage Right. HEROD is seated on throne.)

SOLDIER THREE: Here we are.

SOLDIER TWO *(proudly)***:** Welcome to FOG Government Center, heart of Judean government!

SOLDIER ONE: The throne room of King Herod himself!

(SOLDIER ONE and SOLDIER TWO position selves around the throne, along with other SOLDIERS.)

HEROD: Are these the men I've been hearing about?

SOLDIER ONE: Absolutely, Sire.

HEROD: The ones asking about the newly born King?

SOLDIER TWO: Absolutely, Sire.

HEROD: The ones who brought gifts of gold, frankincense and myrrh?

SOLDIER THREE: Absolutely, Sire.

HEROD: Then bring these men forward!

(WISE MEN approach HEROD.)

WISE MAN ONE: Where is He who is born the King of the Jews?

WISE MAN TWO: We have seen His star—in the East.

WISE MAN THREE: *(Bows.)* And we've come to worship Him.

HEROD: No King has been born here!

WISE MEN: *(Together.)* No?

HEROD: But I asked the priests and scribes about it. They say a King is to be born in Bethlehem. So, go to Bethlehem. Search for the child. When you find Him, come back and tell me. *(Clasps hands together and looks upward.)* I, too, want to worship Him.

(WISE MEN bow and back away from HEROD to exit, Stage Right.)

HEROD *(seeing REPORTER for the first time)***:** And who are YOU?

REPORTER: *(Holds out hand to shake hands with HEROD.)* Marcy Tan. FOG News. You must have seen me on TV. *(Lowers hand since HEROD is ignoring it.)*

HEROD: News? What is FOG News? Is it news about the weather? And what's TV?

REPORTER: *(Claps palm to head, looks up and shakes head in exasperation.)* Sorry. I forgot again. *(Takes out notebook and pencil.)* Sire, could I ask you about Christmas?

HEROD: What's Christmas?

REPORTER: Uh, the birth of the King of the Jews.

HEROD: Oh, THAT. *(Looks around, then motions REPORTER closer.)* Can you keep a secret?

REPORTER: I'm a respected journalist. *(Poises pen to write.)* What's the secret?

HEROD *(happily)***:** When those wise men find the child and tell me where He is, I'm going to send my soldiers to Bethlehem to KILL Him!

REPORTER: Then you're not happy about His birth?

HEROD: *(Begins to rave.)* Happy! Why should I be happy? If a NEW King is born, what happens to ME, the old king? I lose my power, that's what! I want Him dead. *(Catches himself and stops raving.)* Did I invite you for supper?

REPORTER: No. But I'd be happy to stay and have...

HEROD (*interrupting*)**:** Good. Because there's only enough for ME. Don't slam the door when you leave. (*Exits, Stage Left, with SOLDIERS.*)

REPORTER: (*Coming forward to speak to audience, folding notebook closed.*) Hmmm. I think I have all the information I need. (*Points upward.*) To the time machine! (*Exits Stage Right and reenters on time machine, traveling forward around stage. While REPORTER travels, STAGEHANDS break down Scene Six and set up Scene Seven.*)

(*REPORTER exits, Stage Left.*)

(*Audience sings carol while STAGEHANDS set up manger at the back of the stage. If stage cannot be divided front and back by a curtain, keep back area as dark as possible while the front is lighted. While it is dark, MARY enters to sit by the manger; JOSEPH stands beside her.*)

SCENE SEVEN: THE FOG NEWS OFFICE

("FREQUENTLY ODD GLOBAL" NEWS OFFICE)

(*GOFER enters, Stage Left, and tidies news desk. There's a sound of a crash offstage. REPORTER stumbles onstage from Stage Right. Moves to front.*)

REPORTER: (*To audience.*) We've GOT to get those brakes checked.

GOFER: Welcome back. Did you get the story?

(*REPORTER takes out notebook, walks to news desk and sits. Studies notebook.*)

REPORTER: No. I got confused.

GOFER: Why?

REPORTER: Because people don't agree about Christmas.

GOFER: Tell me about it. What happened?

REPORTER: Mary and Joseph were excited. Even though people might laugh at them or say horrible things about them, they were excited.

(*Rear curtain opens, or lights at rear of stage increase to reveal MARY sitting by the manger and JOSEPH standing beside her.*)

GOFER: So, Christmas is an exciting time.

REPORTER: But the innkeeper HATED it. Even though he was making lots of money, he could only complain about it.

(*INNKEEPER enters, Stage Right, walking behind MARY. He mimes that he is complaining, and stops just onstage continuing to mime. He does not look at the child.*)

GOFER: So Christmas is a time when people complain.

REPORTER: But the shepherds were filled with joy! They wanted to tell EVERYONE about Jesus.

(*SHEPHERDS enter, Stage Left, and kneel at manger, looking at the child.*)

GOFER: So Christmas is a joyous time.

REPORTER: But Herod wanted to KILL the baby. He was afraid of losing power.

(HEROD and SOLDIERS enter, Stage Left. HEROD looks furious, mimes being angry; SOLDIERS look worried. They walk across stage, behind MARY, stopping just onstage but looking offstage, not at the child.)

GOFER: So Christmas is a time of hatred and anger.

REPORTER: But later, the wise men came bearing gifts—to celebrate His birth and worship Him.

(WISE MEN enter, Stage Right, and kneel before MARY and the child, offering their gifts.)

GOFER: So Christmas is a time of celebration and worship.

REPORTER: But how can it be ALL those things? They're all so different.

GOFER: Did you see the baby?

REPORTER: Yes. I was actually in the stable!

GOFER: But what did you SEE?

REPORTER: Just an ordinary baby. Nothing special.

GOFER: Maybe that's the difference.

REPORTER: What do you mean?

GOFER: Mary and Joseph, the shepherds, the wise men all looked up. They saw the angels and the star.

(ANGELS enter, Stage Right and Stage Left, to stand around manger scene.)

REPORTER: So?

GOFER: The innkeeper and Herod only looked at the earth, at what was happening to THEMSELVES. Maybe the way you look at Christmas depends on the way you look at the baby! Do you look down at the earth or up to heaven? *(Looks at watch.)* Whoops, we're almost on the air. *(Backs away from REPORTER, moves toward manger. Approaches manger scene and kneels to worship Jesus.)*

REPORTER: *(Brings microphone in front and adjusts papers.)* Good evening. I'm Marcy Tan. Tonight—a FOG News exclusive. We'll be bringing you today's top story, "Don't You Love Christmas?"

(Lights fade to black on REPORTER while lights near manger increase.)

(Audience sings carol.)

THE SIMPLE CHRISTMAS STORY

(APPROXIMATE TIME: 25 MINUTES)

SYNOPSIS

A successful producer shows a writer his plans to "spice up" the Christmas story.

STAGE SETTINGS

PRODUCER'S OFFICE
Table and chairs, Stage Left

MARY'S HOUSE
Simple furnishings (table, chair), Center Stage

CAESAR'S PALACE
- Throne, Center Stage
- Chair beside throne for Scribe
- Lavish furnishings around stage to indicate throne room

BETHLEHEM STREET
- Facade to represent buildings, Center Stage
- Sign reading "Inn" on a door that can be opened

SHEPHERDS' CAMP
- Campfire, Center Stage
- Optional—Tents

HEROD'S PALACE
- Throne, Center Stage
- Lavish furnishings around stage to indicate throne room, different from Caesar's throne room

THE PLAYERS

SHEPHERD ONE (Grade 5 or older)

SHEPHERD TWO (Grade 3 or older)

SHEPHERD THREE (Grade 1 or older)

CHILD (Grade 1 or older)

MARY (Grade 3 or older)

CAESAR (Grade 3 or older)

SPEAKING CLOWN (Grade 3 or older)

SPEAKING ANGEL (Grade 3 or older)

WISE MAN (Grade 3 or older)

WRITER (Grade 5 or older)

PRODUCER (Grade 5 or older)

GABRIEL (Grade 5 or older)

JOSEPH (Grade 5 or older)

INNKEEPER (Grade 5 or older)

HEROD (Grade 5 or older)

STAGEHANDS (All ages)

NONSPEAKING PARTS (Scribe, Wild Animals, Acrobats, Jugglers, Soldiers, Musicians, Clowns, Singer, Dancers, Flunkies, Shepherds, Angels, Wise Men) (All ages)

SUGGESTED PROPS

■ Ascot and beret for Producer

■ Crowns for Caesar and Herod (same crown could be used for both)

■ Wild animal costumes

■ Clown costumes and balloons

■ Large cardboard thermometer

■ Credit card (homemade)

■ Small sheaf of papers (ten to twenty) to represent Writer's script

■ Large sheaf of papers to represent Producer's changes

■ Bible-times costumes

■ Angel costumes

■ Gifts for Wise Men

■ Modern secretary's clothing for Scribe

■ Notebook

■ Bible

DIRECTOR'S TIPS

1. Stage directions indicate that you are to open and close a curtain. If your stage area does not have a curtain, Stagehands can set up and break down sets in view of audience.

2. After noisy scenes, be sure Producer and Writer wait for quiet before continuing with the play.

3. Use any available talents (gymnasts, mimes, etc.) for Caesar's palace scene.

4. Mary and Joseph need a quick change of costume from peasant robes to fancy robes. It may be easiest to use a different Mary and Joseph for the Writer's concept of the scene and the Producer's concept.

5. Jugglers, Dancers, Singers, etc. could also have Angel and Shepherd parts if you need more actors. Stagehands can also be actors.

THE SIMPLE CHRISTMAS STORY

(WRITER is seated at table, waiting nervously, drumming fingers, twiddling thumbs, etc. PRODUCER enters, Stage Left, and crosses to table, carrying script. The WRITER jumps up in anticipation.)

PRODUCER: Sit down, kid. *(Both sit. PRODUCER taps script.)* I LOVE it.

WRITER: You do? Then you'll make my story into a movie?

PRODUCER: Of course I will. It's a natural! It'll be a winner. It DID, however, need a few minor alterations.

WRITER *(nervously)*: Alterations?

PRODUCER: Nothing major, kid. *(Yells offstage.)* Bring in the revised script!

(Two FLUNKIES enter, Stage Left, carrying large sheaf of papers between them and laboriously place it on table, then exit, Stage Left.)

PRODUCER: This is just the Act One revisions, but you get the idea.

WRITER: But what was wrong with MY story?

PRODUCER: It was too SIMPLE. It didn't have any oomph! *(Picks up small script and opens it to first page.)* Look here. This is your Scene One.

(PRODUCER and WRITER consult script while curtain opens on MARY's house. MARY could be sewing, cleaning, cooking, etc.)

WRITER *(reading from script)*: A young woman named Mary is working in her home. Suddenly, an angel of the Lord appears to her...

(GABRIEL enters, Stage Right, startling MARY.)

GABRIEL: Hail! You are blessed among women! The Lord is with you.

MARY *(puzzled)*: Who are you? What are you saying? What do you mean?

GABRIEL: Fear not, Mary. For you have pleased God.

MARY: I have?

GABRIEL: You shall have a child and shall call Him "Jesus."

MARY: Me? Have a baby?

GABRIEL: He shall be called the Son of the Highest, and God will give Him the throne of David. His kingdom will never end.

MARY: But I CAN'T have a baby. I'm not married! I don't have a husband.

GABRIEL: The Holy Spirit will come upon you. The child born of you will be called the Son of God.

(MARY sits down, stunned. GABRIEL exits, Stage Right, as curtain closes.)

WRITER: *(To PRODUCER.)* What's wrong with Scene One?

PRODUCER: Well, in the first place, you have Mary doing HOUSEWORK. What kind of job is THAT for the female lead? She needs something more glamorous, more EXCITING. Corporate vice president, lawyer, something high-powered.

WRITER: But she was a peasant!

PRODUCER: Peasant, schmeasant! No way. That's DULL! *(Turns page of small script.)* Then there's this bit about the baby. Who's going to believe she'd be worried about being a mother before she's married?

WRITER: But she WAS worried! She was concerned. You don't understand!

PRODUCER: But I DO understand, kid. I know what SELLS! Listen kid, the thing's too simple. No production value. It needs some pizzazz! So here's what we'll do. We'll cut that scene. Replace it with Caesar's palace. Color, excitement!

(Curtain opens to reveal Caesar's palace set.)

PRODUCER: We'll have jugglers, acrobats, clowns, musicians...

(Characters enter from both sides of stage as PRODUCER speaks. JUGGLERS enter juggling, ACROBATS do cartwheels, MUSICIANS play, CLOWNS run to give balloons to people in front row, etc.)

PRODUCER *(shouting above noise)***:** There'll be singers, dancers...

(SINGERS enter singing, DANCERS do a simple line dance.)

PRODUCER *(still shouting)***:** ...wild animals!

(Children dressed in animal costumes enter, snarling and growling.)

PRODUCER *(still shouting above noise)***:** Suddenly! *(Noise stops. PRODUCER speaks normally.)* CAESAR enters.

(CAESAR slowly enters, Stage Right. All on stage bow down. CAESAR waves graciously and seats himself on his throne.)

CAESAR: I need to make a decree.

(SPEAKING CLOWN runs up to the throne.)

SPEAKING CLOWN *(holding up large cardboard thermometer)***:** If you had ninety-eight point six decrees, you'd be NORMAL.

CAESAR: Be gone, fool! *(Calls offstage.)* Send me a scribe.

(SCRIBE enters, Stage Right, dressed as modern secretary, carrying notebook. Sits in chair beside throne to take notes in notebook as CAESAR speaks.)

CAESAR: I hereby decree that all people shall go back to their ancestors' towns so that all the world can be counted. AND, of course, TAXED! *(Dismisses SCRIBE with a wave of his hand.)*

(SCRIBE exits, Stage Right.)

CAESAR: Well, THAT'S a good day's work. I think I'll have a nap. *(Yawns regally, then exits, Stage Right. All others follow, exiting as they had entered, ANIMALS snarling, SINGERS singing, DANCERS dancing, etc. Curtain closes.)*

PRODUCER: *(To WRITER.)* Now THAT'S an opening scene. It has everything! The audience will be riveted to their seats.

WRITER: But it spends too much time on Caesar and his palace!

PRODUCER: Too much TIME on Caesar? Kid, Caesar was the most important man there was! Emperor of the World. You can't spend too much time on Caesar.

WRITER: But in this story, there's only one reason he's mentioned! His decree caused prophecy to be fulfilled. It meant that the Messiah would be born in Bethlehem.

PRODUCER: *(Shaking head.)* Kid, kid! Listen to ME! My way is better. Take a little time to think it over. You'll see. Let's look at another scene—the one in Bethlehem.

WRITER: *(Flips through script. Reads.)* "So Joseph took his wife, Mary, and traveled to Bethlehem. But they arrived late. There was no room at the inn..."

(Curtain opens to reveal Bethlehem street scene. JOSEPH and MARY, dressed as peasants, enter, Stage Left.)

MARY: It's awfully late. Do you think we'll find a room?

JOSEPH: We'll find a room. There's the inn. *(JOSEPH knocks on inn door.)*

(INNKEEPER opens door.)

JOSEPH: We need a place to stay.

INNKEEPER: You and a thousand others! Move on. I've got no room.

JOSEPH: But we must have a room. My wife is about to have a baby.

INNKEEPER: We all got problems. You two are having a baby; I'm having a nervous breakdown. Beat it! I got NO room.

JOSEPH: But, any place will do! A small corner.

INNKEEPER: Read my lips. *(Speaks slowly.)* N-O R-O-O-M! *(Closes door).*

(JOSEPH and MARY turn to leave as door opens again.)

INNKEEPER: Hey, mister.

JOSEPH: *(Turns back.)* Sir?

INNKEEPER: This ain't much, but it's all I can do. The stable's just around the corner. You can maybe find some clean straw and a place to lie down there. But it don't smell too good. It IS a stable.

JOSEPH: *(Grabs INNKEEPER's hand and shakes it.)* Thank you! Thank you, sir. We'll take it. *(Exits with MARY, Stage Right. INNKEEPER watches them go, then closes door.)*

WRITER: What's wrong with THAT scene?

PRODUCER: This Joseph, he's supposed to be the HERO, right?

WRITER: Well, kind of.

PRODUCER: You've made him look STUPID. Can you imagine not phoning ahead for reservations?

WRITER: But they didn't HAVE phones!

PRODUCER: Minor detail. HERE'S how the scene should play.

(JOSEPH and MARY enter, dressed in fine robes, Stage Right.)

MARY: It's awfully late. Do you think we'll find a room?

JOSEPH: We'll find a room. There's the inn. *(JOSEPH knocks on inn door.)*

(INNKEEPER opens door.)

JOSEPH: We need a place to stay.

INNKEEPER: You and a thousand others. Move on. I got no room.

(JOSEPH takes out credit card and shows it to INNKEEPER.)

JOSEPH: But I made a reservation yesterday—with my Judean Express Card. *(Grandly hands credit card to INNKEEPER.)*

INNKEEPER: *(Carefully examines card.)* Joseph, son of Heli. Oh, yeah! *(Changes from gruff tone to smooth, gracious speech. Gives a little bow.)* Excuse me, sir, for not knowing YOU. We have the Emperor Suite all ready for you and your charming, eh...wife. Best in the house. *(Returns credit card to JOSEPH.)*

JOSEPH: *(Holds up card, speaks to audience.)* The Judean Express Card. Don't leave Nazareth without it. *(Enters inn in grand fashion, with MARY. INNKEEPER closes door as curtain closes.)*

PRODUCER: Now, isn't that BETTER? Our heroine gets a better place in which to have her baby, and now Joseph looks like a real hero! PLUS—and you got to CONSIDER these things—a certain credit card company will chip in a BUNDLE to help us produce the movie!

WRITER: But that's NOT what happened!

PRODUCER: Hey! We're making a MOVIE, not writing a history book! My way works better. Trust me. I know this business. *(Flips through small script.)* Now HERE'S a scene we REALLY like.

WRITER: Amazing. A scene you plan to leave ALONE?

PRODUCER: Sure, kid! The shepherds out in the field.

WRITER: *(Takes script from PRODUCER and finds place. Reads.)* "And in the same country, there were shepherds staying in the field, keeping watch over their flocks at night..."

(Curtain opens. SHEPHERDS are huddled around camp fire.)

SHEPHERD ONE: It's a cold night. Who has first watch?

SHEPHERD TWO: *(Points at SHEPHERD THREE.)* Him.

SHEPHERD THREE: I ALWAYS have to take first watch! Why ME?

SHEPHERD TWO: Because you're the YOUNGEST.

(ANGEL enters, Stage Left. A bright light shines. All SHEPHERDS scream and hide their faces.)

SPEAKING ANGEL: Don't be afraid! I bring you news of great joy!

SHEPHERD ONE: *(Looks up, shielding eyes.)* Who are YOU?

SPEAKING ANGEL: I am a messenger of the most high God. Today, in the City of David, a Savior has been born.

(Other SHEPHERDS look up, shielding their eyes.)

SHEPHERD THREE: A Savior?

SHEPHERD TWO: How will we know Him? There are THOUSANDS of people in Bethlehem tonight.

SPEAKING ANGEL: This will be a sign to you. You will find the baby wrapped in cloth and lying in a manger.

(Other ANGELS enter, Stage Left.)

OTHER ANGELS: Glory to God in the highest! And on earth, peace and goodwill. *(Other ANGELS exit, Stage Left, except for SPEAKING ANGEL, who exits Stage Right.)*

SHEPHERD ONE: Let's go to Bethlehem and see the child. *(Exits with all SHEPHERDS, Stage Left. Curtain closes.)*

WRITER *(excitedly)*: I can't believe it! You're leaving that scene as it IS?

PRODUCER: Well, we ARE making a few minor changes.

WRITER *(suspiciously)*: Such as?

PRODUCER: Well, we have to tie it in to the changes in the other scenes. *(Takes a deep breath.)* SO...

(Curtain opens. SPEAKING ANGEL enters, Stage Right.)

SPEAKING ANGEL: You will find the baby wrapped in the finest linen money can buy, in a BEAUTIFUL crib at the inn. The EMPEROR suite, of course.

(SPEAKING ANGEL exits, Stage Right. Curtain closes.)

WRITER: But I keep telling you, it didn't HAPPEN that way!

PRODUCER: It will in OUR movie! And you know, if we're going to have angels, we need special effects. I've got some TERRIFIC ones planned!

WRITER: Like what?

PRODUCER: *(Rises to feet to demonstrate.)* First, they'll zoom in like rockets through the sky. Horrible-looking, ghostly faces, fangs. Then, one of the shepherds looks up when he shouldn't, and his face melts! Yes!

WRITER: I SAW that somewhere already. It's been DONE.

PRODUCER: It doesn't matter! It SELLS! We'll do it again!

WRITER: But why would the angels HARM the shepherds? The angels are there to announce good news. The Savior is born! There is JOY, not death!

PRODUCER: *(Lays an arm across shoulders of WRITER in fatherly fashion.)* Listen, kid. NEVER let the facts interfere with good special effects!

WRITER: *(Pulls away.)* I don't know about this...

PRODUCER: Trust me. I know my business. We'll have a HIT! Just listen to this last scene—you'll see what I mean. Here's how YOU'VE written it.

(Curtain opens to reveal Herod's palace. HEROD is seated on throne, SOLDIERS stand behind throne. WISE MEN enter, Stage Left.)

WISE MAN: *(Bowing to HEROD.)* Your Majesty.

HEROD: I certainly AM! What do you want? I'm a busy man, a busy man.

WISE MAN: We've come to present our gifts to the newly born King.

HEROD: WHAT new king?

WISE MAN: The one whose star we've seen in the East.

HEROD: Impossible! If there was a new king born, I would be the FIRST to know.

WISE MAN: But there MUST be a newly born King. We saw His star.

> *(All the WISE MEN nod in agreement.)*

HEROD: Well, you must be mistaken. But I'll find out. Guard!

> *(One SOLDIER moves to front of throne and salutes.)*

HEROD: Go and ask my counselors where some King is supposed to be born.

> *(SOLDIER salutes and exits, Stage Right.)*

HEROD: While we're waiting, why don't you show me the GIFTS you brought?

WISE MAN: We brought gifts fit for the King! We brought gold. *(Shows his gift to HEROD.)*

WISE MAN: Frankincense! *(Shows his gift.)*

WISE MAN: And myrrh. *(Shows his gift.)*

HEROD *(rubbing his hands greedily)*: WONDERFUL gifts. I LOVE them!

> *(SOLDIER enters, Stage Right, and whispers to HEROD.)*

HEROD: *(To WISE MEN.)* Good. I have the information you need. This King is supposed to be born in Bethlehem. Go search for Him. When you have found Him, come and tell me where He is. Then I can...uh...go and worship Him, too.

WISE MAN *(bowing)*: As Your Majesty wishes.

> *(WISE MEN exit, Stage Left.)*

HEROD: Guards!

> *(All SOLDIERS move to front of throne and salute.)*

HEROD: Get all the soldiers together. When those eastern wise men tell me where to FIND this King, I'll give Him MY present—His own personal beheading! *(Laughs maniacally.)* And maybe I'll be able to retrieve all those other gifts as well. *(SOLDIERS salute and exit, Stage Left.)*

> *(Curtain closes.)*

WRITER: That's right. Then the wise men are warned in a dream not to return to Herod. What's wrong with THAT?

PRODUCER: It's not so much THAT part. It's what happens next. All those babies killed in Bethlehem.

WRITER: But you want to kill a bunch of SHEPHERDS!

PRODUCER: That's different. These are BABIES. You can't kill BABIES in a Christmas movie! People wouldn't buy tickets. We need a good, warm, happy ending. Here's what we'll do.

(Curtain opens to reveal Herod's palace with throne facing the opposite direction. HEROD is seated and SOLDIERS are standing behind throne. WISE MEN stand in front of throne.)

WISE MAN: *(Bowing to HEROD.)* Your Majesty.

HEROD: I certainly AM! What do you want? I'm a busy man, a busy man.

WISE MAN: We've come to present our gifts to the newly born King.

HEROD: WHAT new king?

WISE MAN: The one whose star we've seen in the East.

HEROD: Impossible! If there was a new king born, I would be the FIRST to know.

WISE MAN: But there MUST be a newly born King. We saw His star.

(All the WISE MEN nod in agreement.)

HEROD: Well, you must be mistaken. But I'll find out. Guard!

(One SOLDIER moves to front of throne and salutes.)

HEROD: Go and ask my counselors where some King is supposed to be born.

(SOLDIER salutes and exits, Stage Left.)

HEROD: While we're waiting, why don't you show me the GIFTS you brought?

WISE MAN: We brought gifts fit for the King! We brought gold. *(Shows his gift to HEROD.)*

WISE MAN: Frankincense! *(Shows his gift.)*

WISE MAN: And myrrh. *(Shows his gift.)*

HEROD *(thoughtfully)***:** Wonderful gifts. Simply wonderful.

(SOLDIER enters, Stage Left, and whispers to HEROD.)

HEROD: Ah! I have the information you want. This new King is to be born in Bethlehem.

WISE MAN: Thank you so much! We'll go there immediately. *(WISE MEN turn to leave.)*

HEROD: Wait!

WISE MAN: *(Turning back to HEROD.)* Yes, Your Majesty?

HEROD: You brought all these wonderful gifts for the new King.

WISE MAN: Yes, Your Majesty.

HEROD: *(Begins to whine.)* No one ever brings ME gifts anymore. Why not?

WISE MAN: Perhaps, Your Majesty, you have been an evil king.

HEROD *(sniffling)***:** Yes! I have!

WISE MAN: Perhaps your subjects no longer love you.

HEROD *(wiping tears)***:** You're right! They don't!

WISE MAN: *(Points at HEROD.)* You need to CHANGE.

HEROD: *(Stops crying, snaps fingers.)* That's it! Guards!

(SOLDIERS all move to front of throne and salute.)

HEROD *(grandly)***:** Gather all my possessions. Bring me a bag of gold to give to the new King. Then, give EVERYTHING else to all the POOR people in Jerusalem!

(SOLDIERS turn to exit.)

HEROD: Guards!

(SOLDIERS turn and salute.)

HEROD: Tell the royal chef to cook the fattest goose he can find. I'm going to take it to the house of that poor scribe. The one with the lame son.

(SOLDIERS salute, turn and exit, Stage Right.)

WISE MAN: You are most generous to your people, Your Majesty.

HEROD: *(Clasps hands, looks upward.)* I see how WRONG I've been. Come, let's go to Bethlehem TOGETHER. We'll find the new King. Let's try the Emperor Suite at the inn first. Then, we'll ALL come back to Jerusalem and have a happy Christmas dinner together!

(Curtain closes as HEROD and WISE MEN exit, Stage Right.)

PRODUCER: There! That's exactly the kind of heart-warming ending a Christmas movie needs.

WRITER: But IT'S ALL WRONG!

PRODUCER: Nonsense. It'll SELL. My way is best.

(CHILD, carrying Bible, walks up from front of audience to the PRODUCER, tugs on his sleeve.)

CHILD: Mister.

PRODUCER: What do you want, kid?

CHILD: Your movie is all WRONG!

PRODUCER: What do you mean, it's wrong? You're just a little kid. How do YOU know?

CHILD: *(Holds up Bible.)* Because Mommy read the story to me already! From this Book.

(Curtain opens to reveal manger scene. MARY and JOSEPH are seated behind the manger. ANGELS stand in a semicircle behind them. WRITER takes Bible from CHILD and opens it to Luke 2:16.)

WRITER *(reading)*: "So they hurried off and found Mary and Joseph, and the baby, who was lying in a manger."

(SHEPHERDS enter, Stage Left, and kneel to worship Jesus. WRITER turns to Matthew 2:11.)

WRITER *(reading)*: "On coming to the house, they saw the child with his mother Mary, and they bowed down and worshiped him. Then they opened their treasures and presented him with gifts of gold and of incense and of myrrh."

(WISE MEN enter, Stage Right, kneel and present their gifts. WRITER takes CHILD by hand to join the manger scene, kneeling to worship Jesus. CAESAR, HEROD and SOLDIERS enter, Stage Right, and move to the front of the stage. PRODUCER walks over to join them. PRODUCER looks over his shoulder at manger scene, then faces audience and shakes his head.)

PRODUCER: It's too SIMPLE. It'll NEVER sell!

THE SPIRIT OF CHRISTMAS

(APPROXIMATE TIME: 10 MINUTES)

SYNOPSIS
A mad scientist and his assistant concoct Christmas spirit—in their own way.

STAGE SETTING: MAD SCIENTIST'S LABORATORY
■ Work table with scientific equipment (beakers, bottles, etc.) laid on it, Center Stage
■ "Thinking chair" in front of work table
■ "Radio table," Stage Left, behind work table

THE PLAYERS
MAD SCIENTIST (Grade 5 or older)
IGOR (Grade 3 or older)

SUGGESTED PROPS
■ Lab coat for Mad Scientist
■ Large coat for Igor
■ Papers and pencil laid on work table
■ Ruler and protractor laid on work table
■ Tape player to play tape and to represent radio
■ Three photographs to represent "chestnuts"
  (These need not be actual photos of people mentioned in the skit, since no one will see photos.)
■ Cassette tape with recording of "Johnny B. Goode"
■ Small plastic rocket
■ Cardboard cutout of a toe
■ Bottle of Canada Dry ginger ale
■ Cassette tape with recording of someone reading Luke 2:8-17 while instrumental Christmas carol is playing in background
■ Large cooking pot and wooden spoon
■ Matches
■ Bottle of shampoo

DIRECTOR'S TIPS
1. The Mad Scientist is on the verge of insanity (or perhaps several steps over the line). He is always on the point of hysteria.
2. Igor is subservient to, and in awe of, the Mad Scientist.

THE SPIRIT OF CHRISTMAS

(MAD SCIENTIST is busy, mixing chemicals in pot, making notes on paper, etc.)

MAD SCIENTIST: Where is he? I can't complete my work without those items!

IGOR: *(From offstage.)* I'm coming, Master. I'm coming. *(Enters, wearing a large coat.)*

MAD SCIENTIST: It's about time! I need those ingredients! Did you get everything on the list?

IGOR: *(Bows.)* I got everything, Master. I have it all.

MAD SCIENTIST: *(MAD SCIENTIST looks grandly at audience.)* Then, soon it will all be mine. Soon, I shall...dare I say it?

IGOR: Say it, Master! Please! Say it!

MAD SCIENTIST: *(Picks up ruler, waves it as if it were a scepter while he speaks.)* Soon, I shall RULE the WORLD.

IGOR: I LOVE it when you say that.

MAD SCIENTIST: Yes! I shall be the RULER of the world.

IGOR: Oh, Master! Can I be something, too?

MAD SCIENTIST: Let me think. *(Moves to chair and holds position of "The Thinker" for a moment.)* Yes! I shall be Ruler and you can be...

IGOR *(excitedly)***:** Yes? Yes?

MAD SCIENTIST: *(Picks up protractor, shows it to IGOR.)* You can be Protractor!

IGOR: *(Falls to knees and kisses hem of MAD SCIENTIST's lab coat.)* Oh, thank you, thank you, Master!

MAD SCIENTIST: Yes. While I keep my subjects in line, you can think up angles. But enough of this idle chatter! *(Points.)* To work!

(IGOR jumps to his feet. MAD SCIENTIST and IGOR move to work table.)

IGOR: Yes, Master. But what are you making?

MAD SCIENTIST: You've heard people complaining about this time of year! Too much to do! Not enough time! They don't have any... *(Waits for IGOR to answer.)*

IGOR: Credit left on their MasterCards?

MAD SCIENTIST: No! They don't have any Christmas spirit! Well, I shall make it—and patent it. Then, when someone needs some, they'll have to come to me. Yes, with this absolutely potent elixir, I shall be Absolute Potentate (PO-t'n-tayt)!

IGOR: And I shall be your Detractor!

MAD SCIENTIST: That's "Protractor," you imbecile.

IGOR: Yes, Master. Sorry.

MAD SCIENTIST: Now! To work. *(Holds out hand.)* Chestnuts!

(IGOR hands MAD SCIENTIST three pictures.)

MAD SCIENTIST: *(Looking at pictures.)* What are these? I told you to get chestnuts!

IGOR: *(Points to first picture.)* That's Bobby Fischer. To be a world chess champion, you HAVE to be a chess nut.

MAD SCIENTIST: Very well. He qualifies. *(Crumples picture and throws it into pot.)*

IGOR: *(Points to next picture.)* That's a bodybuilder—running around, showing off his chest in the middle of winter with no shirt on.

MAD SCIENTIST: Definitely a chest nut. *(Crumples picture and throws it in pot.)*

IGOR: *(Points to last picture.)* And that's Mark Chesnutt, the country music singer.

MAD SCIENTIST: Excellent! *(Crumples picture and throws it in pot. Rubs hands together.)* Three chestnuts. Excellent! Now, we need to roast them on an open fire. (Strikes match and holds it under the pot to roast "chestnuts.")

IGOR: Oh, Master! Already I can feel the glow of your Christmas Sprite!

MAD SCIENTIST: That's SPIRIT! And we've only just begun. *(Holds out hand.)* Next, holly berries!

(IGOR hands MAD SCIENTIST a cassette tape.)

MAD SCIENTIST: What's this?

IGOR: Oh, Master! I couldn't find holly berries. I got something better!

(MAD SCIENTIST puts tape into tape player and pushes "play." Listens to part of "Johnny B. Goode.")

IGOR: See, Master? I got some classic CHUCK Berry!

MAD SCIENTIST: Let me think. (Moves to thinking chair and assumes "The Thinker" pose for a moment.) Yes! It should work. (Returns to tape player, ejects tape and throws it into pot on work table.) Now! *(Holds out hand.)* Mistletoe!

(IGOR hands MAD SCIENTIST a rocket and a cardboard cutout of a toe. MAD SCIENTIST looks at one item, then the other, shrugs to audience and tosses rocket and toe into pot. IGOR takes spoon and eagerly stirs.)

MAD SCIENTIST: Now for the champagne! A little something to make it bubble!

IGOR: I have it, Master! I have it! *(Pulls bottle of shampoo from under coat.)*

IGOR: Here it is, Master. *(Brings bottle to MAD SCIENTIST.)*

MAD SCIENTIST: Idiot! I said, "Champagne!" Not "Shampoo!"

(IGOR looks shamefaced. IGOR leaves stage and moves through audience, looking carefully at various people.)

IGOR: I don't think we'll find any champagne in this crowd.

MAD SCIENTIST: Let me think! Let me think! *(Goes to chair and assumes "The Thinker" pose briefly.)*

MAD SCIENTIST: I'll find the right substitute even if I have to drink Canada Dry to do it.

IGOR: *(Removes another bottle from coat and holds it under MAD SCIENTIST's nose.)* Would you like some ginger ale while you think, Master?

MAD SCIENTIST: *(MAD SCIENTIST grabs bottle.)* Of course! *(To audience.)* I'm a genius! I'll use the "Champagne of Ginger Ales." *(MAD SCIENTIST pours contents of bottle into pot. IGOR stirs eagerly with spoon.)*

MAD SCIENTIST: Now, we'll just wait for the chemical reaction to happen.

IGOR: How long will it take, Master?

MAD SCIENTIST: It could be hours. Why don't you see if there's anything on the radio? *(IGOR stops stirring, goes to radio tape player, runs finger over it and returns to MAD SCIENTIST.)* There's nothing but dust on the radio, Master.

MAD SCIENTIST: Fool! I meant, turn the radio on so we can hear it.

(IGOR places cassette into tape player as he turns his back to audience and pretends to turn on radio. On cassette, Christmas carol plays in background as a person reads Luke 2:8-17. MAD SCIENTIST turns off tape player.)

IGOR: *(Sighs.)* Doesn't that just make you feel warm all over?

MAD SCIENTIST: Nonsense! Shepherds and angels and baby Jesus have nothing to do with Christmas! Christmas is about—making MONEY! Enough money to...dare I say it?

IGOR: Yes, Master! Say it!

MAD SCIENTIST: Rule the world! That stuff on the radio can't be any good.

IGOR: Why not?

MAD SCIENTIST: Because it's free. My elixir will be VERY expensive. That's how people will know it's good. *(Looks into pot, then yawns.)* Good work, Igor. It's time to get some rest. Take my potion with you and let it work overnight. Today, the lab. Tomorrow, the world!

IGOR: *(Struggles to pick up pot.)* Yes, Master!

MAD SCIENTIST: I'll need a good name and an advertising jingle. Something bouncy. *(Goes to chair and adopts "The Thinker" pose briefly.)*

MAD SCIENTIST: *(Stands, excited.)* Yes! I have it! I'll call it "Supersonic Tonic."

(Sings to tune of "Jingle Bells," as he exits.)

In the dumps? Feeling blue?

Here comes Christmas cheer!

Supersonic Tonic makes

Your Christmas last all year!

IGOR: *(To audience as he exits, carrying pot.)* My master is a genius.

LENT AND EASTER

(LENT ONE)

COMPLETELY IN CHARGE?

(APPROXIMATE TIME: 8-10 MINUTES EACH)

SYNOPSIS
Caesar and his court try to discover what's happening in Judea, who Jesus is and what He is doing.

STAGE SETTING: CAESAR'S PALACE
■ Throne for Caesar with small table beside it, Center Stage

■ Table and chairs for Advisors, Stage Left

■ Lavish surroundings (drapery, wall hangings, pillars, etc.)

THE PLAYERS
ADVISOR TWO (Grade 3 or older)

ADVISOR ONE (Grade 5 or older)

ADVISOR THREE (Grade 3 or older)

SOLDIER ONE (Grade 1 or older)   **SOLDIER TWO** (Grade 3 or older)

SOLDIER THREE (Grade 1 or older)   **SOLDIER FOUR** (Grade 3 or older)

SERVANT GIRL ONE (Grade 1 or older)   **SERVANT GIRL TWO** (Grade 1 or older)

SERVANT GIRL THREE (Grade 3 or older)   **CAESAR** (Grade 5 or older)

OTHER SOLDIERS, ADVISORS (All ages)   **STAGEHANDS** (All ages)

SUGGESTED PROPS
■ Caesar's throne

■ Candle to provide sealing wax

■ Large ring for Caesar

■ Soldiers' uniforms

■ Glass of water, tray

■ Pillow

■ Bible-times costumes

■ Crown for Caesar

■ Scrolls for advisors

■ Soldiers' weapons (swords, shields, spears, etc.)

■ Loaf of bread

■ Notepad and quill pen for Advisor Three

■ Papers for reading and signing; pen, laid on Caesar's table

DIRECTOR'S TIPS
1. This first skit is a comedy. The actors may "ham it up" if they wish.

2. When Soldiers capture Servant Girls, warn players to capture girls in such a way that while it may appear rough to the audience, it is gentle in reality.

3. To salute Caesar, player places right arm across chest and gently thumps chest with fist. This running visual gag will be more effective if it is practiced until it comes naturally.

4. Help Advisor Three practice delivering his line "Something's happening!" in different ways for comic effect.

COMPLETELY IN CHARGE?

(CAESAR is seated on his throne, Center Stage, reading and signing documents. All SOLDIERS stand around him in a semicircle. ADVISORS are seated at a table to CAESAR's left, reading scrolls and discussing the contents with each other.)

ADVISOR ONE: Something's happening! *(Shows scroll to other ADVISORS who nod in agreement. All ADVISORS rise and approach CAESAR.)*

ADVISOR ONE: Hail, Caesar! *(Salutes.)*

ADVISOR TWO: Hail, Caesar! *(Salutes.)*

ADVISOR THREE: Hail, Caesar! *(Salutes.)*

SOLDIERS: Hail, Caesar! *(Salute.)*

CAESAR: *(Stands, saluting.)* Hail, ME! *(Thumps chest so strongly, he knocks himself back into throne. Looks dazed for a moment.)*

ADVISOR ONE: Mighty Caesar, live forever!

CAESAR: If you insist.

ADVISOR ONE: We have something to show you.

ADVISOR TWO: Something MOST important.

ADVISOR THREE: Something's HAPPENING.

CAESAR: Of COURSE something's happening! This is ROME. Something's ALWAYS happening in Rome.

ADVISOR TWO: No. It's NOT happening in Rome.

CAESAR: Nothing's happening in ROME? You're joking.

ADVISOR ONE: Of COURSE things are happening in Rome. But in Judea...

ADVISOR THREE: Something's HAPPENING!

CAESAR: *(Looks bored.)* Is this going to be a long story?

ADVISOR ONE: It may be.

CAESAR: Then I need to have something to drink. *(Yells offstage.)* Water!

(SERVANT GIRL ONE enters, Stage Right, with glass of water on tray. She places it on CAESAR's table and turns to leave. CAESAR takes drink.)

CAESAR: Now that's water fit for... *(Stands and yells.)* CAESAR!

(SOLDIER ONE and SOLDIER TWO stop SERVANT GIRL ONE and escort her back to CAESAR.)

SOLDIER ONE: We have her, Sire.

CAESAR: I can SEE that. WHY do you have her?

SOLDIER TWO: You said, "Seize her!" So we did.

(*CAESAR looks puzzled, then suddenly understands.*)

CAESAR: No, no, no. I didn't say… (*Points to SERVANT GIRL ONE.*) …"SEIZE her!" I said… (*Taps himself on chest.*) "CAESAR!" (*Looks around, peeved.*) Wait a minute. When I say "CAESAR," everyone's supposed to salute!

(*SOLDIERS and ADVISORS salute. SERVANT GIRL ONE takes opportunity to sneak to exit, Stage Right. SOLDIERS return to their stations. CAESAR sits.*)

CAESAR: That's better. (*To ADVISOR ONE.*) Now, what's this about…

ADVISOR ONE (*interrupting*): Judea, Sire.

ADVISOR THREE: SOMETHING'S happening!

CAESAR: Yes, yes, yes. You said that before. What's happening?

ADVISOR TWO: Miracles.

CAESAR: Nonsense. Miracles don't happen.

ADVISOR ONE: They do in Judea!

ADVISOR TWO: We have proof! (*Taps scroll.*) Right here.

CAESAR: (*Points to scroll.*) I suppose you want me to read that.

(*ADVISOR TWO bows and holds out scroll to CAESAR.*)

CAESAR: This looks like a TEDIOUS job. I'll need some food for strength. (*Yells offstage.*) Bread!

(*SERVANT GIRL TWO enters, Stage Right, with loaf of bread on tray. She places it on CAESAR's table and turns to leave. CAESAR takes a bite.*)

CAESAR: (*Smacks his lips.*) Now THAT'S bread fit for… (*Stands and yells.*) CAESAR!

(*SOLDIER THREE and SOLDIER FOUR stop SERVANT GIRL TWO and escort her back to CAESAR.*)

SOLDIER THREE: We have her, Sire.

SOLDIER FOUR: You said, "Seize her!" So we did.

(*CAESAR looks upward in disgust.*)

CAESAR: Not… (*Points to SERVANT GIRL TWO, shaking head, no. Taps himself on chest, nodding his head.*) CAESAR!

(*SOLDIERS and ADVISORS salute reflexively. SERVANT GIRL TWO takes opportunity to exit, Stage Right. SOLDIERS return to their stations. CAESAR sits.*)

CAESAR: Now, then. You expect me to read this?

ADVISOR ONE: Only the relevant parts, Sire.

ADVISOR TWO: Only the parts that show…

ADVISOR THREE: Something's happening!

(*CAESAR opens scroll to read it but looks puzzled.*)

CAESAR: What IS this gibberish? This can't be read!

(ADVISOR TWO walks behind CAESAR to read over his shoulder, then takes scroll and turns it around. CAESAR has been holding it upside down. ADVISOR TWO returns to other side of table.)

CAESAR: Oh, yes. MUCH better. Now let's see... *(Mumbles as he reads.)* Water into wine. Very IMPRESSIVE. BLIND man healed. LEPERS healed. Ooooh...someone raised from the DEAD! VERY impressive. Who is doing all these things?

ADVISOR ONE: A man named Yeshua (Yuh-SHOE-uh).

CAESAR: Bless you! What did you say His name was?

ADVISOR TWO: Yeshua!

CAESAR: Bless you, too. My, my. Is everyone coming down with a COLD?

ADVISOR ONE: No, Mighty Caesar. The man's name is *(Slowly and deliberately.)* Yeshua.

CAESAR: THAT'S a strange name. I've never heard of a name like that.

ADVISOR TWO: That's His name in Hebrew, Sire. In Greek, His name is...

(ADVISORS huddle together to confer in whispers.)

ADVISOR THREE: Jesus!

CAESAR: Well. Jesus, is it? Some magician is doing a few tricks. I don't think that's cause for CONCERN. But this throne—it's DEFINITELY a cause for concern. It's so HARD! *(Yells offstage.)* Pillow!

ADVISOR ONE: But, Mighty Caesar, if this Jesus continues to trick people...

ADVISOR TWO: ...they may begin to believe He is a god.

(SERVANT GIRL THREE enters, Stage Right, with pillow and stands by CAESAR.)

CAESAR: He can't do THAT! Only CAESAR can be a god! Look! *(Removes ring and shows it to ADVISORS and SOLDIERS.)*

CAESAR: See! I have the ring! *(Places ring on table near SERVANT GIRL THREE. He sees her and stands so she can place pillow on throne. CAESAR sits again. SERVANT GIRL THREE sees ring on table and slyly steals it. She turns to leave.)*

CAESAR: Ahhhhh! That's better. A pillow fit for... *(Notices ring is missing. He jumps up and yells.)* SEIZE HER!

(SOLDIERS and ADVISORS snap to attention and salute while SERVANT GIRL THREE flees, Stage Right.)

CAESAR: *(Yells and stomps.)* No, no, NO! She stole my RING! Get it BACK!

(SOLDIERS exit, Stage Right, in hot pursuit.)

CAESAR: Now. *(Taps scroll.)* About this Judean situation. What should I do?

ADVISOR ONE: You must be better informed.

ADVISOR TWO: You must find out what's happening!

CAESAR: You're right. Take a letter.

ADVISOR THREE: *Q?*

ADVISOR TWO: *J?*

ADVISOR ONE: *X?*

CAESAR: No, no, NO! Write something down.

> *(ADVISOR THREE takes notepad and quill pen and pretends to write what CAESAR dictates.)*

CAESAR: To Pontius Pilate, Jerusalem, Judea. Look up the zip code yourself. Dear PP— *(To ADVISORS.)* I always call him PP, you know. Ahem, where was I?

ADVISOR THREE *(reading)*: "Dear PP—"

CAESAR: Right. Dear PP. Am advised of magician calling himself Sneezy or something like that in your neighborhood. Check Him out and stop Him if it seems advisable. Your Emperor and god...ME!

ADVISOR THREE: *(Ends letter with a flourish.)* Me!

CAESAR: Not YOU. *(CAESAR points to himself.)* ME! Ah, well. That's a good day's work. I wonder if they've caught that thief yet. *(Rises and begins to exit, Stage Right.)* Guards! Guards! Have you caught the thief? *(Exits, Stage Right.)*

> *(ADVISOR ONE and ADVISOR TWO follow CAESAR offstage. ADVISOR THREE finishes proofreading letter, folds it and pretends to seal it with candle wax. He places folded letter on CAESAR's table and looks at audience.)*

ADVISOR THREE: Something's HAPPENING.

> *(ADVISOR THREE hurries off, Stage Right, after others.)*

(LENT TWO)

MOTHER'S WORRY

(APPROXIMATE TIME: 5-10 MINUTES)

SYNOPSIS

Mary and Martha talk with their visitors about what's happening in Jesus' life and ministry.

STAGE SETTING: MARY AND MARTHA'S HOUSE

Table and five chairs, Center Stage

THE PLAYERS

MARY ONE (Jesus' mother) (Grade 5 or older)

MARY TWO (Mary Magdalene) (Grade 3 or older)

MARY THREE (Martha's sister) (Grade 1 or older)

MARTHA (Grade 5 or older)

JOANNA (Grade 3 or older)

STAGEHANDS (All ages)

SUGGESTED PROPS

■ Broom for Mary Three

■ Fabric, needles and thread for Joanna, Mary One and Mary Two to sew

■ Loaf of bread

■ Jug of water

■ Plates and cups

■ Butter

■ Bible-times costumes, including aprons for Martha and Mary Three

DIRECTOR'S TIPS

1. The women are seated at the table and work on small sewing projects as they talk.

2. Martha is brusque with her little sister, but she does love Mary. Don't let Martha seem too overbearing.

3. When Mary Two mimics Pilate, have her lower the pitch of her voice to simulate that of a man.

(LENT TWO)
MOTHER'S WORRY

(JOANNA, MARY ONE and MARY TWO are sitting around a table sewing, Center Stage. MARY THREE is dreamily sweeping, Stage Right. MARTHA is being the perfect hostess, coming and going from Stage Left.)

MARY THREE: *(Stops sweeping.)* Something's happening!

JOANNA: *(Looks up at MARY THREE.)* Did you say something, dear?

(MARY THREE stops sweeping and approaches other women.)

MARY THREE: Something's happening.

MARY TWO: What's happening, dear?

MARY THREE: *(Shakes head, no.)* I don't know.

MARTHA: *(Strides in from Stage Left, wiping hands on apron.)* I know what's happening—NOTHING! Mary, get back to work. Sometimes I think you're the LAZIEST sister a woman could have.

(MARY THREE goes back to sweeping the floor, briskly at first, then dreamily again.)

JOANNA: *(To MARTHA.)* You shouldn't be so hard on your little sister, Martha.

MARTHA *(snapping)***:** What do YOU know about it? She always leaves me to do ALL the work! ESPECIALLY when Jesus comes to visit.

(MARY ONE stops sewing and stares at the floor. The others stop and look at her. MARY THREE moves to MARY ONE, squats beside her.)

MARY TWO: *(To MARTHA.)* Now you've done it.

MARY THREE: *(To MARY ONE.)* Don't worry. It'll be all right.

MARTHA: *(Sits down.)* I don't know what all the fuss is about. He's MY friend, too.

JOANNA: Yes. But He's not your son.

MARY ONE: *(To JOANNA.)* No, Martha's right. I shouldn't be upsetting everyone. It's just... *(Looks down again.)*

MARTHA: It's just that you're worried about Jesus. But He's a big boy now, Mary. He knows how to look after Himself.

MARY ONE: Sometimes I wonder. All those things He says. It almost seems that He WANTS to be in trouble with the priests and Pharisees.

MARTHA: So what? What are they going to DO? The same thing they always do. Make a bunch of noise and tell Him not to come to the Temple again. It's not like they're going to KILL Him.

MARY THREE *(shocked)*: Martha!

JOANNA: No, Martha's right.

MARTHA: Thank you, Joanna.

MARY TWO: Sure, she's right. You don't have to worry about Jesus, Mary. After all, He has His friends with Him. They won't let anything happen to Him. Especially Peter. He's as good a friend as a man could have.

JOANNA: He surely is. No matter what, Peter will always be true.

MARY THREE: But what if they DO try to kill Jesus?

MARTHA: They won't. That would be murder. Only the ROMANS can execute someone.

MARY TWO: That's right. And Caiaphas (KAY-eh-fehs) would never do ANYTHING to make the Romans REALLY angry with him.

JOANNA: That's right. He knows which side HIS bread is buttered on!

MARTHA: *(Jumps to her feet.)* Bread! I've been letting you sit here and starve. Mary, come with me. Let's get some lunch for our guests. *(MARTHA and MARY THREE hurry off, Stage Left.)*

MARY ONE: I know I shouldn't worry. But I do.

MARY TWO: It's perfectly understandable. Mothers SHOULD worry about their children.

JOANNA: And Jesus DOES say some outrageous things!

MARY TWO *(chuckling)*: Can you imagine? Calling the Pharisees "white-painted tombs"!

JOANNA: And calling the priests and scribes "snakes"! *(Chuckles.)*

(MARTHA and MARY THREE enter, Stage Left, with bread, a jug of water, plates and cups.)

MARY ONE: *(Shakes her head, no.)* That's what I mean! How can a man say all those things to such important people? You know that they WANT to kill Jesus.

MARTHA: *(Sets down cups and plates.)* Wanting and doing are two different things, Mary.

MARY THREE: *(Sets down bread and jug.)* I'd sure miss Him if anything happened.

MARTHA: *(To MARY THREE.)* Nothing's going to HAPPEN!

MARY THREE: Then why does it SEEM like something's happening?

JOANNA: It's just your imagination, dear. When you get older, you'll know. A young woman can just let her imagination run away with her!

MARY ONE: I'm not so sure it's her imagination. I feel the same way.

JOANNA: But you're a MOTHER. Mothers sometimes let their imaginations run wild, too.

MARY TWO: Besides, how can they really hurt JESUS?

MARY ONE: What do you mean?

MARY TWO: Look at all He's done. He's healed the sick. He's even raised people from the dead.

MARTHA: Which reminds me, where IS Lazarus?

MARY THREE: He said he was going hunting.

MARTHA: *(Rolls her eyes.)* Just like him to disappear when guests are coming—leaving ME to get everything ready. *(Looks around table.)* Mary, we forgot the butter. Go and get it, please.

(MARY THREE exits, Stage Left.)

MARY ONE: I wish I just didn't feel so...so...

JOANNA: Worried?

MARY ONE: That's it. That's it, exactly.

MARY TWO: Worrying is what mothers do. Don't worry about it! *(Chuckles at her joke.)*

MARTHA: *(Calls offstage.)* Mary! Where ARE you? Can't you find the butter?

(MARY THREE hurries onstage from Stage Left, carrying butter that she places on table.)

MARTHA: Where have you been? How long does it take to get a little butter?

MARY THREE: I'm sorry. I was looking out the window, thinking.

MARTHA *(sarcastically)*: I am so blessed! A brother who disappears and a sister who can't find the butter because she's looking out the window!

JOANNA: Oh, Martha. She's still young. She'll grow out of it.

MARY THREE: But what if...what if Jesus IS in real danger? What'll we do? *(Pauses, looks down at her plate.)* Something's happening. I know it!

(MARY ONE stares down at her plate also.)

MARTHA: Now look what you've done! You're upsetting Mary again.

MARY THREE: But you all know that the priests and scribes want to kill Jesus.

MARTHA: *(Rolls eyes.)* How many times must we go THROUGH this?

JOANNA: *(To MARY THREE.)* Mary, the priests and scribes can't kill ANYONE.

MARY TWO: Only the Romans can do that!

MARY THREE *(thoughtfully)*: Maybe the Romans will.

MARTHA: *(Snorts.)* Why WOULD they?

MARY THREE: I don't know. People do strange things sometimes!

JOANNA: Not the ROMANS. They only care about their law.

MARTHA: And they have NO reason to sentence Jesus to DEATH.

MARY TWO: *(Chuckles to herself.)* I can almost see Pontius Pilate if the chief priest asks him to have Jesus killed. *(Stands and looks very officious, imitating Pilate.)* What's the matter with you, anyway? Don't you Jews have better things to do than waste my time? Go back to your sacrifices and leave me alone!

(All laugh, even MARY ONE.)

MARTHA: That's him. That's a perfect imitation of Pilate!

JOANNA *(chuckling)***:** His sneer. His frown. You have him to a *T*!

MARY THREE *(clapping her hands)***:** Do some more!

MARY ONE: *(To MARY TWO.)* I see now that I've been worrying for nothing. Thank you, Mary.

MARY TWO: *(Looks out window. To MARTHA.)* My dear, the sun is getting low. We must be going.

JOANNA: *(To MARTHA.)* We'll just help you clean up before we go.

(MARY ONE, MARY TWO, JOANNA and MARTHA gather up dishes and food from the table. Move to exit, Stage Left.)

MARTHA: *(To MARY THREE.)* Sweep the floor. And THIS time, do a good job. Get all the crumbs.

(MARY THREE starts sweeping while humming a happy tune. Then she stops sweeping and shivers. Walks toward the audience.)

MARY THREE: *(To audience.)* Something's happening.

(MARY THREE runs offstage, Stage Left.)

(LENT THREE)

HE WHO HAS EARS

(APPROXIMATE TIME: 8-10 MINUTES)

SYNOPSIS

Caiaphas and his fellow leaders attempt to understand what's happening in Jerusalem to threaten their control.

STAGE SETTING: CAIAPHAS'S OFFICE

■ Table and chair for Caiaphas, Center Stage

■ Table and chair for Scribe One, Stage Left

■ Filing cabinets, other office furnishings

■ Council chairs for Scribes, Priests and Advisors, set in a semicircle, Stage Right

THE PLAYERS

CAIAPHAS (KAY-eh-fehs) (Grade 5 or older)   **SPY ONE** (Grade 3 or older)

SPY TWO (Grade 3 or older   **SPY THREE** (Grade 5 or older)

SCRIBE ONE (Grade 5 or older)   **SCRIBE TWO** (Grade 5 or older)

PRIEST ONE (Grade 5 or older)   **PRIEST TWO** (Grade 3 or older)

PRIEST THREE (Grade 3 or older)   **STAGEHANDS** (All ages)

NONSPEAKING SCRIBES, ADVISORS, PRIESTS (All ages)

SUGGESTED PROPS

■ Papers for Caiaphas to read

■ Paper and pen for Scribe One

■ Notepad for Scribe One

■ Bible-times costumes, including belts in which to stuff handkerchiefs

■ Four large handkerchiefs for Scribe Two and Spies One, Two and Three

DIRECTOR'S TIPS

1. Scribe Two and the three Spies can be played as comedy parts in this skit.

2. Caiaphas should be very serious at all times. He speaks deliberately, as if he—and his words—are of great importance.

3. Consider using older players in the nonspeaking roles to help younger players know where to move on the stage.

(LENT THREE)

HE WHO HAS EARS

(CAIAPHAS is seated at his table, reading reports. SCRIBE ONE is seated at table to CAIAPHAS's left, writing. Other SCRIBES scurry about, filing reports, taking papers from SCRIBE ONE's table to CAIAPHAS, taking papers from CAIAPHAS's table to other SCRIBES, etc.)

CAIAPHAS *(while reading)*: Something's happening.

(All SCRIBES stop what they are doing to listen to CAIAPHAS.)

SCRIBE ONE: *(Glances up from reading.)* I beg your pardon, Lord Caiaphas? Did you say something?

CAIAPHAS: *(Looks at SCRIBE ONE.)* I SAID, "Something's HAPPENING."

SCRIBE ONE: Why do you say that, Sir?

CAIAPHAS: *(Holds up report he is reading.)* Because of THIS.

(SCRIBE TWO takes report from CAIAPHAS, reading it as he takes it to SCRIBE ONE. SCRIBE ONE reads it briefly and returns it to SCRIBE TWO, who returns it to CAIAPHAS.)

SCRIBE ONE: *(To CAIAPHAS.)* I don't see anything UNUSUAL in it.

CAIAPHAS: Because you read with UNENLIGHTENED EYES. *(Grandly.)* He who has eyes, let him see.

SCRIBE TWO: *(Aside to SCRIBE ONE, imitating CAIAPHAS.)* And he who has a nose, let him blow.

CAIAPHAS: *(Rises, angrily to SCRIBE TWO.)* Have you nothing BETTER to do with your time?

SCRIBE TWO: Uh...no, Sir. I mean yes, Sir. I have a nose. I'm blowing. *(Removes handkerchief from belt, blows nose loudly as he joins other SCRIBES who return to their work.)*

SCRIBE ONE: What IS it about that report, Sir?

CAIAPHAS: Read between the lines. Pontius Pilate's behavior is changing—ever so slightly.

SCRIBE ONE: So?

CAIAPHAS: So, WHY? Why is his behavior CHANGING?

SCRIBE TWO: Bad breakfast?

CAIAPHAS: *(Shakes head, no.)* Perhaps. But maybe, just MAYBE, something is on his mind. Maybe he's received a message from ROME. Maybe something BIG is happening. *(Reads report again.)*

(SCRIBE ONE continues writing. PRIEST ONE enters, Stage Right, shaking his head. He approaches SCRIBE ONE and begins to whisper.)

CAIAPHAS: I have EARS. Speak UP, so I may hear.

PRIEST ONE: Lord Caiaphas, the spies we sent out have returned.

CAIAPHAS: Excellent! Have them come in and report.

PRIEST ONE: *(Rolls eyes.)* If I must. *(Exits, Stage Right.)*

CAIAPHAS: *(Rises, speaks brightly to SCRIBE ONE.)* NOW we'll know what's happening!

(PRIEST ONE and SPIES enter, Stage Right, and approach CAIAPHAS.)

CAIAPHAS: Report! What's Pilate up to?

(SPIES look at each other and measure comparative heights with their hands. They finally agree on a height just a bit taller than they are.)

SPY ONE: He's just about the same height he's always been.

SPY TWO: I don't think you grow much after you reach age twenty.

SPY THREE: *(Grandly waving them off.)* You idiots! Caiaphas knows THAT!

(CAIAPHAS nods his approval to SPY THREE.)

SPY THREE: He KNOWS Pilate isn't getting taller. BUT when you get older, sometimes you SHRINK. *(Conspiratorially, to CAIAPHAS.)* But Pilate isn't shrinking yet.

(CAIAPHAS slaps palm to his head and shakes his head in disgust.)

PRIEST ONE: *(To CAIAPHAS.)* And these were the best spies we could find.

CAIAPHAS: *(To SPIES.)* What is Pilate DOING?

SPY ONE: He gets up in the morning.

SPY TWO: He does a full day's work.

SPY THREE: And then, he goes to bed at night.

(CAIAPHAS looks at PRIEST ONE in disgust. PRIEST ONE shrugs.)

CAIAPHAS: Haven't you been spying on Pilate?

SPY ONE: Not really.

SPY TWO: We've been busy.

SPY THREE: In the marketplace. Watching Jesus!

CAIAPHAS: Aha! So you have a report on HIS activities?

SPY ONE: We do.

SPY TWO: We pretended to be just curious.

SPY THREE: So we went up to Him and said, "We're just curious. What do you think about the tax situation here in Israel?"

CAIAPHAS: And?

SPY ONE: And He tried to ROB us!

CAIAPHAS: He did?

SPY TWO: Yes. He said, "Give Me your money."

CAIAPHAS: *(Rubs hands together eagerly.)* Excellent! A criminal offense.

PRIEST ONE: I'm afraid not.

(CAIAPHAS looks at PRIEST ONE in surprise.)

CAIAPHAS: No?

PRIEST ONE: No.

SPY THREE: I gave Him a penny. And He looked at the image on it. Boy, is He ignorant!

CAIAPHAS: Why do you say that?

SPY THREE: Because He doesn't know whose PICTURE is on the money! He asked me, "Whose image is this?" And I had to tell Him, "That's Caesar." He didn't know! Then He said I should give what is Caesar's to Caesar and what is God's to God. Go figure!

CAIAPHAS: *(Angrily, to SPIES.)* Fools! All of you! Do you have eyes?

(SPIES all nod, yes.)

CAIAPHAS: Then USE them to SEE. Do you have EARS?

(SPIES all nod, yes.)

CAIAPHAS: Then USE them to HEAR. Do you have NOSES?

(SPIES all nod, yes.)

CAIAPHAS: *(CAIAPHAS points to exit, Stage Right.)* Then BLOW!

SCRIBE TWO: *(To other SCRIBES.)* I gave him that one.

(SPIES pull out and fumble with handkerchiefs, blowing noses loudly.)

CAIAPHAS: *(Shouts to SPIES.)* Find out what Pilate is DOING!

(SPIES exit, Stage Right, still blowing noses.)

CAIAPHAS: *(To PRIEST ONE.)* Bring in the council.

(PRIEST ONE exits, Stage Right. CAIAPHAS and SCRIBE ONE move to council chairs. CAIAPHAS sits in center chair, SCRIBE ONE sits on one end. Other SCRIBES move to positions behind chairs as PRIEST ONE and rest of ADVISORS enter, Stage Right. They take the remaining council chairs. SCRIBE TWO takes his position directly behind CAIAPHAS. As ADVISORS speak, SCRIBE ONE takes notes.)

CAIAPHAS: We have a serious situation, gentlemen.

(ADVISORS look at each other, look back at CAIAPHAS and ask, "What is it? What's happening?" etc.)

CAIAPHAS: You will recall that I warned you before of someone named Yeshua, also known as Jesus.

PRIEST TWO: We remember.

PRIEST ONE: *(To ADVISORS.)* He's still at it.

PRIEST THREE: More miracles?

PRIEST ONE: Worse than THAT. More preaching and teaching. And all our traps have FAILED!

CAIAPHAS: Every time we think we have Him cornered, He wriggles out.

PRIEST ONE: He's making a mockery of us!

PRIEST TWO: Are more people believing in Him?

CAIAPHAS: Yes. And you know what THAT means.

PRIEST THREE: The Romans.

CAIAPHAS: Precisely.

PRIEST ONE: If we can't control the religious fervor of our people, the Romans will remove us from power—and replace us with people who CAN.

PRIEST TWO *(alarmed)***:** They wouldn't do that! Would they?

CAIAPHAS: They WOULD. And I think it might possibly be in the works.

PRIEST THREE: What do you mean?

CAIAPHAS: Pilate's behavior has changed slightly.

PRIEST TWO: So?

CAIAPHAS: So what if he received a letter from Rome?

SCRIBE TWO: *(To other SCRIBES.)* I like this game. What if wishes were horses? Then beggars would ride instead of walk.

(CAIAPHAS reaches up, grabs SCRIBE TWO by the collar and pulls his head down.)

CAIAPHAS: If MY wishes were horses, a certain SCRIBE would be TRAMPLED. *(Releases SCRIBE TWO and looks at other ADVISORS.)* Do you remember my words at our previous meeting?

(SCRIBE ONE flips back through notes and reads from minutes of previous meeting.)

SCRIBE ONE *(reading)***:** "You know nothing at all! You do not realize that it is better for you that one man die for the people than that the whole nation perish."[1]

CAIAPHAS: *(To ADVISORS.)* Have you EARS? Then listen. We MUST find a way to capture Jesus and bring Him to the council!

PRIEST ONE: What good will that do? We have no charge against Him.

CAIAPHAS: Have we no BRAINS? We'll FIND one.

PRIEST TWO: STILL no good. WE can't execute Him.

CAIAPHAS: Leave that to me. I'll find a way.

SCRIBE TWO: *(Aside, to other SCRIBES.)* Maybe he'll trample Jesus to death with his wish horses.

CAIAPHAS: *(Reaches up, grabs SCRIBE TWO's collar and pulls his head down.)* If you have something POSITIVE to CONTRIBUTE, DO so. Otherwise, BE QUIET!

SCRIBE TWO: *(Still held by the collar.)* Well, there is ONE possibility.

CAIAPHAS: *(Releases SCRIBE TWO.)* And that is...?

SCRIBE TWO: I understand that one of Jesus' disciples might be open to a little BRIBE.

PRIEST TWO: Which one?

SCRIBE TWO: One by the name of Judas. Judas Iscariot.

PRIEST ONE: Why would he betray his Master?

CAIAPHAS: Who CARES? Get him. If he can help us destroy Jesus, we'll USE him. Does anyone have anything further?

(ADVISORS all shake their heads and say, "No. Nothing.")

CAIAPHAS: Then let's adjourn—and await our OPPORTUNITY.

(PRIESTS, ADVISORS and SCRIBES all exit, Stage Right.)

CAIAPHAS: *(Returns to table, picks up report. Turns to exit, Stage Right, then stops to speak to audience.)* SOMETHING'S happening. But I WILL control it. *(Exits, Stage Right.)*

[1]John 11:49,50

(LENT FOUR)
LUCIFER'S LABORS

(APPROXIMATE TIME: 8-10 MINUTES)

SYNOPSIS
Satan and his demons take stock of their efforts to control what's happening.

STAGE SETTING: SATAN'S OFFICE
- Table and chair for Satan, Center Stage
- Chair on each side of desk
- Red lighting to give appearance of flames
- Five council chairs in semicircle, Stage Right, for Maleficent, Cowardice, Greed, Nonsequitur and Satan

THE PLAYERS
SATAN (Grade 5 or older)

GREED (Grade 5 or older)

NONSEQUITUR (non-SEK-wih-tur) (Grade 5 or older)

MALEFICENT (me-LIH-fe-sent) (Grade 5 or older)

COWARDICE (Grade 5 or older)

STAGEHANDS (All ages)

NONSPEAKING DEMONS (All ages)

SUGGESTED PROPS
- Filing cabinets, other office implements
- Reports for Satan to read
- Business suits, briefcases for Demons
- Papers for Demons to carry back and forth

DIRECTOR'S TIPS
1. Satan is a very deadly, dangerous enemy. There is no comedy in his character. He should be under-played to increase the menace when his anger shows. Because of the nature of this skit, teens and adults may be best suited for these parts.

2. All Demons are afraid of Satan and jealous of each other.

(LENT FOUR)

LUCIFER'S LABORS

(SATAN is seated at table, Center Stage, reading a report. DEMONS scurry about, bump into each other, drop papers, snarl at each other, etc.)

SATAN *(looking up at audience)*: Something's HAPPENING.

(GREED enters, Stage Left, laughing evilly.)

SATAN: I LIKE the sound of that laugh. Something EVIL is happening!

(GREED sits down to right of SATAN's desk.)

GREED: I DID it. I've worked long and hard, and I DID it!

SATAN: ANOTHER success for US? You, Greed, are my most faithful lieutenant. Again and again, where others fail, you succeed. Tell me of our LATEST triumph.

GREED: *(Laughs again.)* It's Judas! I've got him tied up with his own money belt.

SATAN *(interested)*: Yes? Yes?

GREED: First, I started him dipping into Jesus' disciples' traveling funds. But that was only the beginning. *(Laughs evilly as NONSEQUITUR enters, Stage Left.)*

NONSEQUITUR *(suspiciously)*: What's so funny?

SATAN: Greed was just about to relate MY newest TRIUMPH.

GREED: *(Looks at SATAN.)* YOUR—?

SATAN *(staring at GREED)*: Yes. MINE!

GREED *(nervously)*: Yes. Of course. YOUR latest triumph.

NONSEQUITUR: *(Sits.)* What triumph?

SATAN: Yes, tell us.

GREED: Well, I started with Judas coveting the disciples' traveling funds.

SATAN *(impatiently)*: You told me that.

GREED: Well, after I got him thinking that stealing from those funds wasn't so bad...

NONSEQUITUR: *(Interrupts, leaping up.)* You? YOU? What about ME? *(Shakes finger in GREED's face.)* You had nothing to DO with it! It was MY work!

GREED: *(Rising.)* Nothing? You call my work NOTHING? I made him think that HE could use the money more wisely than the others! I did THAT!

SATAN *(sharply)*: Sit down, both of you! This is MY triumph.

(GREED and NONSEQUITUR sit and glare at each other.)

SATAN: Continue, Greed. *(To NONSEQUITUR.)* And if I want YOUR opinion, I'll GIVE it to you. Understand?

(NONSEQUITUR nods.)

GREED: As I was saying before being so RUDELY interrupted, after I had Judas believing that STEALING was OK, I had him right where I wanted him. It was just a SHORT step to BETRAYAL.

SATAN (*sighing with pleasure*): Betrayal. What a lovely word.

GREED: Thirty pieces of silver should be enough to make him hand Jesus over to the priests and scribes. (*Laughs.*)

SATAN (*annoyed*): You call this a TRIUMPH?

GREED (*confused*): Of course.

SATAN: (*Rises, gesturing.*) I have such incompetents working for me! Nonsequitur, you'll have to bail out this fool—again.

NONSEQUITUR: What do you want me to do?

SATAN: Is this a KINDERGARTEN? Must I spell everything out?

GREED: If you spell, he won't understand.

NONSEQUITUR: Better than you. You only understand money!

SATAN: Quiet! Both of you. We need to give Judas more motivation than money. Something he can tell himself to excuse his unpardonable behavior.

NONSEQUITUR: Hmmm. An excuse. I'm good with those. (*Thinks hard.*) YES!

SATAN: (*Sits, eager.*) You have something?

NONSEQUITUR: Judas CAN'T believe he's greedy.

SATAN: True. (*Points upward.*) HE did give all men a conscience.

NONSEQUITUR: So, I get him thinking NOBLE thoughts. Start with patriotism.

SATAN: Good. I like it. Turn something good to evil.

NONSEQUITUR: I'll keep repeating, "The Romans are evil. Jesus will overthrow Rome."

SATAN: Yes. I did a good job on all of Israel, making them think HE (*SATAN points upward.*) plans to destroy Rome soon.

NONSEQUITUR (*indignantly*): YOU?

SATAN (*snarling*): Me!

NONSEQUITUR: Yes. Of course. YOU. Anyway, I got him telling himself, *Since Jesus will certainly overthrow Rome, why shouldn't I help things along—and make a profit? I'll lead them to Jesus. Once He's arrested, He'll HAVE to destroy Rome to set up His government.*

SATAN: I LIKE it. Take an evil act and pretend it's NOBLE. This is one of MY best ideas. Unfortunately, the two of you will have to...

GREED (*horrified*): Don't say it!

NONSEQUITUR: Not the *C* word!

SATAN: (*Smiles and leans toward them.*) Yes. COOPERATE.

(*GREED and NONSEQUITUR scream and cover their ears.*)

SATAN: (*Rises, pointing.*) Now go and MAKE IT HAPPEN! If it doesn't work, BOTH of you will be blamed.

GREED: (*Stands.*) I'll try. But he messes up everything.

NONSEQUITUR: *(Stands.)* ME? I'm the only one who THINKS around here. *(Both exit, Stage Left, arguing.)*

SATAN: Arguing. I LOVE that sound.

(MALEFICENT and COWARDICE enter, Stage Left. MALEFICENT points in the direction of GREED and NONSEQUITUR, laughing.)

SATAN: Maleficent, do I detect YOUR hand in this?

(MALEFICENT and COWARDICE run to the chair at right of SATAN's table and fight over who will sit there. MALEFICENT wins and sits in the chair. COWARDICE stares at MALEFICENT, hands on hips. SATAN motions COWARDICE to other chair.)

SATAN: Sit here. In the less-favored chair.

(COWARDICE sits.)

SATAN: What have you got to report?

MALEFICENT: I have done a MAGNIFICENT job.

COWARDICE: *(To MALEFICENT.)* You! Yours was easy. MINE was the tough job.

SATAN: As much as I love to hear arguing, get on with it!

MALEFICENT: The priests are in a murderous rage. They'll do ANYTHING I tell them if it will harm Jesus.

SATAN: Excellent! *(To COWARDICE.)* What have YOU done, Cowardice?

COWARDICE: I've been working on Pontius Pilate. He's the key.

MALEFICENT: Nonsense! MY work is the key. The priests must hate Jesus.

COWARDICE: What good is hate without power? Only Pilate can sentence Jesus to death. *(Grandly.)* Now, we all know that Pilate doesn't care about the Jews.

MALEFICENT *(proudly)***:** I did that!

COWARDICE *(scornfully)***:** As if THAT would be difficult.

SATAN: Pilate's attitude will pose a problem. *(To MALEFICENT.)* And you were responsible. Why don't the two of you change chairs?

(MALEFICENT and COWARDICE switch places. As they pass each other, MALEFICENT snarls at COWARDICE, who swaggers to the favored chair.)

SATAN: *(To COWARDICE.)* What's your plan?

COWARDICE: Simplicity itself. Pilate fears only one man—Caesar! So I had Caesar send a letter to Pilate.

SATAN: Excellent! No governor likes a letter from Caesar unless it's full of praise for his work.

COWARDICE: Which this letter ISN'T. It suggests that Caesar is watching Pilate carefully— just WAITING for him to slip!

SATAN: Beautiful! How do I come up with these plans?

COWARDICE *(indignantly)***:** You?

SATAN *(snarling)***:** ME!

COWARDICE: Of course. You. YOUR plan.

SATAN: Go and keep up the evil work. Maleficent, keep the priests angry. But don't stop with them. Work on the crowds as well.

MALEFICENT: But how? They love Jesus!

SATAN: I don't CARE how. Just DO it! Failure will not be tolerated.

MALEFICENT: Of course.

SATAN: And Cowardice, keep working on Pilate. Trouble his dreams. And work on his wife as well. A troubled household helps keep the ball rolling.

COWARDICE: An excellent suggestion.

SATAN: A SUGGESTION? From ME? No! It was an ORDER.

COWARDICE: Yes. Of course. Excellent ORDER, sir.

SATAN: Before you go, we need a council meeting. Call my other lieutenants!

(One NONSPEAKING demon runs to exit, Stage Left. SATAN, MALEFICENT and COWARDICE move to council chairs. SATAN takes the middle seat while MALEFICENT and COWARDICE fight over the seat to his immediate right. COWARDICE wins this time. GREED and NONSEQUITUR enter, Stage Left, and approach council chairs. They glare at MALEFICENT and COWARDICE who have taken the best seats and sit in the other chairs. NONSPEAKING Demons in the background sneak forward to listen.)

SATAN: We all know something's happening.

GREED: Of course.

SATAN: Did I ask you to speak?

GREED: No.

SATAN: Then don't. Now, where was I? Oh, yes. We all know something's happening. We can feel it. *(Points upward.)* HE is up to something. Jesus is not walking the earth for nothing. *(Looks at ADVISORS.)* WELL?

(ADVISORS nod and say, "Of course." "Naturally." etc.)

SATAN: Once again, we don't know HIS...*(points upward)*...plan. But we DO know we don't like it. We must STOP it. And the best way to block HIM...*(points upward)*...is to kill Jesus as soon as possible.

(ADVISORS nod and say, "Of course," "Naturally," etc.)

SATAN: I have made a brilliant plan that you will carry out. Jesus will die—and die SOON. Any failure will be SWIFTLY punished. Is that understood?

(ADVISORS rise, salute and say, "Yes, sir!")

SATAN: Then go and DO it. But remember, HE...*(points upward)*...will not stand by idly while we work. Have the army with you at all times. Michael and his warrior angels will attack. They MUST not stop us. Now, GO!

(GREED, NONSEQUITUR, MALEFICENT and COWARDICE all flee from SATAN's presence, Stage Left. They are followed by the other NONSPEAKING DEMONS.)

SATAN: *(Standing, to audience.)* Something's HAPPENING. And for once, I'M in control. *(Exits, Stage Left.)*

(LENT FIVE)

HEAVEN WAITS

(APPROXIMATE TIME: 8 MINUTES)

SYNOPSIS

The angels prepare for action—although they don't understand what's happening.

STAGE SETTING: HEAVEN

■ Table and chair for Michael, Center Stage, to the left
■ Table and chair for Gabriel, Center Stage, to the right

THE PLAYERS

ANGEL SOLDIER ONE (Grade 3 or older)

ANGEL SOLDIER TWO (Grade 3 or older)

ANGEL MESSENGER ONE (Grade 3 or older)

ANGEL MESSENGER TWO (Grade 3 or older)

MICHAEL (Grade 5 or older)

GABRIEL (Grade 5 or older)

STAGEHANDS (All ages)

NONSPEAKING ANGELS (All ages)

SUGGESTED PROPS

■ Maps and charts for Michael
■ Musical scores for Gabriel
■ Angel costumes

DIRECTOR'S TIPS

1. Heaven is harmonious. The players should be happy but not silly.

2. Michael and Gabriel do not always understand God's plan, but they are never worried. Don't let them sound excessively concerned when they express a desire to know what's happening.

3. Because of the difficulty of play, older students and adults may want to be involved.

(LENT FIVE)

HEAVEN WAITS

(MICHAEL and GABRIEL are seated at their tables. MICHAEL studies maps and charts; GABRIEL studies musical scores. In the background, ANGELS are moving about quietly. All is peaceful. If two ANGELS approach the same place, one politely motions the other ahead. From time to time, one of the NONSPEAKING ANGELS brings another map to MICHAEL, music to GABRIEL or takes something from one of the other ANGELS to file it, etc. NONSPEAKING ANGELS continue with their duties throughout skit.)

MICHAEL: *(Lays down maps, frowning.)* Something's happening.

GABRIEL: *(Looks up from work.)* What?

MICHAEL: I said, "Something's happening."

GABRIEL: And I said, "What?" What's happening?

MICHAEL: I don't KNOW.

GABRIEL: Then don't worry about it! If you need to know, He'll tell you.

MICHAEL: You're right. But all the same...

GABRIEL: Something's happening. *(They both laugh.)*

MICHAEL: And I'm worrying. *(Shakes head.)* What's the matter with me?

GABRIEL: I don't know. But if I need to know what's wrong with you, He'll tell me that, too! *(Chuckles, rises, holding music.)* Choir practice. Care to join us?

MICHAEL: No, I'll just continue my work, thanks anyway.

GABRIEL: If we'll be disturbing you, we can practice elsewhere.

MICHAEL: Disturb me? Your choir soothes me!

GABRIEL: Assemble the choir!

(NONSPEAKING ANGELS assemble as choir in an orderly fashion. GABRIEL leads them in a chorus of "Fairest Lord Jesus" or some other familiar song about Jesus. When choir is finished, ANGELS go back to their tasks and GABRIEL returns to his seat.)

MICHAEL: *(Sighs.)* Beautiful, as always.

GABRIEL: In heaven, perfection is easy.

MICHAEL: True. But on earth...

GABRIEL: *(Interrupts.)* Something's happening?

(ANGEL SOLDIER ONE approaches MICHAEL and salutes.)

ANGEL SOLDIER ONE: Sir, Greed is continuing to work on Judas Iscariot. What shall I do?

MICHAEL: Do nothing until the time. Continue to monitor the situation. Dismissed. *(Salutes.)*

ANGEL SOLDIER ONE: Yes, Sir! *(Salutes and exits, Stage Right.)*

MICHAEL: *(Goes back to checking maps. Points to map. To GABRIEL.)* Look here. *(Shows map to GABRIEL.)* Satan is working in Rome.

GABRIEL: That's not surprising! It's one of his FAVORITE places to work. Sin City!

MICHAEL: But his demon Cowardice is having Caesar send a message to Pilate. Why would he want to make Pilate afraid?

GABRIEL: God knows!

MICHAEL: But I don't. Why doesn't He tell me to DO something? I keep telling the other angels, "Do nothing until the time." But I'm beginning to feel like the TIME will never COME!

GABRIEL: He will tell us what to do. The time WILL come. Rest easy, my friend!

(ANGEL MESSENGER ONE approaches GABRIEL.)

GABRIEL: Yes? What is it?

ANGEL MESSENGER ONE: We're supposed to prepare for darkness at midday. And an EARTHQUAKE in the area of Jerusalem at about the same time!

GABRIEL *(concerned)*: What is this about?

ANGEL MESSENGER ONE: *(Hands paper to GABRIEL.)* We weren't given full details, Sir. But I've been told it involves great sorrow—sorrow like the earth has never seen.

GABRIEL: *(Reading message.)* Hmm. Thank you very much.

ANGEL MESSENGER ONE: Yes, Sir. *(Exits, Stage Left.)*

MICHAEL: Apparently, I'm not the only one who doesn't know what's happening.

GABRIEL: Obscure messages. That's all I've been getting lately. Deep sorrow. It sounds like events are coming together soon. *(Returns to his table, reading message over, shaking his head.)*

(ANGEL SOLDIER TWO approaches MICHAEL and salutes.)

MICHAEL: *(Salutes.)* Yes. What is it?

ANGEL SOLDIER TWO: *(Hands MICHAEL a message.)* Maleficent, Sir. That despicable demon! He continues to work on making the priests hate Jesus, Sir. But now, he's started working to create hatred and jealousy of Jesus in some unsuspecting citizens of Jerusalem. What shall I do?

MICHAEL: *(Sighs.)* You know the answer. Do nothing until the time. Continue to monitor the situation.

ANGEL SOLDIER TWO: Yes, Sir! *(ANGEL SOLDIER TWO salutes and exits, Stage Left.)*

GABRIEL: More activity. More STRANGE activity.

MICHAEL: Yes. The Messiah stands in the middle of a gathering storm. And I'm doing NOTHING.

GABRIEL: Yes, you ARE! You're waiting for the word of the Lord. His timing has never been wrong, in all of eternity!

MICHAEL: True.

(ANGEL MESSENGER TWO approaches GABRIEL.)

GABRIEL: Yes. What is it?

ANGEL MESSENGER TWO: (Hands paper to GABRIEL.) We have a message to send, Sir. But I'm not sure how we should send it.

GABRIEL: Who's it for?

ANGEL MESSENGER TWO: Caiaphas (KAY-eh-fehs), Sir. The High Priest in Jerusalem.

GABRIEL: Caiaphas?

ANGEL MESSENGER TWO: Yes, Sir.

GABRIEL: He'd never listen to any angel who came to talk to HIM! Simply send the idea. Make him think it's his own thought. That man won't take advice from anyone.

ANGEL MESSENGER TWO: Yes, Sir. (Exits, Stage Right.)

MICHAEL: So, you're sending messages you don't understand. I'm monitoring a situation I don't understand.

GABRIEL: (Gestures impatiently.) So what do we DO?

MICHAEL: What we ALWAYS do.

GABRIEL and MICHAEL: (Half laugh, half sigh.) WAIT—for the word of the Lord!

MICHAEL: (Picks up map, points.) Meanwhile, I'll position soldiers here, here, here and here. That way, we'll be in a perfect position to counter any move Satan might make and still be ready to launch our own offensive.

MICHAEL: (To GABRIEL.) SOMETHING'S happening.

GABRIEL: (Pats MICHAEL's shoulder.) And God's in control of it.

(GABRIEL and MICHAEL nod to each other. MICHAEL gathers up his maps and exits, Stage Left, followed by the ANGEL SOLDIERS. GABRIEL gathers up his music and exits, Stage Right, followed by the ANGEL MESSENGERS.)

(PALM SUNDAY)

EARTHLY TRIUMPH

(APPROXIMATE TIME: 8-10 MINUTES)

SYNOPSIS

Jesus' disciples anticipate future happenings as they wait for Jesus' arrival at the Upper Room.

STAGE SETTING: THE UPPER ROOM

■ Large table with chairs for Disciples, Center Stage

■ Small table, Stage Right

THE PLAYERS

CHILDREN (Grade 1 or older)   **JAMES ONE** (Grade 3 or older)

JAMES TWO (Grade 3 or older)   **PHILIP** (Grade 3 or older)

ANDREW (Grade 3 or older)   **SIMON** (SY-mun) (Grade 3 or older)

NATHANIEL (Grade 3 or older)   **MATTHEW** (Grade 3 or older)

THOMAS (Grade 3 or older)   **JUDAS** (Grade 3 or older)

JOHN (Grade 5 or older)   **PETER** (Grade 5 or older)

BARTHOLOMEW (bahr-THOL-eh-mu) (Grade 3 or older)

STAGEHANDS (All ages)

NONSPEAKING PEOPLE IN CROWD (All ages)

SUGGESTED PROPS

■ Food on table

■ Palm branches for children to wave

■ Money bag and ledger for Judas

■ Large bowl and towel for small table, Stage Right

■ Bible-times costumes

DIRECTOR'S TIPS

1. This skit can be played on Palm Sunday as part of the Lent series or may be produced independently.

2. The Disciples are not perfect. They should not be played as comedy characters, but their foibles, petty jealousies, etc., should be played realistically.

3. Because of the complexity of the characters, use some teen and adult players.

EARTHLY TRIUMPH

(The DISCIPLES, except for PETER and JUDAS, are seated around a table, Center Stage, prepared for a meal with Jesus.)

JAMES ONE: *(Leans forward, excited.)* Something's happening!

JOHN: I'll say it is! We're about to become PRINCES.

PHILIP: *(Points.)* And I suppose you two still want to be CHIEF princes?

ANDREW: *(Nudges PHILIP.)* Knock it off, Philip! That's over. We'll ALL be princes. Nobody will be chief.

SIMON: *(Rises, gesturing excitedly.)* Jesus will be King, and we'll be His princes. Everyone will bow down to us. We'll be famous!

NATHANIEL: *(Leans back, arms folded.)* What makes you think we'll be princes? *(SIMON sits, thoughtful.)*

MATTHEW: We HAVE to be. Jesus will be King! Of COURSE we'll be His princes!

BARTHOLOMEW: Things will be GREAT!

JAMES TWO: Everything we want will be ours.

THOMAS: Gold, fine clothes, spices!

NATHANIEL: Excuse me, gentlemen, but how can we be princes? Princes are sons of kings.

JAMES TWO: *(To the others.)* He has a point.

JOHN: Come on, Nathaniel! Jesus will make us princes. He can change ALL the rules when He becomes King.

ANDREW: *(Shaking head, no.)* I don't know. Maybe Nathaniel is right.

PHILIP: *(Thinking aloud.)* He COULD be. Sure! He's right.

JAMES TWO: *(Irritated, waving.)* You two brothers always stick together. I WANT to be a PRINCE.

MATTHEW: Strictly speaking, Nathaniel IS right. We CAN'T be princes.

THOMAS: *(To MATTHEW.)* Who put YOU in charge? Jesus can make EVERYTHING different.

MATTHEW: I didn't say things wouldn't be different. We can still be important people in Jesus' kingdom. We just can't be princes.

NATHANIEL: That's what I was saying!

PHILIP: What could we be if we're not princes?

MATTHEW: We could be important government officials.

JAMES TWO: You mean, like governor of a country?

MATTHEW: Possibly.

JOHN: What about Minister of the Treasury?

MATTHEW: That's a distinct possibility.

THOMAS: *(Chuckles.)* You'd be PERFECT for that job, Matthew. After all, you had a lot of experience collecting taxes for the Romans.

BARTHOLOMEW: *(Chuckling, shakes head, no.)* But you'll have to fight Judas for the money bag. And I doubt he'll let it go!

(JUDAS enters, Stage Right, as his name is spoken.)

JUDAS: Is somebody talking about me?

BARTHOLOMEW *(To JUDAS)***:** We were just saying that either you or Matthew will be Minister of the Treasury when Jesus sets up His new government.

NATHANIEL: *(Aside, to others.)* Or maybe they could share the job. Just to keep each other honest. *(Chuckles.)*

JUDAS *(angrily)***:** Are you accusing me of being a thief? *(Throws money bag and ledger onto table.)* Go ahead! Check my books! You won't find anything wrong in them! *(Aside, to audience.)* I'm much too clever to be caught by THESE bumpkins.

THOMAS: Calm down. Nobody's accusing you of ANYTHING. We're just talking, that's all.

ANDREW: *(To JUDAS.)* Pull up a chair. You look tired. What have you been doing?

JUDAS: *(Sits, avoiding ANDREW's gaze.)* A little of this, a little of that.

SIMON: When do you think Jesus will set up His kingdom, Judas?

JAMES TWO: I hope it's soon. I'm tired of waiting to be important.

JUDAS: *(Leans back, wisely.)* I wager it will be sooner than later. Things are in motion.

JOHN: *(Leans forward, a bit suspicious.)* You speak as if you know something we don't. What KINDS of things?

JUDAS: Oh, uh, I'm just thinking of the political climate. Things are happening!

SIMON: Just so the Romans get what's coming to them.

ANDREW: And what's that?

SIMON: Nothing! *(All laugh.)* They think they're so important. Well, we'll show THEM. We'll kick them out of power and leave them with nothing.

(PETER enters, Stage Right, as SIMON speaks.)

PETER: That's pretty big talk for someone who can't seem to take care of the simplest details!

SIMON: What? What is it? What are you complaining about now?

PETER: *(Walking to table.)* When I come in, I expect to have my feet washed. *(Looks around.)* Where's the servant? *(Sits.)*

SIMON: That wasn't my responsibility. JUDAS should have done it.

JUDAS: What are you talking about? I have nothing to do with servants.

BARTHOLOMEW: You arranged for the room.

JUDAS: I only RENTED it. Someone else should have seen about servants.

PHILIP: Well, don't look at me. Nobody told ME to do it.

ANDREW: Me, either.

(All the disciples murmur, "It wasn't my fault, either.")

MATTHEW: Relax, Peter. I expect you've eaten with dirty feet before.

PETER: Not at Passover! SOMEONE should have had a servant here to do it.

ANDREW: *(Grins slyly.)* YOU could do it, Peter.

THOMAS: Do what? Get a servant or wash our feet?

PETER: *(Leaps up, grabs THOMAS by the collar.)* Do I look like the lowliest servant to YOU?

(ANDREW, JOHN and JAMES ONE pull PETER off of THOMAS.)

ANDREW: Take it easy, Peter. It was just a joke.

PETER: *(Sits again, insulted.)* Not a very good one.

JAMES TWO: I know what the perfect job for Peter will be. He can be Minister of Defense.

PETER *(puzzled)*: What?

JAMES TWO: We were trying to decide what jobs we would have in the new government. With YOUR temperament, you'd be perfect to lead the army!

PETER *(thinking)*: General Peter. It has a nice ring to it.

PHILIP: We'll need someone to be in charge of pageantry.

BARTHOLOMEW: Then we can have parades. Like the one the other day.

(The DISCIPLES sit back, thinking about the parade as lights on them dim. Lights rise on Stage Left to show CHILDREN entering, waving palm branches. They shout, "Hosanna! Blessed is the King of Israel who comes in the name of the Lord!" over and over. Lights dim on Stage Left, and CHILDREN exit, Stage Left. Lights rise on the DISCIPLES.)

SIMON: That's how I want to be treated. Every day, to have people bowing down...!

PETER: Well, first—find a servant to wash our feet!

SIMON: I'm not your SLAVE. If you want your feet washed, find your own servant.

BARTHOLOMEW *(sarcastically)*: Don't fight, children. Play nice.

JOHN: Oh, leave them alone, Bart. If they want to fight during Passover, let them.

PETER: All I'm saying... *(All chime in with whining voices.)* ...is that I want my feet washed.

PETER: It's UNTHINKABLE to eat Passover with dirty feet. That's all.

SIMON: Well, better unwashed feet than unwashed hands.

JAMES TWO: He's right. You may have to wash your own feet as well as your hands, Peter. There doesn't seem to be any servant around who is lowly enough to do it.

PETER: Well, what happens when Jesus gets here? Who's going to wash HIS feet?

JOHN: You have a point! We DO need to find a servant. Who'll volunteer?

ANDREW: Not me. It's cold out.

PHILIP: And where will we start looking? It's night!

THOMAS: Judas should do it. He forgot in the first place.

JUDAS: I did NOT! I was only supposed to rent the room.

SIMON: Peter's the one who's anxious to have it done.

BARTHOLOMEW: That's right! Let HIM go.

JAMES ONE: Look. It's not exactly part of the Law or anything. And no one's going to put his feet on the table.

NATHANIEL: And supper's ready anyway. Let's eat first and worry about foot washing after.

(PETER looks offstage, Stage Right.)

PETER: Here comes Jesus. *(Rises.)* Jesus! There's no one here to wash our feet. Send one of these friends of Yours out to find a servant. *(To others.)* There. Now Jesus knows there's no one to wash our feet. Now something will HAPPEN.

(Curtain closes or lights dim as JESUS enters Stage Right and moves to towel and water bowl.)

(GOOD FRIDAY)
SOMETHING'S WRONG

(APPROXIMATE TIME: 10 MINUTES)

SYNOPSIS
Jesus is crucified. All give their views of what's happening.

STAGE SETTINGS

SCENE ONE: CALVARY
No sets. Steps to right of platform may be used to give impression of people standing on hill. Optional—Crucifixion scene backdrop.

SCENE TWO: HEAVEN
Platform near the Calvary area, Stage Right

SCENE THREE: CAIAPHAS'S OFFICE
Table and chair for Caiaphas, Center Stage

SCENE FOUR: SATAN'S OFFICE
Table and chair for Satan, Center Stage

THE PLAYERS

MARY ONE (Jesus' mother) (Grade 5 or older)

MARY TWO (Mary Magdalene) (Grade 3 or older)

MARY THREE (Martha's sister) (Grade 3 or older)

PRIEST ONE (Grade 5 or older)

PRIEST TWO (Grade 3 or older)

PRIEST THREE (Grade 1 or older)

JOANNA (Grade 3 or older)

SCRIBE ONE (Grade 3 or older)

SCRIBE TWO (Grade 5 or older)

ANGEL SOLDIER ONE (Grade 3 or older)

ANGEL MESSENGER ONE (Grade 3 or older)

MARTHA (Grade 5 or older)

CAIAPHAS (KAY-eh-fehs) (Grade 5 or older)

SATAN (Grade 5 or older)

GREED (Grade 5 or older)

NONSEQUITUR (non-SEK-wih-tur) (Grade 5 or older)

MALEFICENT (me-LIH-fe-sent) (Grade 5 or older)

COWARDICE (Grade 5 or older)

MICHAEL (Grade 5 or older)

GABRIEL (Grade 5 or older)

JOHN (Grade 5 or older)

STAGEHANDS (All ages)

NONSPEAKING SCRIBES, ADVISORS, ANGELS, DEMONS, PEOPLE IN CROWD, PRIESTS
(All ages)

SUGGESTED PROPS

■ Business suits for demons
■ Palm branches
■ Notebook for Scribe One
■ Bible-times costumes
■ Angel costumes

DIRECTOR'S TIPS

1. This skit is set up to be the culmination of the Lent series. It is best played out on Good Friday. The use of the same costumes for each character as in the previous skits in the series will help the audience immediately identify characters.

2. Because of the large number of parts and difficulty of play, involve teen and adult players.

3. As an alternative to using platform steps for the Calvary area, consider having the Calvary action take place at the front of Stage Right and the heaven action take place on risers to the rear of Stage Right.

4. Mary One and Mary Three should sob throughout Scene One.

5. Jesus' offstage voice is not powerful. It is the voice of someone suffering an excruciatingly painful death. The voice must also be loud and clear enough to be heard. An adult would handle the role best.

6. In Scenes Three and Four, Caiaphas and Satan are somber and reflective while the others around them are all jubilant.

(GOOD FRIDAY)
SOMETHING'S WRONG

SCENE ONE: CALVARY

(MARY ONE stands in the center of the group. JOHN is beside her, supporting her with his arm around her. MARY TWO, MARY THREE, MARTHA and JOANNA stand in a semicircle about them. MARTHA supports MARY THREE with her arm around her. Others in the crowd move silently behind them. CAIAPHAS, PRIESTS and SCRIBES move back and forth through crowd.)

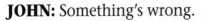

JOHN: Something's wrong.

MARY ONE *(crying)***:** Why? Why? Why? Why? *(Continues to cry softly.)*

JOHN: *(Looks around, bewildered.)* We were supposed to be high government officials. People of importance.

MARTHA: Where are His friends? Where's Peter?

MARY TWO: How can this be happening?

JOANNA: It's all wrong. It can't HAPPEN!

PRIEST ONE: *(Shouts derisively.)* He saved OTHERS. Let Him save HIMSELF! *(Other PRIESTS and SCRIBES echo his shout and laugh.)*

CAIAPHAS: *(Points to top of Jesus' cross. Speaks angrily)* That sign. Calling Jesus KING of the JEWS? It's BLASPHEMOUS!

SCRIBE ONE: It should be removed.

CAIAPHAS: *(Shouts.)* He's not OUR king! *(Other PRIESTS and SCRIBES echo CAIAPHAS's shout.)*

MARY THREE: *(To MARTHA.)* He was always so gentle, so kind. Why do they hate Him?

MARTHA: Hush, little sister. Evil ones always hate good.

JESUS' VOICE: *(From offstage.)* My God, My God, why have You forsaken Me?

PRIEST ONE: Listen! He's calling for Elijah to save Him! *(All PRIESTS and SCRIBES except for SCRIBE TWO repeat PRIESTS ONE's words and laugh, shouting, "Save Him, Elijah!")*

SCRIBE TWO *(thoughtfully, to audience)***:** He's not calling for Elijah. He's quoting Scripture. Psalm 22. Did we make a mistake? What have we DONE?

JOHN: Where are all the others? Where's James, Matthew, Thomas?

JOANNA: Has Jesus no friends except for us?

MARY TWO: I've seen Nicodemus (NICK-uh-DEE-mus). He's somewhere in the crowd.

MARY THREE: Somebody DO something! Save Him!

MARTHA: Hush, little one. No one can do ANYTHING now.

MARY TWO: Joseph of Arimathea (air-im-uh-THEE-uh) is around, too.

JESUS' VOICE: *(From offstage.)* Woman, behold your Son.

PRIEST ONE: Yeah! Look at what happens to blaspheming sons.

SCRIBE TWO *(thoughtfully)*: That's not what He meant, is it? He can't be asking His own mother to watch Him suffer.

JESUS' VOICE: *(From offstage.)* Son, behold your mother.

JOHN: Yes, Jesus! I'll look after her. *(To MARY ONE.)* You'll come and live in my house.

SCRIBE TWO: That's what He meant. He's dying on a cross and He still thinks of taking care of His mother. What kind of Man is this?

MARY THREE: *(Sobbing, screams.)* I hate them! I HATE them!

MARTHA: Don't say that, little one. He never taught us to hate.

MARY THREE: I don't CARE! He didn't hurt them. Why are they so cruel?

MARY TWO: It is easy to hate them.

JOANNA: *(Bitterly, fists clenched.)* They deserve our hatred. They've EARNED it.

JESUS' VOICE: *(From offstage.)* Father, forgive them. They don't know what they're doing.

MARTHA: Hear that, Mary? HE forgives them. He doesn't hate. We mustn't, either.

MARY THREE: How can I forgive them? Look what they've DONE!

MARTHA: Remember Him. Ask Him to let His love live in you.

SCRIBE TWO: *(Falls to his knees.)* Forgive me, Lord. I didn't know.

(Light fades on Scene One. All players for Scene One quietly exit.)

SCENE TWO: HEAVEN

(Light increases on area where ANGELS look on.)

MICHAEL: Something's wrong.

GABRIEL: Something's DEFINITELY wrong.

MICHAEL: Soldier!

(ANGEL SOLDIER ONE approaches MICHAEL and salutes.)

ANGEL SOLDIER ONE: Yes, Sir.

MICHAEL: *(Salutes.)* Has any further order come in?

ANGEL SOLDIER ONE: No, Sir. Just the same message. Stand by.

MICHAEL: *(Shakes head, no.)* Very well. Dismissed.

(ANGEL SOLDIER ONE salutes and returns to ranks.)

GABRIEL: *(Paces back and forth.)* How can this be happening? How can the creation kill the CREATOR?

MICHAEL: *(Slams fist into palm.)* We could STOP this. We have the power. Those puny humans wouldn't stand a chance. In the twinkling of an eye, we could have Him off that cross and here, where He belongs.

GABRIEL: Yes, we could.

MICHAEL: *(Takes a deep breath.)* But we won't. We'll wait for the word of the Lord.

(ANGEL MESSENGER ONE approaches GABRIEL.)

GABRIEL *(eagerly)*: Yes. What is it? What's the message?

MICHAEL: Hurry! Tell us. Do we go?

ANGEL MESSENGER ONE: He says, "Listen closely. The most important words in history are about to be spoken."

GABRIEL: That's IT?

MICHAEL: *(Lays a hand on GABRIEL's shoulder.)* He said to listen, not speak. *(All ANGELS listen attentively. There is a moment of silence.)*

JESUS' VOICE: *(From offstage.)* It is finished!

(Light fades as Scene Two players exit, Stage Right.)

SCENE THREE: CAIAPHAS'S OFFICE

(Light increases on Center Stage, CAIAPHAS's office. CAIAPHAS is seated behind table. PRIESTS and SCRIBES are congratulating each other. SCRIBE TWO is not present.)

CAIAPHAS: *(Shaking head, no.)* Something's wrong.

PRIEST ONE: NOTHING'S wrong. It all went like clockwork!

SCRIBE ONE: We did it! We got rid of Him!

CAIAPHAS: I keep thinking we've forgotten something.

PRIEST TWO: You worry too much.

PRIEST THREE: We won! He's DEAD!

CAIAPHAS: Something He said. What was it? *(Tries to remember.)* Something He said.

PRIEST ONE: He said, "Save Me, Elijah."

SCRIBE TWO: *(Entering, Stage Right.)* You weren't listening. He said, *Eli, Eli, lama sabachthani!* Don't you know your Scripture?

CAIAPHAS: Ah, you've finally arrived! Come, celebrate with us!

SCRIBE TWO: I've only arrived to say I'm through. I can't work with you people anymore. *(Exits, Stage Right.)*

PRIEST TWO: *(Looks after SCRIBE TWO, shaking head.)* Even in death, Jesus causes trouble.

CAIAPHAS: *(Snaps fingers.)* That's it!

PRIEST THREE: What's it?

CAIAPHAS: Don't you remember? That blasphemer said something about being dead three days and then coming back to life.

SCRIBE ONE: *(Checks his notes.)* Sign of Jonah. Three days in the fish...

CAIAPHAS: *(Interrupts.)* We MUST have a guard set up to make sure the body stays put. We'll go to Pilate and get a guard. Better yet, we'll see to it that he seals the tomb.

PRIEST ONE: You think Pilate will give you a guard and seal the tomb?

CAIAPHAS: Leave Pilate to me. Does anyone know where the tomb is?

PRIEST: Sure. Joseph of Arimathea took the body and put it in his tomb.

PRIEST THREE: Everyone knows where that is.

CAIAPHAS: *(Rises, starts to walk to Stage Right.)* Let's go—before it's too late. *(Exits, Stage Right, with PRIESTS and SCRIBES.)*

SCENE FOUR: SATAN'S OFFICE

(Lights increase. SATAN enters, Stage Left, and sits behind table, Center Stage. GREED, NONSEQUITUR, MALEFICENT, COWARDICE and DEMONS follow. DEMONS are jumping, high-fiving each other and celebrating their victory.)

SATAN: *(Rises, begins to pace.)* Something's wrong.

GREED: Wrong? NOTHING'S wrong.

NONSEQUITUR: We've WON! We're the champions!

MALEFICENT: *(Rubs hands in glee.)* Killed on a cross. Like a lamb led to slaughter.

COWARDICE: No opposition. Winners by acclamation—us!

SATAN: *(Stops pacing. Slams his fist into open palm.)* That's just it! Where was Michael? Where was the heavenly Host?

GREED: Sleeping?

NONSEQUITUR: Eating?

MALEFICENT: *(Giggles.)* Choir practice?

COWARDICE: *(Chuckles.)* Bible study? Who CARES? We know where they WEREN'T.

SATAN: *(Starts pacing again.)* It was too easy. It shouldn't have been that easy. *(Looks at DEMONS, who are still celebrating. SATAN turns to audience, shakes head, no.)* It was TOO easy. Something's WRONG!

(Lights dim. All exit, Stage Left.)

(EASTER)

HE'S ALIVE!

(APPROXIMATE TIME: 25 MINUTES)

SYNOPSIS

Those who witnessed Jesus' resurrection tell their stories in the form of a dramatic reading.

STAGE SETTING

■ Stage is bare, except for an empty cross in the background
■ A podium may be set up for the readers, Stage Left

THE PLAYERS

PRIEST ONE (Grade 1 or older)

SOLDIER (Grade 1 or older)

JOANNA (Grade 3 or older)

MICHAEL (Grade 5 or older)

SATAN (Grade 5 or older)

JOHN (Grade 5 or older)

PEOPLE IN CROWD (All ages)

MARY TWO (Mary Magdalene) (Grade 3 or older)

MARY THREE (Martha's sister) (Grade 3 or older)

NONSPEAKING DEMONS, PRIESTS (All ages)

CAIAPHAS (KAY-eh-fehs) (Grade 5 or older)

ANGEL CHORUS (Grade 1 or older)

THOMAS (Grade 3 or older)

GABRIEL (Grade 5 or older)

MARTHA (Grade 5 or older)

PETER (Grade 5 or older)

MARY ONE (Jesus' mother) (Grade 5 or older)

SUGGESTED PROPS

■ Weapons and uniforms for soldiers
■ Angel costumes
■ Bible-times costumes
■ Palm branches
■ Business suits for demons

DIRECTOR'S TIPS

1. This skit is in the form of a dramatic reading. In a dramatic reading, the action is limited and the script is often read rather than memorized and performed. The action is mainly symbolic.

2. This piece works best as the final skit for the Lent series. However, it may be performed alone as well.

3. If used after the Lent series, "Something's Happening," the parts do not have to be portrayed by the same actors. However, for easy audience identification, characters should be wearing the same costumes as worn in the series.

4. Demons are trapped beside the empty cross by the Angel Chorus. They are not allowed freedom to work their evil on Easter. While Demons may try to escape at times, the movements of Demons and Angels should not become a distraction.

5. Angels should outnumber Demons two-to-one.

(EASTER)
HE'S ALIVE!

(Stage is dark except for dim light on empty cross. DEMONS are standing, looking at the cross, pointing and laughing softly. ANGEL CHORUS enters from both sides of stage and forms large semicircle around demons. As ANGEL CHORUS enters, lights are raised on the scene. DEMONS become terrified and try to hide their eyes from the light. From time to time, a DEMON will try to escape from the circle, but is prevented by the ANGELS.)

SCENE ONE

(SATAN, MICHAEL and GABRIEL enter, Stage Left, and move to speaking area.)

SATAN *(bitterly)*: HE'S ALIVE!

MICHAEL *(joyously)*: HE'S ALIVE!

GABRIEL *(joyously)*: HE'S ALIVE!

SATAN: I knew it was too easy! How could I have expected to kill the only Man who never sinned? Death is the wages of SIN. He completely fooled me! I was prepared for an all-out battle; I could have met His companies of angels. But who would have thought He would do THIS—sacrifice Himself for these puny sheep He calls humans!

GABRIEL: For God so loved the world that he gave his one and only Son, that whoever believes in him shall not perish but have eternal life.[1]

SATAN *(puzzled and outraged)*: How can that much LOVE exist in one being? How can the Eternal One care about these mortals, who live their lives and never give HIM a second thought? How could He take their sin upon Himself and pay the price His righteousness requires?

MICHAEL: The blood of Jesus, the righteous Lamb of God, was foreshadowed in the days of slavery in Egypt. When God saw the blood of lambs painted across the tops and down the sides of the door frames, death passed over those houses, and God did not let the plague of death enter their houses.[2]

SATAN: But the wages of sin is death.[3] And all have sinned and come short of the glory of God![4] He should allow them to DIE for their sin—to be given over to ME for eternal PUNISHMENT!

GABRIEL: From before the beginning of time, God knew people would sin. From the very beginning, He prepared the way of redemption. From the millions of people on the earth, He chose Abram, and promised that in Abram all the people of the earth would be blessed.

SATAN: But it's not FAIR! I worked and I schemed to destroy His creation. Didn't I convince people that God was a liar? "Eat!" I told the woman. "You won't die! When you eat, you will be like God." I KNEW He would have to destroy them![5] The wages of sin is DEATH!

MICHAEL: And God gave mercy instead. While you were disguised as the serpent, He told you that Eve's offspring would crush your head and you would strike His heel.[6] Today, that prophecy is fulfilled.

SATAN: But how can He allow it? How could He permit a man like DAVID to bring blessing to the earth? He coveted his neighbor's wife. That led to adultery and murder. Right THERE, David broke THREE of the commandments! How can God FORGIVE these grasshoppers He calls people, when they ignore Him and follow their own desires?

GABRIEL: The Lord is merciful and kind. To those who recognize their wrong, forgiveness is always possible. David knew this. He talked of God's mercy and unfailing love, and His great compassion to blot out sins. He asked God, "Create in me a pure heart, O God, and renew a steadfast spirit within me."[7] And so God called David a man after His own heart.

SATAN (scornfully)**:** Forgiveness! If I were God, I would NEVER forgive. Let them be DESTROYED for their sin! Give them over to me and I will see them PUNISHED for their sin! But no! ALL who I thought were mine have been given the chance to be HIS!

MICHAEL: In heaven, in the midst of the throne and the elders, stood a Lamb looking as if it had been slain. He came and took the scroll from the right hand of Him who sat on the throne. And all those around Him sang a new song: "You are worthy to take the scroll and to open its seals, because you were slain, and with your blood you purchased men for God from every tribe and language and people and nation."[8]

SATAN: (Growls.) Even now, my demons are trapped around an EMPTY cross. The cross that should have been the symbol of my greatest TRIUMPH is now the symbol of my DEFEAT. But we shall break free again and resume our deceit on the people of the earth.

GABRIEL: For God so loved the world, that he gave his only begotten Son, that whoever believes in Him should not perish but have everlasting life.

(SATAN leaves podium and joins DEMONS inside circle of ANGELS.)

ANGEL CHORUS: Why do you seek Him here? He is not here; He is risen!

(GABRIEL and MICHAEL exit, Stage Left.)

(CAIAPHAS, PRIEST ONE and other PRIESTS enter, Stage Left, and move to speaking area.)

SCENE TWO

CAIAPHAS: He's alive?

PRIEST ONE *(disbelieving)*: He's ALIVE?

CAIAPHAS: The nonsense I feared is coming to pass. Didn't we go to Pilate? Didn't we say, "Remember that deceiver you put on a cross? He said He would rise again in three days. Put a guard around the tomb. Don't let His followers come and steal the body. If they do, they will go to the people and say..."

PRIEST ONE: *(Interrupts.)* "He's alive!"

CAIAPHAS: So what has happened? Those Roman soldiers slipped up! Somehow the body disappeared. It's not there! I checked myself. And now, do you know what will happen? His disciples will go around proclaiming...

PRIEST ONE: *(Interrupts.)* He's alive!

CAIAPHAS: This has been an expensive week for the treasury. First, we had to pay that traitor, Judas, thirty pieces of silver to betray Jesus. True, he gave the money back...

PRIEST ONE *(insulted)*: He THREW it at us!

CAIAPHAS: But it was blood money. It isn't LAWFUL to put that kind of money back into the treasury. It would make the whole treasury UNCLEAN. So we used it to buy a potter's field for a graveyard where we could bury strangers.

PRIEST ONE: Isn't there something in Zechariah (zek-eh-RYE-eh) about buying a potter's field...

CAIAPHAS *(angrily interrupting)*: Don't go quoting Scripture to ME! I know it better than you! We're not talking religion; we're talking politics. If people believe Jesus is the Messiah, that makes us His enemies. The people will revolt against us. There could be panic, confusion, unrest, rioting. We won't be able to stop it, because the people will no longer FEAR us. Rome will move in—and we'll lose our exalted position.

PRIEST ONE: We can't let THAT happen! We must stop any rumors!

CAIAPHAS: Which we've already started to do. *(Sighs.)* MORE money from the treasury. The guards were smart enough to come to us first to tell us the body was gone. If they had gone directly to Pilate, he would have had them executed, according to Roman law.

PRIEST ONE: Which he SHOULD do. After ALL, how can you lose a dead body that's been put into a grave and had a huge stone rolled up against the opening?

CAIAPHAS: I don't care how it happened—I only care about what WILL happen. This MUST NOT affect my role as high priest! I must maintain my political presence in Jerusalem. I must KEEP my position of IMPORTANCE.

PRIEST ONE *(thinking)*: But if He IS alive...

CAIAPHAS: Don't SAY that! We spent good money bribing those soldiers! They will admit to falling asleep on duty and letting the disciples steal the body. And it WASN'T cheap! A soldier who is risking execution won't lie without a large bribe. Never, never must anyone be allowed to say...

PRIEST ONE: *(Interrupts.)* He's alive!

(MICHAEL and GABRIEL enter, Stage Left, and move to speaking area as CAIAPHAS continues.)

CAIAPHAS: Don't say that! He's DEAD. He MUST be dead. I will not believe that He's alive. I will NOT!

GABRIEL: For God so loved the world, that he gave his only begotten Son, that whoever believes in Him should not perish but have everlasting life.

MICHAEL: And every creature in heaven and on earth will sing, "To Him who sits on the throne and to the Lamb be praise and honor and glory and power, for ever and ever!"[9]

CAIAPHAS: I WON'T believe it!

PRIEST ONE: I won't believe it, either. He's dead, not alive.

(CAIAPHAS, PRIEST ONE and other PRIESTS move to cross saying, "He's dead, not alive. He's dead, not alive." ANGELS allow them to pass through their ranks and join the DEMONS.)

ANGEL CHORUS: Why do you seek for Him here? He is not here; He is risen!

(GABRIEL and MICHAEL exit, Stage Left, while MARY ONE, MARY TWO, MARY THREE, MARTHA and JOANNA enter, Stage Left, and move to speaking area.)

SCENE THREE

MARY THREE *(softly, in wonder)***:** He's ALIVE!

MARY TWO *(joyously, laughing)***:** He's ALIVE!

MARTHA *(certainly)***:** HE'S ALIVE!

JOANNA *(thankfully)***:** HE'S ALIVE!

MARY ONE *(announcing)***:** HE'S ALIVE!

MARY THREE: For three days, I've done nothing but cry.

MARTHA: That's the truth. I couldn't convince her to eat. The only time she slept was when her crying made her so tired that she slept. But she cried in her sleep and awoke crying.

JOANNA: We were all sad. We might have SHOWN it in different ways, but we all felt like crying. Who could have believed it would HAPPEN? Jesus, dead! Crucified!

MARTHA: We all cried. *(Firmly.)* But there were things to do.

MARY ONE: I was totally lost, totally bewildered. My Son had been executed on a cross; killed as if He were a common criminal. What had He done to hurt anyone? Hadn't He given the blind back their sight? The lame walked; the lepers were made clean; the deaf heard and the poor had the gospel preached to them! It was as if the words of Isaiah had come to life. Suddenly, He was gone!

MARY TWO: Killed on a cross and hurriedly laid in a tomb. Joseph of Arimathea (AIR-im-uh-THEE-uh) and Nicodemus (NICK-uh-DEE-mus) did their best to give the body a quick burial, but they didn't have time to do the job properly.

JOANNA: That's why we had to take the burial spices and go to the tomb. How could we live with ourselves if we knew that our best Friend had been put into His final resting place without a proper burial?

MARTHA: But you never thought about how you would move the stone. You should have known you could never have moved it yourselves.

MARY TWO: We knew. We talked about it on the way.

MARY ONE: I appreciate everything you all did for my Son. Martha, you always saw that He was well fed when He visited you. All of you were so kind to Him. I was so thankful to John for taking me to his home after...after Jesus died. I don't know what I would have done if I had been alone that night.

MARY THREE: I cried. All that night and the next day, I cried.

MARTHA: I know you did. And who could blame you?

JOANNA: We all cried. While we prepared the spices, while we walked to the tomb, we all cried.

MARY TWO: But as we approached the tomb—what a surprise!

JOANNA: The stone was rolled away from the mouth of the tomb!

MARY TWO: We went into the tomb and saw the grave clothes!

JOANNA: But the BODY was GONE. And whoever had taken the body had left the grave clothes, all neatly folded.

MARTHA (drily)**:** Very uncommon, finding considerate and tidy grave robbers.

MARY TWO: We couldn't understand it. What had HAPPENED here? Where was the body? Suddenly, we weren't ALONE.

(GABRIEL and MICHAEL enter, Stage Left, and join the women.)

JOANNA: Suddenly, two men in shining robes were with us.

GABRIEL: Why do you seek the living among the dead?

MICHAEL: He is not here. He is risen.

GABRIEL: Remember what He said to you in Galilee.

MICHAEL: "The Son of man must be delivered into the hands of sinful men, and be crucified, and on the third day, rise again."[10]

(GABRIEL and MICHAEL exit, Stage Left.)

JOANNA: We hurried back to tell the disciples, especially Peter and John.

MARY TWO: But on the way, we had doubts. What did we see? Was it REAL? After we told the disciples, I went back to the tomb.

MARTHA: *(Chuckles.)* A complete waste of time. The tomb was empty.

MARY TWO: But I HAD to look again. And there it was—an EMPTY tomb. I began to cry, thinking of all the things that had happened. And now, His body was gone. I would never see Him again and I would never know where His body was laid.

MARY THREE: But He was alive! You heard it, from angels!

MARTHA: The dead don't come back to life, little one.

MARY THREE: Our brother did!

MARTHA: But that's because Jesus was there.

MARY THREE: Well, Jesus was in His TOMB, too!

MARY ONE: (Chuckles.) You can't argue with her, Martha. Jesus was there!

MARY TWO: But not when I returned.

JOANNA: I should have gone back with you.

MARY TWO: And when I looked into the tomb, the two men were there, asking me why I was crying. I told them, "Because they've taken my Lord away and I don't know where they have put Him." And then I turned around. I nearly bumped into the gardener. At least I THOUGHT it was the gardener! And He asked me, "Why are you crying?" When I told Him, He simply said, "Mary." I couldn't believe it. I KNEW that voice! Through my tears, I looked again. It was Jesus. He IS alive!

MARY THREE: You should have believed before. When the angels told you.

(GABRIEL and MICHAEL enter, Stage Left, and join the women.)

GABRIEL: Why do you seek the living among the dead?

MICHAEL: He is not here. He is risen.

GABRIEL: Remember what He said to you in Galilee.

MICHAEL: "The Son of man must be delivered into the hands of sinful men, and be crucified, and on the third day, rise again."

(MARY ONE, MARY TWO, MARY THREE, MARTHA and JOANNA approach the ANGEL CHORUS, saying to each other, "He's alive! He's alive!" GABRIEL and MICHAEL exit, Stage Left.)

ANGEL CHORUS: Why do you seek for Him here? He is not here; He is risen!

(PETER, JOHN and the other DISCIPLES except THOMAS enter, Stage Left, and approach speaking area.)

SCENE FOUR

PETER: (Shouts.) HE'S ALIVE!

JOHN: (Laughs.) HE'S ALIVE!

PETER: What a weekend!

JOHN: You wouldn't believe all we went through.

PETER: The Passover supper with Jesus should have been the highlight of the year. For three years, we had traveled with Him, listened to Him. We knew something special was going to happen.

JOHN: We had been faithful. And soon, we would be rewarded. When Jesus became King, we would all have important jobs in the Kingdom. We wouldn't just be fishermen anymore.

PETER: Then, disaster!

JOHN: Jesus, taken by an angry mob, right in front of us. We could hardly believe our eyes. These were the same people who greeted us with palm branches less than a week before!

(PEOPLE waving palm branches and saying, "Hosanna!" enter from both sides of stage and join WOMEN and ANGEL CHORUS.)

PETER: And we ran! Just like scared rabbits, we ran!

JOHN: But curiosity made us creep up to the judgment house...

PETER: Where I lived the most humiliating moments of my life. Hadn't I been the loud and boastful fool! "Don't worry about me, Jesus! The others may all desert You, but I will always be by Your side." But in the space of a few short hours, I denied that I had even heard of Him. Not once, not twice. THREE times I denied knowing Jesus.

JOHN: Then, the morning after the Sabbath, we were roused by a bunch of screaming women. They were trying to tell us the most unbelievable thing we had ever heard. They had been to the tomb...

PETER: And the body was gone. But it hadn't been stolen.

JOHN: "He's alive!" they told us. "We've been told He's alive!"

PETER: Well, we quickly put a stop to THAT nonsense. After all, dead is dead. We saw Him crucified. *(Shudders.)* We saw the nails being driven through His hands and feet.

JOHN: We saw the spear driven into His side. We saw the blood and water pour out of His body. He was dead!

PETER: One very strange thing happened at the Cross that day. Remember?

JOHN: You mean the centurion.

(SOLDIER enters, Stage Left, and joins PETER and JOHN.)

PETER: He must have seen hundreds of crucifixions.

JOHN: But this time, something must have seemed different to him.

PETER: Remember what he said?

SOLDIER: Surely, this was a righteous man.

JOHN: That alone would have been strange enough.

PETER: He could have been accused of treason for suggesting that the Roman governor had signed the death warrant for an innocent man. But he said something else.

SOLDIER: Truly, this man was the Son of God. *(Leaves speaking area and joins WOMEN and ANGEL CHORUS.)*

JOHN: And now, after all THAT, Mary and Joanna and the others came running to tell us that the body had disappeared.

PETER: And to tell us about Jesus being ALIVE. We soon set them straight. Obviously, someone had moved the body. But who?

JOHN: And why? So we went to investigate.

PETER: The most obvious answer was that nobody had done anything. The women just went to the wrong place. So we approached it cautiously.

JOHN: After all, there were guards around that tomb.

PETER: But when we got to within seeing distance, we found out the women were partly right.

JOHN: The stone HAD been moved. The guard was gone!

PETER: So we ran to get a better look.

JOHN: I looked into the tomb, but I couldn't see anything. You pushed past me...

PETER: Well, I had to. You were blocking the entrance! And it was just like the women had said. Except for one thing—the grave clothes were all neatly folded, but the linen for the head was in a different place from the other clothes, also neatly folded. That's when you went crazy.

JOHN: I didn't go crazy! I just said maybe the women were right. Maybe He IS alive.

PETER: Like I said, crazy! Then, we went home. But it wasn't over.

JOHN: Mary came back. This time she had a better story!

PETER: This time, she'd SEEN—and talked to—Jesus. What an imagination!

JOHN: Later, that night, the others joined us. All except for Thomas. We carefully locked the door. We knew that Caiaphas and the others would gladly have us killed, too. We told the others what the women had said.

PETER: They all seemed to think the women were imagining things. Then, it happened.

JOHN: JESUS appeared to us. It was HIM. He had nail holes in His hands and feet. He had the spear wound in His side. But He was ALIVE!

PETER: I didn't know if I should be more happy or ashamed. Jesus—alive! But I had failed Him. I ran off. I denied Him. What would He say to me? Would He throw me out for denying Him? I would deserve it. But who could have imagined what He did? He FORGAVE me! Jesus—alive. And me—FORGIVEN!

JOHN: We were all forgiven. Although He did rebuke us for not believing the women in the first place.

PETER: We all saw Him, except Thomas.

(THOMAS enters, Stage Left, and joins PETER and JOHN.)

THOMAS: I thought the entire world had gone mad. A bunch of women claiming that Jesus was alive. And the other ten acting even crazier. "He's alive!" they kept yelling at me. So I told them, "You want me to believe? I will, but I won't only believe my eyes. If I see the nail holes myself AND put my fingers into them AND if I can put my hand into the wound in His side, then I'll believe. But not until."

(GABRIEL and MICHAEL enter, Stage Left, and move to speaking area.)

THOMAS: And He appeared to me. I STILL find it hard to believe. Not that He's alive, but that He cared so much to show me that He is alive. Only me. The others already knew. He didn't have to show Himself to me. He could have let me continue doubting. But He didn't! He's so good!

PETER: Now, we believe.

JOHN: All of us.

THOMAS: Blessed are they who have not seen, and yet have believed.

(PETER, JOHN, THOMAS and other DISCIPLES join others with ANGEL CHORUS.)

ANGEL CHORUS: Why do you seek Him here? He is not here; He is risen!

GABRIEL: For God so loved the world, that he gave his only begotten Son, that whoever believes in Him should not perish but have everlasting life.

MICHAEL: Jesus! You are worthy to take the scroll and to open its seals, because you were slain, and with your blood you purchased men for God from every tribe and language and people and nation.

GABRIEL: And never again will they hunger. Never again will they thirst, for the Lamb will be their Shepherd. He will lead them to springs of living water. And God will wipe away every tear from their eyes.[11]

MICHAEL: And every creature in heaven and on earth will sing, "To Him who sits on the throne and to the Lamb be praise and honor and glory and power, forever and ever."

GABRIEL: Behold! The Lamb of God, who takes away the sin of the world!

MICHAEL: Behold! Now the Tabernacle of God is with men, and He will dwell with them. They shall be His people, and God Himself will be with them and be their God.

(GABRIEL and MICHAEL join the ANGEL CHORUS.)

ANGEL CHORUS: Why do you seek Him here? He is not here; He is risen!

GABRIEL: Seek Him where you are.

MICHAEL: Seek and you shall find.

ALL: HE'S ALIVE!

(Lights dim, then rise on cast.)

[1]John 3:16
[2]See Exodus 12.
[3]See Romans 6:23.
[4]See Romans 3:23.
[5]See Genesis 3.
[6]See Genesis 3:15.
[7]Psalm 51:10
[8]Revelation 5:9
[9]Revelation 5:13
[10]See Matthew 26:2.
[11]See Revelation 22.

WHAT DO I DETECT?

(APPROXIMATE TIME: 60 MINUTES)

SYNOPSIS

Detective Sam Shovel digs up reasons to believe in Jesus.

STAGE SETTINGS

SCENE ONE: SAM'S OFFICE
- Desk and chair for Sam, Center Stage, facing Stage Right
- Chair for client on other side of desk
- Sign on desk, reading "SAM SHOVEL"
- Coat rack behind desk
- Filing cabinets

SCENE TWO: PASTOR'S OFFICE
- Desk and chair for Pastor, Stage Right
- Chair for visitors on other side of desk
- Filing cabinets
- Bookcases and books

SCENE THREE: SAM'S OFFICE
Same as Scene One

SCENE FOUR: FOG NEWSROOM
- News desk, Stage Right, facing audience
- Two chairs behind news desk
- Optional—Backdrop with world map on wall, clocks showing various times around the world, etc.

SCENE FIVE: PAUL'S HOUSE
- Table, Center Stage, facing Stage Right
- Chair behind table for Paul
- Chair beside table for visitors

SCENE SIX: JOSEPHUS'S HOUSE
- Table, Center Stage, facing Stage Left
- Chair behind table for Flavius Josephus
- Chair beside table for visitors
- Bookcases with scrolls

SCENE SEVEN: JERUSALEM NIGHT
- Bonfire, Stage Left
- Building facade

SCENE EIGHT: JERUSALEM DAY
- Platform for Disciples, Stage Right
- Building facade

SCENE NINE: SAM'S OFFICE
Same as Scene One

THE PLAYERS

SAM SHOVEL (detective)

TRACY (client)

PASTOR

SIGN CARRIER

MARCY TAN (news reporter)

PAUL

PETER

NEWSROOM FLUNKEY

NEWSROOM MONKEY

NEWSROOM WORKERS

GIRL ONE (speaking to Peter)

GIRL TWO (speaking to Peter)

MAN (speaking to Peter)

SOLDIERS (guarding Paul)

OTHER APOSTLES

CROWD

STAGEHANDS (All ages)

NARRATORS' VOICES:

MALE ONE	**MALE TWO**
MALE THREE	**MALE FOUR**
FEMALE ONE	**FEMALE TWO**

FLAVIUS JOSEPHUS (FLAY-vee-us) (jo-SEE-fus) (noted historian)

NOTE: Because most of the skit is narrated, the acting parts can be played by people of any age. Voices (Narrators) should have good reading skills and expressive voices. If possible, invite your pastor to play the Pastor's role.

SUGGESTED PROPS

- Trench coat and hat for Sam
- Bible for Pastor
- Papers, etc. for desk in newsroom
- Headphones to represent translation equipment
- Quill pen for Paul and Flavius Josephus
- Painting
- Bottle of lemonade
- Large handbag for Tracy filled with:
  - a) flashlight
  - b) head of lettuce
  - c) play money
  - d) box of tacks
- Chain to manacle Paul to soldiers
- Telephone, lamp, papers, empty glasses, etc. for Sam's desk
- Signs lettered "TROUBLE" to be attached to Tracy
- Time machine (one of the following): tricycle, pogo stick, skateboard—anything that the detective can use to move forward (ahead in time) or backward (back in time)
- File folder with papers inside for Sam's report

- Baseball
- Large sign lettered "IT"
- Veil
- Monkey suit (or mask)
- Soldiers' uniforms
- Bible-times costumes
- Package of gum

DIRECTOR'S TIPS

1. To give players more lines, they may repeat appropriate lines read by Narrators.

2. Players should mime what Narrators are saying.

3. Male One should speak matter-of-factly without very much emotion, in the manner of Sam Spade. Other Narrators should read with emotion.

4. Narrators' parts can be read.

5. Narrators should stand where they are able to see stage action.

WHAT DO I DETECT?

SCENE ONE: SAM'S OFFICE

(SAM SHOVEL sits at desk covered with papers, pencils, empty glasses, etc. Holds his head in his hands. He is chewing gum. He is obviously not feeling well.)

MALE ONE: It was another dark and dismal day in a life FILLED with dark and dismal days. I had a bitter taste in my mouth that I couldn't identify. Maybe it was too many glasses of lemonade and too many sticks of gum last night. I hadn't had a case for nearly a week. Then, the phone rang... *(Phone rings.)*

SAM SHOVEL: *(Picks up phone.)* Sam Shovel—we dig up the dirt!

MALE ONE: I was hoping for an interesting case, but it was just another call from the phone company telling me they'd cut my phone off if I didn't pay my bill. I was about to make a quick joke, but my attention was diverted. My office door opened and SHE walked in.

(TRACY enters, Stage Right. Wears a dress covered with signs reading "TROUBLE." She could also wear a hat with a "TROUBLE" sign on it.)

The moment I saw her, I knew she was trouble. It was written all over her. But when you're desperate for a case, you ignore the warning signs.

(SAM SHOVEL hangs up phone, rises and motions TRACY to a chair. TRACY sits.)

She was the kind of girl you automatically offer a stick of gum...

(SAM pulls out pack of gum and offers stick to TRACY. She accepts and removes gum from pack but does not unwrap it.)

I offered her a light...

(SAM SHOVEL picks up lamp from desk and offers it to TRACY.)

...but she said she had her own.

(TRACY removes flashlight from handbag, turns it on and places it on SAM's desk. She holds the stick of gum in the flashlight beam and unwraps it. She begins to chew gum and looks for a place to put the wrapper. Seeing none, she crumples it and tosses it onto the mess on SAM's desk. She picks up flashlight, turns it off and returns it to handbag.)

She asked me if I was Sam Shovel. I gave her my line.

SAM SHOVEL: Sam Shovel. We dig up the dirt.

MALE ONE: She didn't think it was very clever. I told her I had planned to change my name to Sam Hammer. I wanted to open an agency with a man named Peacock. Then I could have said, "Peacock and Hammer. We tail 'em and nail 'em." But it fell through. I didn't know anyone named Peacock. She looked at me like I was something my name had dug up. I squirmed under her glare.

(TRACY glares at SAM SHOVEL. SAM shifts uncomfortably.)

MALE ONE: I asked her what she wanted, and she told me...

FEMALE ONE: I need a detective in the worst way possible.

MALE ONE: It would have been tough to find a detective in a worse way than me, but I didn't tell her that. Instead, I asked her to tell me her problem.

FEMALE ONE: It's Christians...

MALE ONE: ...she told me.

FEMALE ONE: They keep telling me I should believe! I want them to stay AWAY from me.

MALE ONE: I wasn't in the body guarding business and I told her so.

SAM SHOVEL: *(Points at TRACY.)* So!

MALE ONE: But a body guard wasn't what she had in mind. She continued...

FEMALE ONE: What I want is to have you find out that Christianity is false. Then, when they start bothering me again, I can take out your report and show them how WRONG they are.

MALE ONE: I said I'd take the case. But I told her I didn't work cheap. It was a lie. But in my business, you can make a few extra bucks that way. She told me...

FEMALE ONE: I have lots. Your fee will be no problem.

MALE ONE: She reached into that bag of hers and pulled out the biggest wad of lettuce I'd ever seen...

(TRACY takes large head of lettuce out of handbag.)

...but I told her, "No dice. I work for money, not vegetables." She said it was no problem.

FEMALE ONE: That's no problem. I carry money as well.

(TRACY returns lettuce to handbag, pulls out a large wad of bills. SAM SHOVEL stares open-mouthed at the money.)

MALE ONE: That wad could have choked a horse. But it wasn't choking me. The gum I inhaled when I saw all that CASH was choking me well enough.

(SAM begins to choke and cough. TRACY drops money on desk and pats him on the back to help.)

Having saved my life, she began to appeal to my better nature.

FEMALE ONE: You will help me, won't you, Sam? If you don't stop these crazy Christians, they'll drive me NUTS. You're my only hope! Say you'll do it! You MUST do it! Oh, PLEASE help me!

(During speech, TRACY tugs at SAM's jacket, pulls her hair and finally sinks into chair, burying her face in her arms on the desk and weeping. She sneaks a peak at SAM to see if her act has had any effect, then buries her face and weeps some more. SAM concentrates hard while looking at audience.)

MALE ONE: Unfortunately for her, I don't have a better nature. Fortunately for her, I do have a greedy one. And that pile sitting on my desk wasn't play dough. I told her I'd do it.

(TRACY jumps up from chair. She has her handbag hooked over her right arm and shakes SAM's hand vigorously with her right hand while her left hand picks up the pile of money.)

FEMALE ONE: Oh, thank you, thank you, thank you, THANK you! A million, trillion thanks couldn't be enough. You've saved my LIFE. Thank you, thank you, thank you, THANK you!

(TRACY turns her back to SAM to shield SAM's view of the money. Returns money to handbag as she exits, Stage Right. SAM SHOVEL watches her go, then sits down to look at the money on his desk and sees it's gone.)

MALE ONE: Obviously, she wasn't so overcome with gratitude that she forgot the material things in life. But that's OK. When I got what she wanted, she'd pay any price I asked. The first thing I needed to do was to refresh my memory on what Christians believe.

(SAM places head in hands and begins thinking hard.)

All I could come up with is something about a guy who wears a red suit in the winter and becomes a rabbit in the spring. Obviously, I needed a better source of information than my own memory. I decided to go out and pound the pavement.

(SAM SHOVEL gets hat and trench coat and exits office, Stage Right.)

INTERMEZZO

(While STAGEHANDS break down Scene One and set up Scene Two, SAM enters, front of Stage Right, crawling on his hands and knees. As he crawls, he hits the floor with the sides of his fists. He continues as NARRATOR speaks.)

MALE ONE: I had pounded the pavement for six blocks. No luck. All I had were sore knees, scuffed shoes and aching hands. There had to be a better way to get information. Then, I saw it...

(SAM looks up and stares offstage, Stage Left.)

MALE ONE: A church. Of course! Somebody there should know something about Christianity. There was my answer.

(SAM SHOVEL rises and exits, running, Stage Left. STAGEHANDS finish setting up Scene Two.)

SCENE TWO: PASTOR'S OFFICE

(PASTOR is at desk studying Bible, making notes, etc. SAM enters, Stage Left.)

MALE ONE: It looked like any other office. Just like mine, except tidier and it had books. But what can you learn from books? Experience! That's what you need to learn anything. The person at the desk looked friendly enough, like someone you could talk to, someone who was willing to help.

(PASTOR looks up.)

PASTOR: May I help you?

(SAM looks around as though he thinks the PASTOR has spoken to someone else, then realizes the PASTOR means him. Points to himself. PASTOR nods. SAM approaches desk and sits.)

MALE ONE: I hoped the pastor could help me, but how could I say what I really wanted? How do you say to someone, "Why are you such an idiot to believe Christianity?" You won't get the answer you want. I had to be sneaky. I said I was searching. The pastor seemed interested in what I was saying.

(SAM pantomimes speech. PASTOR listens intently, occasionally nodding.)

I said, "I need answers. I need to know what Christians believe." The pastor opened a big Book on the desk that seemed to be filled with other books.

(PASTOR opens Bible to the book of Genesis.)

He showed me how this Book, "The Bible," says that God created the world and everything in it. God made it and said it was good. "Then why do I feel so rotten? Why is there pain and suffering?" I asked.

(PASTOR shows SAM the Creation story. SAM mimes asking questions.)

The pastor showed me where it said that people disobeyed God and the world began to change. Instead of being a place of perfect beauty, it became a place where there was evil. Things went wrong, people did bad things. "So that's it," I said. "God abandoned the world."

(The PASTOR shows SAM the story of the Fall. SAM mimes asking questions. The PASTOR shakes head, chuckling gently.)

The pastor said...

PASTOR: No. God never forgot His creation. Even when people became extremely evil, God continued to show mercy and love.

MALE ONE: That pastor showed me places in Genesis where God made promises to different people, like Abraham, Isaac and Jacob. He told how God had always stayed with His people, helping them in times of trouble. Then he went to the next book, Exodus. There, God made promises to a man named Moses and gave him God's law. "So," I said. "You obey God's law. Then God will help you." That's the, the, the...

(SAM gropes for the right word.)

PASTOR: Arrangement?

MALE ONE: Yeah. Quite an arrangement.

PASTOR: It's not exactly like that! Let me show you.

(The PASTOR shows SAM other parts of Bible. SAM mimes asking questions.)

MALE ONE: The pastor showed me how people COULDN'T obey God's law. Something called sin made it impossible. People kept breaking God's law but God kept loving them anyway. He gave them a special system of sacrifices as a way to say they were sorry for their sins and to ask God to forgive them. Then, the pastor showed me where God made a promise to a king named David. David would always have a descendant who would rule Israel. "There's something wrong," I told him. "Israel doesn't have a king. It has a prime minister."

(The PASTOR shows SAM more Bible passages. SAM mimes arguing. The PASTOR answers gently.)

PASTOR: The kingdom God promised was not of this world. Be patient. You'll see.

MALE ONE: He showed me how God kept making promises to His people. God promised to send a guy called a Messiah. The promises were fulfilled when a baby named Jesus was born. I didn't understand that. How could a baby do the things that this, this, this...

(SAM gropes for the right word.)

PASTOR: Messiah?

MALE ONE: Yeah. How could a baby do the things Messiah was supposed to do?

PASTOR: A baby COULDN'T. But Jesus grew to be an adult. *(The PASTOR shows SAM more Bible passages. SAM continues to question.)*

MALE ONE: The pastor showed me how this, this Messiah Jesus did amazing things. He preached the truth to people, healed the sick, even raised people from the dead. "So everybody believed He was the Messiah?" I asked.

PASTOR: Unfortunately, no. Many didn't. And some of them hated Jesus so much that they had Him killed. *(The PASTOR shows SAM the Crucifixion narrative. SAM is horrified.)*

MALE ONE: He showed me where the Bible said that Jesus was nailed to a cross. Killed like a common criminal. "That explains the pain and suffering in the world," I said. "God must hate people for killing Jesus."

PASTOR: No, He doesn't. This was all part of God's plan.

MALE ONE: He showed me where Jesus didn't stay dead. He rose on the third day. Defeated death, as they say. Jesus died as the perfect sacrifice to forgive sin and the, the, the...

(SAM scratches his head, trying to think of the word.)

PASTOR: Resurrection?

MALE ONE: Yeah, that was the word. It meant the end of death. Somehow, this was all making sense. I thought Christians just believed things without proof.

PASTOR: Oh, no. God asks us to use our intelligence. Look at this verse, Isaiah 1:18. "'Come now, let us reason together,' says the Lord. 'Though your sins are like scarlet, they shall be as white as snow.'"

MALE ONE: This pastor had a verse for every occasion. Hallmark would love it. I had enough information. Now I just had to figure things out.

(SAM SHOVEL rises and shakes hands with PASTOR.)

The pastor invited me to stay and pray. To ask Jesus into my life and forgive my sins. He was beginning to make sense, but I think that's because he's more, more, more...

(SAM scratches head, trying to think of the word he wants.)

PASTOR: Articulate?

MALE ONE: No. It had nothing to do with art. He just knows more words than I do. That's it. I had to think things over. So I left.

PASTOR: Come back any time.

(SAM waves as he exits, Stage Left.)

INTERMEZZO

(As STAGEHANDS remove Scene Two and set up Scene Three, SAM enters, Stage Left. He walks slowly, hands in pockets; he is obviously thinking hard.)

MALE ONE: That pastor had given me a lot to think about. Why was my life so messed up? Could Jesus be the answer? What should I do? Then it hit me.

(A person carrying a sign marked "IT" runs onstage, hits SAM with the sign, and runs off. SAM looks up and snaps his fingers.)

I was thinking about the wrong things. I didn't want answers to life. I wanted to get ammunition to prove Christians were wrong. That was the only way I could get my hands on that money. Besides, how much does a pastor know about anything? That pastor never once mentioned anybody in a red suit or bunnies.

(SAM casually exits, Stage Right, smiling.)

SCENE THREE: SAM'S OFFICE

(SAM enters, Stage Right, hangs up hat and coat and sits behind desk. He begins writing his report. As he writes, TRACY enters, Stage Right.)

MALE ONE: Little Miss Trouble walked in, but that was OK with me. I had what she wanted, and she had what I wanted. I had her proof, and she had my money. I told her to sit down. I gave her my report.

(SAM motions TRACY to chair and hands her the report. SAM sits back, satisfied. As TRACY reads the report, she begins to frown.)

I sensed that she was upset.

(TRACY glares at SAM and throws report on his desk.)

FEMALE ONE *(furiously)***:** What are you trying to do? CONVERT me?

MALE ONE: ...she screamed at me. I knew what she was trying to do. She was trying to get out of paying me. She was trying to, to, to...

(SAM and TRACY are arguing. Suddenly SAM stops and scratches head, trying to find the right words.)

FEMALE ONE: Stiff me?

MALE ONE: Yeah! That's it.

(SAM and TRACY continue argument.)

MALE ONE: I told her we had a deal. Now I had delivered. I had proof that Christians were wrong so she had better cough up the loot she had promised. She didn't agree. She said...

(TRACY picks up report.)

FEMALE ONE: We had a bargain, but this isn't a bargain at any price! There's nothing here but a summary of Christian beliefs! I've HEARD all this stuff. I KEEP hearing it from Christians. I HIRED you to get proof that they're WRONG!

(TRACY throws report back on desk. SAM and TRACY glare at each other.)

MALE ONE: I knew she was trouble. She figured she could get out of paying me by starting an argument. And she figured she'd win the argument because she's more, more, more...

FEMALE ONE: Articulate?

MALE ONE: No. It has nothing to do with drawing. But she knows more words. Well, it won't work, and I told her so.

SAM SHOVEL: *(Points at TRACY.)* So!

MALE ONE: I delivered the goods. She had to deliver the cash.

(SAM and TRACY continue to glare at each other. Suddenly, TRACY collapses into her chair, drops her face into her hands and begins to weep. She glances up to see if her tears are having any effect on SAM, then drops her face back into her hands and weeps some more.)

MALE ONE: I hate to see a dame cry. "Look, kid," I told her. "It's nothing personal. But when I do a job, I expect to get paid."

FEMALE ONE *(pleading)***:** Oh, Sam, don't you see? I came to you for help. You're the only one who can help me. I didn't mean to yell at you. But I need proof, Sam. I know you tried, but I need MORE than this. You can do it, Sam. I know you can.

MALE ONE: I didn't see what she was getting at. That report shows that Christians believe a lot of weird stuff. I told her so.

SAM SHOVEL: *(Points at TRACY.)* So!

MALE ONE: She agreed but disagreed.

FEMALE ONE *(pleading)***:** Oh, Sam! YOU know they believe weird things. And I know they believe weird things. But THEY won't see it, Sam. We have to PROVE it. We need more than just words. We need FACTS. Oh, Sam. You can do it if you try.

(TRACY points her finger at SAM.)

MALE ONE: I saw her point.

(SAM watches finger carefully.)

MALE ONE: And I knew she was right. Some people will believe anything if you don't have facts to prove them wrong. "I'll do it," I told her. "But it's going to be expensive, and I'll need an advance on expenses." She broke into the wad and peeled off a few bills.

(TRACY takes money from purse and gives SAM three or four bills. SAM reaches over and takes three or four more, puts them all in his jacket pocket. TRACY returns the rest to her purse.)

MALE ONE: I told her to go. I had work to do.

FEMALE ONE: Oh, thank you, thank you, thank you, THANK YOU! A million, trillion thanks couldn't be enough. You've saved my life. Thank you, thank you, thank you, THANK YOU!

(TRACY shakes SAM's hand vigorously and tries to remove the money from SAM's jacket pocket with her left hand. SAM removes his hand from hers and grabs her left wrist and removes her hand from his pocket. He shakes his finger at her. TRACY exits, Stage Right. SAM gets hat and coat and also exits, Stage Right.)

INTERMEZZO

(As STAGEHANDS remove Scene Three and set up Scene Four, SAM enters, Stage Right, smiling.)

MALE ONE: I was feeling good. I had liberated a few slices of bread from the loaf that Tracy was carrying. Now I had some dough to dangle in front of the occasional informant. That Tracy thinks she's one tough cookie. But I know how to get my cake and eat it, too. Hmm... Something about this case was making me hungry. I decided to have a bite to eat. Then I'd visit my old friend Marcy Tan. She was the investigative reporter for "Frequently Odd Global" News. So, it was on to the Fog City Diner, then to the FOG newsroom.

(SAM rubs his stomach because of hunger and exits, Stage Left.)

SCENE FOUR: FOG NEWSROOM

(Newsroom has lots of people moving around, handing memos to one another, reading memos, etc. All the time, people in the newsroom are saying, "Bzzz. Bzzz. Bzzz." MARCY TAN is seated at news desk, proofreading copy. SAM enters, Stage Left, and waves at MARCY TAN.)

MALE ONE: The FOG newsroom was buzzing with activity. This was the information hot spot of the free world. But they had something even more important to me than information. They had a time machine. Now, if I could just find a way to borrow it...

(SAM crosses to the news desk and sits down.)

I hadn't seen Marcy for a long time. She was pleased to see me and told me so...

MARCY TAN: *(To SAM SHOVEL.)* So.

MALE ONE: I told Marcy that I was working on a case and needed her help. She asked me...

FEMALE TWO: What sort of help do you need, Sam? We've got all kinds of information available.

MALE ONE: I knew I couldn't just come out and ask for the loan of FOG's time machine. I had to make Marcy think she was offering it to me. I pussyfooted around...

(SAM walks around news desk on his tiptoes and returns to his chair.)

...but she misunderstood me. She told me...

(MARCY TAN looks through papers on her desk.)

FEMALE TWO: Sorry, Sam, but we don't have anything on a cat burglar.

MALE ONE: That wasn't working so I gave her some veiled hints.

(SAM holds veil in front of his face and mimes speaking to MARCY TAN. MARCY looks through papers on desk and shows one to SAM.)

FEMALE TWO: We do have one story about Women's Liberation in the Middle East...

(SAM throws up hands in air and MARCY TAN looks through papers again.)

MALE ONE: She wasn't seeing my point...

(SAM points while Marcy Tan looks through papers. MARCY does not look at SAM.)

...so I decided to be more direct.

(SAM looks directly at MARCY TAN.)

I told her I was working on a case that had its roots buried in ancient cultures. I needed reliable information about the people of the time; but how could I trust information that was two thousand years old, if I couldn't check it myself? Then I tossed her the curve ball and waited.

(SAM takes baseball from pocket and gently tosses it to MARCY TAN.)

I think she caught my drift. She said to me...

FEMALE TWO: You know, Sam, it sounds like you could use a time machine.

(SAM SHOVEL turns to audience, signals "thumbs up" and smiles.)

It's too bad ours is broken.

(SAM's smile turns to a frown and his "thumbs up" slowly rotates to "thumbs down.")

FEMALE TWO: We had a little accident with it last Christmas.

MALE ONE: It seems the accident had caused a problem with the space-time continuum thingamabobby that runs the quantum mechanics of the do-hickey gizmo. Sorry about all that scientific mumbo jumbo, but some things can't be explained in layman's language. I asked her if it worked at all. She told me...

FEMALE TWO: The only time that works perfectly is the present. The past times can only get you to an approximate position.

MALE ONE: I told her that would be better than nothing and begged her to let me use it.

(SAM falls to his knees and pleads.)

FEMALE TWO: I can let you borrow it for tonight. But it's scheduled to be in the shop at eight o'clock tomorrow morning. It HAS to be back by then.

MALE ONE: I promised her...

(SAM rises and crosses his heart.)

...and she called in a flunkey.

MARCY TAN: *(Yells offstage.)* Flunkey!

(Actor in MONKEY costume enters, Stage Right, and runs to news desk.)

MALE ONE: She had called for a flunkey, not a monkey, but the mess was soon straightened up...

(MONKEY tidies up all papers on news desk and makes one neat pile. MONKEY exits, Stage Right.)

...and then the flunkey brought in the time machine.

(NEWSROOM FLUNKEY enters, Stage Right, with time machine and gives it to MARCY TAN. FLUNKEY exits, Stage Right.)

MALE ONE: Before she let me have it, Marcy brought up one problem of time travel. Language difficulties. She asked me...

FEMALE TWO: How are you going to speak to the people you meet?

MALE ONE: I told her I had been practicing my ancient languages. I demonstrated my proficiency.

SAM SHOVEL: Ho, varlet! Hie thee hence and speaketh to me!

MALE ONE: She wasn't impressed. She told me...

FEMALE TWO: That's only old English. You'll need to speak other languages to talk to people two thousand years ago. Greek, Latin, Aramaic (ar-eh-MAY-ik), Hebrew. But there's a solution.

MARCY TAN: *(Yells offstage.)* Flunkey!

(MONKEY and FLUNKEY both enter, Stage Right. FLUNKEY is carrying translator headphones. FLUNKEY looks at MONKEY, who then exits, Stage Right. FLUNKEY takes headphones to MARCY TAN and then exits, Stage Right.)

MALE ONE: She explained the function of this strange gadget.

(MARCY TAN hands headphones to SAM SHOVEL.)

FEMALE TWO: These headphones will automatically change everything anyone else says into English and will change your words into their language. That way, you'll be able to communicate with each other.

(SAM tries on headphones and then lets them hang around his neck.)

MALE ONE: They weren't very comfortable, but I could see they would be useful. She reminded me that I had to be back by eight tomorrow morning. I assured her I would, thanked her for her assistance and left.

(SAM exits with time machine and headphones, Stage Left.)

(MARCY TAN gathers papers off desk, then exits, Stage Right.)

INTERMEZZO

(As STAGEHANDS break down Scene Four and set up Scene Five, SAM enters, Stage Left, on time machine. He travels rapidly backwards across stage to indicate traveling back in time. SAM exits, Stage Right.)

SCENE FIVE: PAUL'S HOUSE

(PAUL is seated, chained between two SOLDIERS. PAUL speaks to the two SOLDIERS. SAM enters, stumbling, Stage Right. The headphones are still around his neck.)

MALE ONE: I had no idea where—or when—I was. Time travel is tougher than I thought. I was in some guy's house, but there were soldiers there. This guy was chained between them. I listened to them speak...

(PAUL and SOLDIERS speak gibberish.)

...but it was all Greek to me.

(SAM moves close to PAUL, listens and shakes head, no. He scratches head and touches headphones. Light dawns. He puts on headphones. PAUL is speaking; but as SAM puts on the headphones, PAUL's words change to English.)

PAUL: *(To SOLDIERS.)* ...which is why the Resurrection is so important.

MALE ONE: I had heard that word, Resur...Resur...what was it?

PAUL: Resurrection?

MALE ONE: Yeah. Resurrection. I'd heard it before. Where was it?

(SAM stops and turns to audience. Looks thoughtful, trying to remember. Snaps fingers.)

MALE ONE: That was it. That pastor had used it. This guy with the soldiers knew about the Resurrection, too. Maybe he could help me. But he sounded sympathetic to Christianity. I would have to be careful. I introduced myself.

(SAM holds out hand to shake hands.)

SAM SHOVEL: Sam Shovel. We dig up the dirt.

(SAM lowers his hand since it is being ignored. PAUL motions him to a chair, and he sits.)

MALE ONE: He said his name was Paul. He said that he was a pistol, or something like that. He thought my translator headphones were some kind of strange hat and told me so.

PAUL: So.

MALE ONE: I told him they were special equipment to help translate all that Greek he was using into something recognizable. He told me...

MALE TWO: We were speaking Latin. But we could use Greek if you prefer.

MALE ONE: I told him Latin was fine. Then I asked about this word he had used. Resurrection. What exactly was he talking about?

MALE TWO: Why, the resurrection of our Lord Jesus Christ. What else would it mean?

MALE ONE: I asked him why he was telling the soldiers that the Resurrection was so important. What kind of significance did it have to anyone? He replied...

MALE TWO: It's only the most important fact of history! If Christ did not rise from the dead, then all our preaching is false. If Christ did not rise from the dead, our sins are not forgiven!

MALE ONE: I got the picture.

(SAM walks over and picks up painting leaning against wall.)

This gave me something to do while I was thinking. Did I have the answer or was this just the beginning?

(SAM returns to PAUL's table and sits.)

I had to be sure I had this right. I questioned him closely.

(SAM leans directly into PAUL's face.)

So, the Resurrection is the central teaching of Christianity?

MALE TWO: That's correct.

MALE ONE: If it's false, all Christianity is false.

MALE TWO: But it's not false.

MALE ONE: But hypo...hypo...hypo...

MALE TWO: Hypothetically?

MALE ONE: Another person who was more...more...more...

MALE TWO: Articulate?

MALE ONE: Why is everyone so critical of my art? I happen to have a lot of talent in that area. No, he just knew more words than I did. So, hypothetically, if the Resurrection was false...

MALE TWO: Then all of Christianity is false. We are still in our sin and are sentenced to death.

MALE ONE: I thanked him and prepared to leave. I had my answer. I didn't need to slave over every little bit of Christian teaching. I just had to demonstrate that Jesus did not come back from the dead. What could be easier? This case would soon be completed.

(SAM takes off headphones and places them around his neck. He exits, Stage Right.)

INTERMEZZO

(As STAGEHANDS break down Scene Five and set up Scene Six, SAM enters, Stage Right, on time machine. He moves in a zigzag pattern to indicate that he doesn't know if he's traveling forward or backward in time. As he travels, PAUL and SOLDIERS exit, Stage Right. SAM exits, Stage Left. JOSEPHUS enters, Stage Right, and sits at table.)

SCENE SIX: JOSEPHUS'S HOUSE

(JOSEPHUS writes at table. SAM enters, Stage Left, with the headphones around his neck. JOSEPHUS is muttering in gibberish as he writes.)

MALE ONE: I had no idea where I was. Had I gone forward or backward in time? I would get some information from this stranger. I introduced myself.

(SAM walks over to JOSEPHUS. Puts out hand to shake hands.)

SAM SHOVEL: Sam Shovel. We dig up the dirt.

(JOSEPHUS looks up but doesn't understand SAM. JOSEPHUS says something in gibberish. SAM lowers his hand, since it is being ignored. Scratches his head, realizes he doesn't have on the headphones and puts them in place.)

MALE ONE: That helped. Now we could communicate and his words wouldn't be all Greek to me. He told me...

MALE THREE: I was speaking Latin. But we could use Aramaic (ar-eh-MAY-ik) or Hebrew, if you prefer.

MALE ONE: I assured him that Latin was fine. I introduced myself again and learned that his name was Flavius Josephus. I looked at what he was writing. But the headphones only worked on speech. His writing was still all Greek...

FLAVIUS JOSEPHUS: Latin.

MALE ONE: ...Latin to me. I asked him what he was doing. He explained...

MALE THREE: I'm writing a history of Palestine for the Roman government.

MALE ONE: An official government history, eh? We've all seen those before. Nothing that might embarrass the powers that be. A whitewashed version that bears little resemblance to the truth.

MALE THREE *(indignantly)*: You do me an injustice, sir! I write truth. Look here!

(FLAVIUS JOSEPHUS points to his manuscript.)

MALE THREE: If I wanted to only please the government, would I write about Jesus of Nazareth? No! I would make up some silly story about a fictional character. But do I? No! Jesus of Nazareth lived, and so I write about Him!

MALE ONE: Just my luck. I had met up with another Christian fanatic.

MALE THREE *(indignantly)*: How dare you associate me with THEM?

MALE ONE: At last! I had met someone who didn't believe Christianity. We sat down and talked turkey.

(SAM sits. He and FLAVIUS JOSEPHUS both say, "Gobble, gobble. Gobble, gobble, gobble.")

MALE ONE: I asked him what had happened when Jesus was alive. He told me almost exactly the same thing that the pastor had said. Born in Bethlehem, grew up in Nazareth and became a preacher. For three years or so, Jesus went around teaching and doing things that people called miracles. Jesus' fame grew, and soon the Jewish religious authorities got jealous of Him. So they had Him executed. End of story. But Flavius Josephus explained.

MALE THREE: That SHOULD have been the end of the story. But His body disappeared. This led to the ridiculous rumor that Jesus was ALIVE, resurrected from the dead. All nonsense, of course.

MALE ONE: Naturally, it was nonsense. But what HAD happened? Jesus had been born and grew to be a man. So He was real. Maybe He didn't die. I put this possibility to Flavius Josephus, but he just laughed.

(FLAVIUS JOSEPHUS laughs, loud and long.)

MALE THREE: You must never have seen a crucifixion. The Romans make SURE that the victim is dead.

MALE ONE: But just suppose, hypo...hypo...hypo...

FLAVIUS JOSEPHUS: Hypothetically?

MALE ONE: That's it. But don't start bad-mouthing my art just because you know more words than me. Suppose—hypothetically—that they messed up. This one was taken down before He was dead. He just seemed to be dead. Then He wakes up in the tomb and leaves.

(FLAVIUS JOSEPHUS laughs, loud and long.)

That was twice he laughed in my face! But he explained...

MALE THREE: Suppose that was true. He has been on the Cross all day. He is so close to death that experienced soldiers can't tell the difference. He is weak from His ordeal. Now His friends take His body and prepare it for burial. They take a cloth and cover it with strong-smelling burial spices and put this over His face. Then, they cover cloths with the same spices and wrap His body. After that, they roll a huge stone across the opening to protect the body from wild animals.

MALE ONE: I hadn't known this was how bodies were buried here. It was very interesting, but it didn't answer my question. Flavius Josephus went on...

MALE THREE: Now, you want me to believe that a man who is near death would wake up? He would be easily smothered by the burial spices pressed against His face. But suppose, somehow, He didn't smother. He wakes up, works Himself free from His burial bonds, walks to the door of the tomb and moves a stone that needs three or four strong men to put it into place. Does this sound reasonable?

MALE ONE: He had a point. There was a body. And it was dead. What happened? Did the disciples go to the wrong tomb and think the body was gone? Maybe the body was still resting peacefully.

MALE THREE: No! Many people know where the tomb is. If there was a mistake like that, it would have been discovered years ago. The Pharisees would have opened the correct tomb and shown that He was still dead. His disciples stole the body. It's the only explanation.

MALE ONE: Of course! The simplest explanation. I thanked Flavius Josephus and was ready to go back to my own time. My fee was as good as earned.

(SAM stands and shakes JOSEPHUS's hand. Removes headphones, hangs them around his neck and exits, Stage Left. FLAVIUS JOSEPHUS exits, Stage Right.)

INTERMEZZO

(As STAGEHANDS break down Scene Six and set up Scene Seven, SAM enters, Stage Left, on time machine. He travels backward to show he is moving back in time. SAM exits, Stage Right.)

SCENE SEVEN: JERUSALEM NIGHT

(SAM enters, Stage Right, headphones around his neck. People are grouped around fire, trying to keep warm. PETER stands away from the group, Center Stage. People are all speaking gibberish.)

MALE ONE: Something was wrong. I thought I set the time machine for the present, but I had traveled BACK in time. Where was I? What was happening? What were these people saying? It was all Greek... OK, maybe it was Latin or Aramaic or Hebrew. Why couldn't I understand? Of course.

(SAM slaps forehead. Puts on headphones. GIRL ONE approaches PETER.)

GIRL ONE: I saw you. You're one of the people who followed the prisoner.

PETER *(angrily)*: I don't know what you're talking about.

(PETER stalks away and GIRL ONE returns to the fire. GIRL TWO approaches PETER.)

GIRL TWO: Hey, everyone! Here's someone who knows what's happening. He's one of the prisoner's followers.

PETER *(angrily)*: You're crazy! I never met the man!

(PETER moves away, and GIRL TWO returns to the fire. MAN approaches PETER.)

MAN: Listen to you. Your accent tells us you're one of them. You're from Galilee!

PETER *(angrily)*: How many times do I have to tell you? I don't know what you're talking about! I never met the man! I don't know Him!

(Offstage, a rooster crows. PETER cries out and runs offstage, Stage Right, past SAM.)

MALE ONE: There's nothing to be learned here. Just a typical, sad scene of one criminal pretending he never knew his former friend who's been captured. Well, back to the present—to collect my fee.

(SAM removes headphones, places them around his neck and exits, Stage Right. Others exit, Stage Left.)

INTERMEZZO

(As STAGEHANDS break down Scene Seven and set up Scene Eight, SAM enters on time machine, Stage Right. Time machine moves slowly, indicating moving forward in time, but very slowly. SAM mutters at machine, "C'mon, c'mon, c'mon." SAM exits on time machine, Stage Left.)

SCENE EIGHT: JERUSALEM DAY

(People are milling about PETER and other DISCIPLES. SAM enters, Stage Left, with headphones around his neck. People are speaking gibberish. One man shouts gibberish at PETER.)

PETER: That's where you're wrong! We're not DRUNK. It's only nine o'clock in the morning!

MALE ONE: The time machine was definitely having problems. I hadn't come very far forward in time, but at least I was remembering to put on my translator headphones. I understood every word this man was saying. But there must have been some kind of malfunction. I couldn't understand anyone else.

(SAM reaches to take off headphones and finds they are not on his head. They're still around his neck. He takes them off and looks at them in wonder. Puts them around his neck again.)

Something strange was happening here. Everybody seemed to understand what this man was saying, but nobody here spoke English. In fact, they didn't seem to even speak the same language as each other. That speaker looked familiar. What was he saying?

MALE FOUR: Yes, men of Israel. Hear my words. You know that Jesus of Nazareth was a man approved by God. You saw the wonders and miracles He performed among you. You know that He was killed by wicked men. But now, I say to you, He has been raised up from the dead. He lives, as the Scriptures prophesied.

MALE ONE: He was speaking of the resurrection of Jesus. What luck! I just happened to hit the right time. Wait a minute. Now I know where I've seen that man before. He was the one who denied knowing some criminal.

(SAM puts on headphones to listen to crowd.)

CROWD: What shall we do? What shall we do?

(SAM removes headphones.)

PETER: Repent and be baptized in the name of Jesus Christ for forgiveness of sin.

MALE ONE: Something very strange was happening here. I had to speak to that man, find out what was happening. How could he speak English? How could everyone else understand him when THEY don't speak English? I drew him aside and put these questions to him.

(SAM waves to PETER, motions PETER aside. PETER leaves crowd and joins SAM.)

MALE FOUR: It is the work of the Holy Spirit. All must hear the good news, and so the Holy Spirit gives understanding.

MALE ONE: I asked him about the criminal life he used to live. I let him know that I had seen him one night and that I heard him deny he knew some horrible person who was scheduled to be executed. He laughed at me.

(PETER laughs, loud and long.)

MALE ONE: What is it about me that inspires laughter? Maybe I should stop being a detective and become a comedian instead. But Peter explained...

MALE FOUR: That so-called horrible person was Jesus Christ. He was taken by the Romans to be executed—crucified. I was frightened for my life and denied knowing Him. The only reason I can speak to you now about that night is that I have been forgiven. Because Jesus lives, I live and can speak boldly.

MALE ONE: The poor, deluded man. I thought I had better wise him up. So I told him that Jesus hadn't been resurrected. I had it on good authority that Jesus' disciples had stolen the body.

(PETER laughs, loud and long.)

There was no doubt about it. I was in the wrong line of work. Comedy was where I should be working. Look at the laughs I was getting—without even trying. Then, he explained...

MALE FOUR: But I am one of His disciples. Why do you think we would steal His body? What would we gain?

MALE ONE: He had me there. What WOULD they gain? Power, prestige, wealth?

MALE FOUR: Let me tell you what will happen. We know that most of the world does not want to hear the good news. Our Messiah, the Lord Jesus Christ, was crucified. We who preach in His name face a similar fate. Most of us will probably be killed for saying that Jesus is the Christ. We will certainly be beaten, thrown in prison, and who knows what else.

MALE ONE: I was perplexed. If the disciples stole the body, then they now were telling a lie, and they knew it. If it was a lie, all they would gain were beatings, imprisonment and death. Why would they lie? What do they have to gain?

(SAM exits, Stage Left. PETER goes back to the crowd. All exit, Stage Right. SAM enters on time machine, Stage Left. Time machine moves smoothly forward to indicate it is functioning perfectly as SAM moves forward in time. SAM rides in large circle around the stage and exits, Stage Left.)

INTERMEZZO

(As STAGEHANDS break down Scene Eight and set up Scene Nine, SAM enters, Stage Left. He strolls across the stage, whistling with hands in pockets, as NARRATOR speaks.)

MALE ONE: I had returned the time machine and translator headphones to Marcy at the FOG newsroom. We talked about my experiences in time travel—and a little bit about what they meant. And now I was ready to report to my client.

(SAM exits, Stage Right.)

SCENE NINE: SAM'S OFFICE

(SAM enters, Stage Right. He hangs up his hat and coat and sits behind desk.)

MALE ONE: I was waiting for the Trouble Lady. I had my report ready, but somehow, I didn't think she would find it comforting.

(TRACY enters, Stage Right, and sits in chair.)

She breezed in like a gentle zephyr (ZEF-er). She was anxious but tried to appear calm. I was her last hope. But I had good news for her, and I told her so.

SAM SHOVEL: *(Points at TRACY.)* So—I have good news for you.

MALE ONE: She was DE-lighted.

(TRACY gets up, takes flashlight from handbag and puts it on SAM's desk.)

FEMALE ONE: Oh, Sam, I knew you could do it! What do I tell those horrid Christians when they start to talk to me?

MALE ONE: You say, "Thank you for sharing the truth with me. What must I do?" And they'll tell you, "You must repent and be baptized in the name of Jesus Christ for the forgiveness of your sins." She was no longer delighted.

(TRACY stands angrily, grabs flashlight from desk and stuffs it in handbag.)

The breeze was no longer a zephyr. It was an Arctic gale. Her look could have chilled a polar bear to the bones. She reminded me of our agreement.

FEMALE ONE *(furiously)*: You were supposed to give me ammunition to SHOOT DOWN Christians. Now you tell me I should THANK them!

MALE ONE: She saw her rage wasn't having any effect on me so she tried another tack.

(TRACY takes box of tacks from her purse, chooses one and shows it to SAM. SAM shakes his head. TRACY returns that tack to the box, removes another one and shows it to SAM. SAM shakes his head again. TRACY returns that tack to the box and returns box to her handbag.)

When that failed, she tried turning on the charm. But she must have been using the wrong kind of batteries because it soon turned to cold fury again.

(TRACY tries to smile at SAM but her look soon returns to a frown.)

She soon let me know that she was displeased with my work.

FEMALE ONE: How could you BETRAY me after all we've meant to each other? You sold me out! I'll never FORGIVE you for this!

MALE ONE: I tried to calm her. I told her that I had investigated the claims of Christianity and found—to my surprise—that they were true. She should listen to those Christians. They were the best friends she could have. But she wasn't listening.

(SAM reaches into pocket and takes out money. He returns it to TRACY.)

Even when I returned the fee she'd paid me, she wouldn't listen. She was so upset that she wouldn't listen to anything or anyone. She was not so upset, however, that she forget the money I had returned.

(TRACY stuffs money in handbag and stomps out of office. She exits, Stage Right.)

She stormed from the office like a hurricane. I could only hope that someday she'd listen to someone who wanted to tell her about the love of Jesus. It didn't matter that I didn't get a dime from that case. I got more out of it than I could ever have hoped to receive—forgiveness of sin.

(Phone rings. SAM picks it up.)

SAM SHOVEL: Sam Shovel. We dig up—the truth.

(Lights dim.)

A Pilate's Tale

(APPROXIMATE TIME: 25 MINUTES)

SYNOPSIS

Pontius Pilate, some of his friends and some of his enemies tell about the events surrounding Jesus' death and resurrection.

STAGE SETTINGS

SCENE ONE: JERUSALEM STREET

Tables piled with fruit, vegetables, sacks of grain, rubber chicken, etc. to represent marketplace, about halfway between front and rear of stage

SCENE TWO: CAIAPHAS'S OFFICE

■ Chairs for Priests and Scribes, Stage Left, at front of stage
■ Chair for Jesus, Stage Right, at front of stage

SCENE THREE: PILATE'S JUDGMENT HALL

■ Table at front of Stage Right, facing Stage Left
■ Large chair for Pilate's judgment seat, behind table, facing Stage Left

SCENE FOUR: HEROD'S OFFICE

Same as Scene Three

SCENE FIVE: PILATE'S JUDGMENT HALL

Same as Scene Three

THE PLAYERS

CROWD (All ages)

SOLDIERS (All ages)

PRIESTS and SCRIBES (All ages)

DISCIPLES (All ages)

STAGEHANDS (Grade 1 or older)

HEROD (Grade 3 or older)

NARRATOR (Grade 5 or older)

PILATE (Grade 5 or older)

CAIAPHAS (KAY-eh-fehs) (Grade 5 or older)

JESUS (Grade 5 or older)

SPEAKING SOLDIER (Grade 5 or older)

SUGGESTED PROPS

■ Laurel wreaths for Pilate and Herod to wear

■ Soldiers' uniforms and weapons (swords, spears, shields, etc.)

■ Papers to represent documents to be read by Pilate

■ Jug of water and a glass for Herod

■ Handkerchief for Pilate's wife

■ Poster board signs, lettered "Dead"

■ Poster board signs, lettered "He's Alive!" and "And We're Forgiven!"

■ Bible-times costumes

DIRECTOR'S TIPS

1. Narrator's part may be read. Consider using an adult for the Narrator. The Narrator need not be seen but should be able to see the action. Narrator must allow time for the action to happen before speaking again.

2. Marketplace should be full of activity, but the noise level must remain low to allow the speeches to be heard.

3. Jesus speaks with authority. He is not unsure of Himself. Caiaphas and Pilate are also sure of themselves and speak accordingly.

4. Speaking Soldier is unsure of himself and uncomfortable in the presence of someone as important as Pilate.

5. If your group or your stage is not large enough, use fewer than twelve Disciples.

6. Stagehands can take other roles.

7. Signs ("DEAD," "HE'S ALIVE!" etc.) can be lettered with the entire word or phrase on one sign, or phrases can be made up of one-word signs, or even signs lettered with the individual letters. Let some of the younger children participate as sign holders. If you are using individual words or letters on the signs, make sure actors know where to stand so that signs have the right messages.

8. Make the audience a part of this play. For instance, the Priests can move around the outside edges of the audience from Stage Left to Stage Right to arrest Jesus. They then could bring Him from Stage Right to Stage Left to be ready for the judgment scene.

A Pilate's Tale

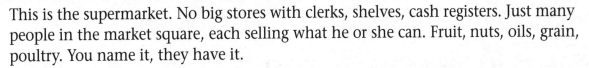

SCENE ONE: JERUSALEM STREET

(Stage area is completely dark.)

NARRATOR: Long, long ago in a land far, far, away, strange events occurred—events that would forever change history. This land was very different from yours. See if you can picture it in your mind.

(Lights rise to show marketplace. People are milling about, buying and selling goods.)

This is the supermarket. No big stores with clerks, shelves, cash registers. Just many people in the market square, each selling what he or she can. Fruit, nuts, oils, grain, poultry. You name it, they have it.

(People in the marketplace continue their business. It becomes noisy with people haggling over prices.)

This is the place where I live and work. Not in the market, of course. I am MUCH too important to work there. Look! There I am, coming into the market square.

(PILATE and SOLDIERS enter, Stage Left, and stop just onstage.)

As you can see, I am a VERY important person. Everywhere I go, people stand aside to let me pass. If they don't, my guard PUSHES them aside.

(PILATE and SOLDIERS begin moving to Center Stage. As they walk, people get out of the way or the SOLDIERS push them aside. As PILATE moves through the crowd, the noise dies down. At Center Stage, PILATE and SOLDIERS stop.)

Perhaps I should introduce myself. My name is Pontius Pilate. I am the governor of Judea; the single most important man in the area.

(PILATE stands with arms folded, looking important. One SOLDIER goes to a table and takes a piece of fruit. The VENDOR starts to argue, but the SOLDIER snarls, goes back to PILATE and gives him the fruit. PILATE eats.)

Everyone fears me. I have the power of life and death over ALL these people. But there is ONE man whom I dislike intensely. Here he comes now.

(CAIAPHAS, PRIESTS and SCRIBES enter, Stage Right, and stop just onstage.)

Those are the religious leaders of the Jews. They are all a royal pain, but the biggest pain is the one in the middle. The chief priest. Caiaphas.

(PILATE looks over at the PRIESTS and sees CAIAPHAS. PILATE looks at audience and grimaces with disgust. He is not happy to see CAIAPHAS. CAIAPHAS, PRIESTS and SCRIBES begin to move toward Center Stage.)

Outwardly, they are polite to me. They have to be. But I suspect that they say DIFFERENT things about me behind my back.

(CAIAPHAS approaches PILATE, bows respectfully. PRIESTS and SCRIBES bow also. PILATE acknowledges bows with a curt wave of his hand and slight nod of his head. PILATE and SOLDIERS continue to walk across stage toward Stage Right. CAIAPHAS, PRIESTS and SCRIBES step toward back of stage to let them pass. When PILATE is about half way to the exit, CAIAPHAS snarls and makes a clawing motion with his hands at PILATE's back. PRIESTS and SCRIBES begin to laugh. PILATE whirls around, PRIESTS and SCRIBES stop laughing and bow to PILATE. PILATE turns and exits, Stage Right, followed by SOLDIERS. CAIAPHAS, PRIESTS and SCRIBES continue their journey across stage, laughing and talking. They exit, Stage Left.)

(Lights begin to dim to indicate night is approaching. People onstage hurry off. Vendors take their wares and tables with them. Lights dim as STAGEHANDS set up Scene Two.)

I have never been to one of Caiaphas's council meetings. But I can certainly guess what goes on at one.

SCENE TWO: CAIAPHAS'S OFFICE

(Lights rise on Scene Two. CAIAPHAS, PRIESTS and SCRIBES enter, Stage Left, and sit.)

NARRATOR: They HATE me. I know they do.

CAIAPHAS *(angrily, but controlled)*: Oh, how I hate Pontius Pilate! Having to bow and scrape to HIM—a ROMAN! But I'll FIX him. I don't know HOW, I don't know WHEN. But I'll GET him.

(CAIAPHAS, PRIESTS and SCRIBES all lean forward and mumble in undertones, plotting something.)

NARRATOR: Yes, they hate me. But it's understandable. I am governor over them and they hate me because I have power. Power that they WANT. But in spite of that, there is SOMEONE they hate even more than ME.

CAIAPHAS: But there's someone I hate even MORE than Pontius Pilate.

(JESUS and DISCIPLES enter, Stage Right. JESUS sits on chair with DISCIPLES forming a semicircle behind him. A CROWD of people enter, Stage Right, and sit on floor in front of JESUS. JESUS begins to mime talking to the CROWD. The CROWD does not acknowledge CAIAPHAS, PRIESTS and SCRIBES; the scene is separate.)

CAIAPHAS *(scornfully)*: Jesus! Jesus of Nazareth!

(CAIAPHAS, PRIESTS and SCRIBES continue to mumble in undertones.)

NARRATOR: I don't pretend to know everything about Jewish religion. It has some odd notion about there being only one God and that He cares for His people. And the priests and Pharisees have made up a whole bunch of rules to decide what is holy and what isn't.

CAIAPHAS: Jesus is destroying the LAW! He must be STOPPED.

(PRIESTS and SCRIBES nod in agreement.)

JESUS: *(Speaks to CROWD.)* Don't think I've come to destroy the Law. I've come to fulfill it!

NARRATOR: The Pharisees keep all these RULES—religiously, you might say.

JESUS: *(Speaks to CROWD.)* Unless you are more righteous than the scribes and Pharisees, you will not enter into the Kingdom of Heaven.

NARRATOR: I suppose these Pharisees MIGHT be good men, but they are extremely concerned about RULES.

CAIAPHAS: Jesus HEALS people on the SABBATH!

(PRIESTS and SCRIBES gasp, shocked by this disregard for the Law.)

NARRATOR: But Jesus seems to make things simpler.

JESUS: *(Speaks to CROWD.)* Two sparrows are sold for a penny. But not even one little sparrow can fall to the ground without God knowing it.

CAIAPHAS: He doesn't keep himself pure—He eats with tax collectors and sinners.

JESUS: *(Speaks to CROWD.)* You have heard it said, "Love your neighbor and hate your enemy." But I say to you, love your enemies. Bless them and do good to them. Pray for them.

CAIAPHAS: And people LISTEN to Him! That's the worst part. He will destroy our place and our nation. He must DIE!

(PRIESTS and SCRIBES nod in agreement.)

JESUS: *(Speaks to CROWD.)* I tell you a truth: Unless a grain of wheat falls into the ground and dies, it remains alone. But if it dies, it brings forth a great deal of fruit.

(JESUS rises and exits, Stage Right, followed by DISCIPLES. The CROWD follows behind.)

CAIAPHAS: It is better for ONE man to die for everyone than to have an entire NATION perish!

NARRATOR: Caiaphas hates me because I have power over him. But he hates Jesus because he is JEALOUS of Jesus.

(CAIAPHAS sits back in chair and rubs his chin thoughtfully. PRIESTS and SCRIBES look at him expectantly.)

CAIAPHAS: If we do this right, maybe we can destroy BOTH of them—Jesus AND Pilate!

(CAIAPHAS, PRIESTS and SCRIBES all laugh. CAIAPHAS rises and exits, Stage Left. PRIESTS and SCRIBES follow.)

(Lights dim. STAGEHANDS remove Scene Two and set up Scene Three.)

NARRATOR: Yes, I can imagine them plotting against Jesus and me. But what can they DO? Nothing! They don't have any REAL power. I'm the ONLY one who can REALLY make things happen.

SCENE THREE: PILATE'S JUDGMENT HALL

(Lights rise to show judgment hall. SOLDIERS are standing by the hall entrance, Stage Left. PILATE enters, Stage Right. Sits in chair and begins reading documents on table. Some he likes— these he sets to his right. Others he doesn't like and sets them to his left.)

NARRATOR: The day began just like any other. Complaints about soldiers' conduct.

(PILATE reads memo and puts it on his left.)

Arguments about property.

(PILATE reads memo and puts it on his left.)

The newest rules from Rome about stopping violence.

(PILATE reads memo and puts it on his right.)

Then something extraordinary happened.

(Noise is heard offstage. SOLDIER exits, Stage Left, then returns, approaches PILATE and salutes.)

SPEAKING SOLDIER: Begging your pardon, Pontiac Piler...

PILATE *(regally)*: That's PONTIUS PILATE.

NARRATOR: Most Roman soldiers are excellent guards, but occasionally there's one...

SPEAKING SOLDIER: Right! *(Salutes again.)* But there's lots of people to see you.

PILATE: Who?

SPEAKING SOLDIER: That priest guy. Cacophonous? (Kak-AW-fun-nus)

PILATE: Caiaphas?

SPEAKING SOLDIER: Right! *(Salutes again.)* He and his gang have a prisoner. It's that Jesus, the one they're always upset about.

NARRATOR: This was nothing new. Caiaphas was ALWAYS trying to find a way to catch me making a mistake in law. He would drag in any dispute he could THINK of. I didn't have time for him. But on the other hand, I couldn't refuse to see him. I was Roman law and he was the top man in Jewish law.

PILATE: Bring them in.

SPEAKING SOLDIER: Begging your pardon, Porky Pigness...

PILATE: That's PONTIUS PILATE!

SPEAKING SOLDIER: Right! *(Salutes again.)* But they WON'T come in. They want you to go out.

PILATE: WHAT?

SPEAKING SOLDIER: Something about you being unclean and then they can't eat, uh, persimmons (per-SIM-mens).

PILATE: You mean Passover?

SPEAKING SOLDIER: That's the one.

PILATE (sighing): Very well. I'll come.

(SOLDIER salutes and exits, Stage Left. PILATE follows him. Other SOLDIERS follow PILATE.)

NARRATOR: MORE of their rules and regulations. Such a nuisance! But I have to appear to respect their silly customs. More than anything else, Rome expects me to keep the peace. And keeping peace is so DIFFICULT here in Judea! Every crackpot in the WORLD seems to live here. And every one of them wants to overthrow the government!

(The following exchange between PILATE and CAIAPHAS is heard from offstage.)

PILATE (irritated): What's the problem?

CAIAPHAS (shouting): This man is a lawbreaker and needs to be punished.

PILATE: Then take Him and judge Him by your law.

CAIAPHAS: We can't! He must be executed! Only you can do that!

NARRATOR: So THAT was it. They thought they had found a way to have this Jesus killed by the Roman government. Well, TWO can play at that game. We don't kill just anybody. They told me Jesus said He was the King of the Jews. So I called Him into the Judgment Hall.

(PILATE enters, Stage Left, followed by JESUS and SOLDIERS. PILATE sits in judgment seat. JESUS stands in front of table.)

PILATE: (To JESUS.) Are you a king?

JESUS: Do you say this of your own knowledge or did others tell you?

PILATE: Do I look like a Jew? Your own people want you killed.

JESUS: My kingdom is not of this world. If it were, my servants would fight to protect me.

(PILATE sits back, folds his hands and considers the case.)

NARRATOR: That was it. Another trumped-up charge, but a serious one. Claiming to be a king is treason. But this fellow was no threat to Rome. He was perhaps a little crazy, but not guilty of any crime.

(PILATE rises and exits, Stage Left. The following exchange happens offstage.)

PILATE: He's not guilty of any crime.

CAIAPHAS (amazed): Not GUILTY? He's been stirring up all the Jews, starting from up in Galilee, all the way to Jerusalem!

(PILATE enters, Stage Left, and returns to judgment seat. He folds his hands and considers Jesus again.)

NARRATOR: I had the perfect solution. No matter what judgment I made, I could get in trouble. But Jesus was from Galilee. Herod is the governor for Galilee. I never have liked Herod. He's a pompous little man who thinks himself better than anyone else. And Herod just HAPPENED to be in Jerusalem. So I sent Jesus to HIM! Let Herod make the decision. Let HIM take the heat!

(PILATE dismisses the SOLDIERS and JESUS with a wave of his hand. SOLDIERS escort JESUS out, Stage Left. PILATE rises and exits, Stage Right, as lights fade. STAGEHANDS set up Scene Four.)

NARRATOR: Because Herod's accomodations in Jerusalem were not an official Roman building, the Pharisees and priests could enter without defiling themselves. Off they went! How they keep track of all their laws is beyond me.

SCENE FOUR: HEROD'S OFFICE

(HEROD enters, Stage Right, and sits. SOLDIERS enter, Stage Left, with JESUS. CAIAPHAS, PRIESTS and SCRIBES follow.)

NARRATOR: I knew Herod would see Jesus. Herod is a thrill-seeker. He had heard about Jesus performing miracles. No doubt he would want to see one firsthand.

HEROD: *(Rises from chair, curious.)* Are you really Jesus?

(JESUS remains silent.)

HEROD: *(Claps impatiently.)* Come! Do a miracle! Guard! A glass of water!

(GUARD pours a glass of water, hands it to HEROD. HEROD holds it up, points to it, looking expectantly at JESUS. He looks at it, smells it, tastes it, but it is still water. Disappointed, he makes a "yuk" face, sets the glass down on the table again.)

HEROD: It's still water! Are you SURE you're Jesus? Do you REALLY think you're a KING?

(CAIAPHAS, PRIESTS and SCRIBES all yell, "Of course He does! He said so!" Herod silences them with a wave of his hand.)

NARRATOR: Herod continued questioning Jesus, but Jesus wouldn't answer.

(HEROD mimes asking questions. JESUS remains silent. CAIAPHAS, PRIESTS and SCRIBES mime yelling accusations.)

NARRATOR: Nothing Herod did could persuade Jesus to speak—or the others to shut up. *(Disgusted.)* So Herod sent them back to ME.

(HEROD waves his hands in disgust at the others and exits, Stage Right. SOLDIERS escort JESUS out, Stage Left. CAIAPHAS, PRIESTS and SCRIBES follow. Lights fade to black. STAGEHANDS set up Scene Five.)

NARRATOR: What could I do? I TRIED to have Jesus released. I had Him scourged to show that I would punish Him for saying ridiculous things. But the priests had OTHER plans. They had aroused the crowd against Jesus. When I asked whom I should release...well, first I should explain. To help keep the peace, we Romans have GRACIOUSLY agreed to acknowledge Passover by releasing one prisoner. There were only two possible choices this year: Jesus or Barabbas (beh-RAB-ehs), a notorious murderer. When I asked whom I should release, the people yelled for the release of Barabbas and demanded that I crucify Jesus. The yelling was led by that despicable Caiaphas and his cohorts. But that left me no choice. I had to do it. It wasn't MY fault. But then, a MIRACLE happened.

SCENE FIVE: PILATE'S JUDGMENT HALL

(PILATE and HEROD enter, Stage Right. They talk, laugh, etc. They behave like the best of friends.)

NARRATOR: THAT was the miracle! Up to now, Herod and I had been bitter enemies. But now, we've become the best of friends. Who would have believed it could HAPPEN?

(PILATE and HEROD smile broadly and look out at audience. Their smiles become expressions of puzzlement.)

NARRATOR: Is something wrong? Were you people expecting something else? A DIFFERENT kind of miracle?

(PILATE and HEROD continue to look at the audience in bewilderment. Suddenly, it hits them. They both slap their palms to their heads and smile again.)

NARRATOR: Oh, of course! You're thinking about those silly rumors. The rumors that there was a REAL miracle—that Jesus rose from the dead. That dozens of people have seen Him! Believe me, there's nothing to them. When we Romans execute someone, he STAYS dead. If you don't believe me, ask Caiaphas!

(CAIAPHAS, PRIESTS and SCRIBES enter, Stage Left. STAGEHANDS bring in chairs, placing them in same position as Caiaphas's Office Scene. CAIAPHAS, PRIESTS and SCRIBES all hold up signs that say "DEAD." Then CAIAPHAS, PRIESTS and SCRIBES are seated.)

NARRATOR: So, as you can see, it's unanimous. Jesus is dead.

(JESUS enters, Stage Left, behind PILATE, HEROD, CAIAPHAS, PRIESTS and SCRIBES. DISCIPLES enter, Stage Right, and stand behind Him. All other cast members enter from both sides of stage and gather near JESUS. They hold up signs reading "HE'S ALIVE!" on JESUS' right and others reading "AND WE'RE FORGIVEN!" on JESUS' left.)

(Lights dim on PILATE, HEROD and PRIESTS. Lights intensify on JESUS and CROWD, especially on the signs, then snap to black.)

SHOWDOWN AT THE EASTER CORRAL

(APPROXIMATE TIME: 30 MINUTES)

SYNOPSIS

The story of Jesus' death and resurrection is told in true "Old West" style by Marshal Pilate.

STAGE SETTINGS

SCENE ONE: MARSHAL PILATE'S OFFICE

■ Desk and chair, Stage Left

■ Rack on wall containing numerous scrolls, left of desk

■ Trash can to left of desk

■ Hat rack slightly behind and to right of desk

■ Chair to right of desk

■ Door with sign lettered "To Cells" behind desk

■ Dividers to represent walls

■ Wanted posters on walls

SCENE TWO: STREETS OF CHRYSLER CITY

■ Facade representing old western town

■ Hitching posts (optional—use sawhorses)

SCENE THREE: MISS COYOTE'S BOARDING HOUSE

■ Tables and chairs set to represent dining room, Stage Right

■ Registry desk, Stage Left

■ Stool behind desk

SCENE FOUR: THE EASTER CORRAL

■ Corral fencing, Center Stage

■ Facade of hill with three crosses at rear of stage

SCENE FIVE: MARSHAL PILATE'S OFFICE

Same as Scene One

THE PLAYERS

THOMAS (Grade 1 or older)

ANNAS (Grade 1 or older)

TOUGH GUYS (All ages)

BOARDING HOUSE RESIDENTS (All ages)

BOARDING HOUSE RESIDENT ONE (Grade 3 or older)

TOWNSPEOPLE (All ages)

CHICHESTER (MARSHAL PILATE's deputy) (Grade 3 or older)

JESUS (Grade 5 or older)

PETER (Grade 3 or older)

MAGGIE DALENE (Grade 5 or older)

TOWNSPERSON ONE (Grade 3 or older)

TOWNSPERSON TWO (Grade 5 or older)

MARSHAL PILATE (Grade 5 or older)

COLT CAIAPHAS (KAY-eh-fehs) (Grade 5 or older)

MISS COYOTE (Grade 5 or older)

JUDAS (Grade 5 or older)

JOHN (Grade 5 or older)

STAGEHANDS (All ages)

NARRATOR (Grade 5 or older)

SUGGESTED PROPS

- Badges for Marshal Pilate and Deputy Chichester
- Scroll holsters for all scroll-toting characters
- Scrolls of various sizes
- Cowboy hats
- Hitching posts
- Corral fences
- Wanted posters—one boldly lettered "BARABBAS"
- Trash can
- Hat rack
- Handkerchief
- Dishes and cutlery
- Western-style clothing

DIRECTOR'S TIPS

1. Marshal Pilate is calm and under control. He is polite to everyone.

2. Chichester limps noticeably. He does not wear a scroll belt.

3. Miss Coyote is fond of Marshal Pilate and vice versa.

4. Narrator's part may be read.

5. Younger players may be able to handle more difficult roles. Include older players in the nonspeaking groups to help guide younger players.

6. For final scene, Judas can become part of Townspeople/Boarding House Residents group.

7. Use the audience in the play. If actors need to move from one side of the stage to the other, they can move through the audience, staying in character while they do.

8. Narrator should stand where he or she can see stage action.

SHOWDOWN AT THE EASTER CORRAL

SCENE ONE: MARSHAL PILATE'S OFFICE

(PILATE is seated at desk, going through papers. His hat is on the hat rack. He picks up wanted poster and hangs it on wall. He removes wanted poster for Barabbas, crumples it up and throws it in trash can beside desk. He returns to desk and continues paperwork.)

NARRATOR: It was a peaceful day in Chrysler City. The peace had been kept for some time under my authority, and I was glad of that. The folks back at the capitol don't like trouble. And if there was any trouble, I would be in the center of it. No, the peaceful life is the only one to lead.

(CHICHESTER enters, Stage Right. He removes hat and places it on hat rack.)

CHICHESTER: Howdy, Marshal Pilate.

MARSHAL PILATE: Howdy, Chichester.

CHICHESTER: It sure is hot out today. Man, it's a scorcher. *(Takes handkerchief from pocket and wipes his brow.)*

MARSHAL PILATE: Just so long as it's peaceful.

CHICHESTER: Oh, it's peaceful. For now, anyways. But Colt Caiaphas is talking up a storm.

NARRATOR: Now, Colt Caiaphas was the big man in Chrysler City. For years, he'd had his way. Talk was, he was responsible for getting rid of the past three or four marshals. Well, I was different. I knew my way around small-town politics as well as he did. Maybe even better. I wondered what was bothering him now.

MARSHAL PILATE: What's his problem NOW?

CHICHESTER: Well, you recollect that fellow who rode into town on that donkey?

MARSHAL PILATE: Yeah, He had a funny kind of a name. What was it? Jesus?

CHICHESTER: Well, ol' Colt kind of figures He's planning to be a rival for power.

MARSHAL PILATE: Well, just so long as there's no fireworks, they can feud all they want.

(TOWNSPERSON ONE enters, Stage Right.)

TOWNSPERSON ONE: You better come quick, Marshal. There's trouble brewing.

(PILATE looks annoyed. CHICHESTER looks worried.)

NARRATOR: That was the last thing I needed—trouble. But if there was trouble, I knew where to start looking. Colt Caiaphas. Something about him seemed to INSPIRE trouble.

(PILATE gets up from desk and gets his hat.)

CHICHESTER: You're not going out armed with just that little old hand scroll, are you?

(PILATE removes scroll from holster.)

MARSHAL PILATE: Regulations for handling minor disputes. I won't need anything more powerful.

CHICHESTER: Well, you can go out with that puny scroll. But I'M taking something stronger. *(Goes to scroll rack and removes large scroll.)*

MARSHAL PILATE: *(Chuckles.)* You think you'll need the whole federal law, Chichester?

CHICHESTER: Call me fussy if you like. But I believe in being careful.

(CHICHESTER limps to hat rack and jams hat on his head. PILATE exits, Stage Right, followed by CHICHESTER and TOWNSPERSON ONE. Lights snap to black. STAGEHANDS remove Scene One and set up Scene Two.)

SCENE TWO: STREETS OF CHRYSLER CITY

(COLT CAIAPHAS, ANNAS and TOUGH GUYS are grouped together, Stage Left, facing THOMAS, JUDAS, JOHN and PETER who stand nearer Center Stage. CAIAPHAS is carrying a very large scroll; ANNAS is carrying a slightly smaller scroll. All are wearing scroll belts with small scrolls in them. TOWNSPEOPLE enter and exit in the background. PILATE and CHICHESTER enter, Stage Right, and stop. TOWNSPEOPLE stop to see what will happen.)

NARRATOR: I was right. Colt Caiaphas was at the center of the trouble, as usual. His gang of tough guys was with him, ready to follow wherever he led. I didn't recognize the fellows he was facing. They were new in town. Chichester and I went over to see what the problem was.

(PILATE and CHICHESTER walk over to COLT CAIAPHAS's group and stand between the combatants, slightly behind them, facing the audience.)

MARSHAL PILATE: What seems to be the trouble here?

COLT CAIAPHAS: No problem, Marshal—as soon as these BLASPHEMERS leave town.

PETER *(angrily)***:** We aren't blasphemers!

ANNAS *(shouting)***:** You are, too!

THOMAS *(shouting)***:** I doubt it!

(All combatants look as if they're ready to draw their scrolls.)

NARRATOR: Some powerful emotions were running through this crowd. It was my job as keeper of the peace to calm them down and find out what was going on. Apparently, these new fellows were from some place called Blasphemy (BLAS-fuh-me). I'd never heard of it myself, but I knew that Colt Caiaphas hated anybody from that place. He often talked about Blasphemers and how they should all be strung up. Funny thing was, I thought I recognized their accents. I would have thought they came from Galilee county, up north of here.

Showdown at the Easter Corral ☆ *Holiday Skits* ☆ 149

MARSHAL PILATE: Are you sure they're Blasphemers? They sound like Galileans (gal-uh-LEE-ans) to me.

COLT CAIAPHAS: I don't care what they SOUND like. They're BLASPHEMERS.

PETER: We are not!

JUDAS: Take it easy, Peter. Nobody wants a showdown. Not yet.

JOHN: Well, if he keeps calling us blasphemers, there'll BE one.

PETER: That's right! We're not blasphemers!

ANNAS: You are, too!

THOMAS: I doubt it!

JUDAS: Take it easy, Thomas. You're getting as bad as Peter.

THOMAS: I doubt it!

(All combatants look as if they're ready to draw their scrolls.)

NARRATOR: The situation was becoming more complicated. Apparently, nobody liked anyone from Blasphemy. It must have been one rough town. I'd have to wire the capitol and get some information on it. But in the meantime, I had to cool down these hotheads before someone got hurt. All of them were armed. All of Colt Caiaphas's crowd were carrying their usual sidearm—*The Law and the Prophets*, they called it. But Annas and Colt Caiaphas were carrying heavier artillery. Annas had the *Commentary on the Law and the Prophets*, and Caiaphas was carrying the biggest weapon he had—*The Tradition of the Rabbis*. He often threatened the townspeople with it to keep them in line. That was fine by me. As long as there was no trouble, these people could do anything they wanted to settle their own disputes. But they all knew I didn't allow any killing in this town—unless I ordered it myself.

MARSHAL PILATE: *(To JUDAS.)* You seem to be a levelheaded fellow. What's your name?

JUDAS: It's Judas. That's Peter, John and Thomas.

MARSHAL PILATE: So what are you boys doing in town?

JOHN: We just rode in for the Passover, if you must know.

MARSHAL PILATE: I wasn't speaking to you, son. You should mind your manners. I'm the law in this town. You, Judas.

JUDAS: Yes?

MARSHAL PILATE: Mind if I take a look at that sidearm of yours? I've never seen one like it before.

JUDAS: Be my guest, Marshal. As long as I get it back. *(Reaches for scroll. TOUGH GUYS all get ready to draw. JUDAS then slowly removes scroll from holster and hands it to PILATE.)*

NARRATOR: I looked the weapon over.

(PILATE carefully unrolls and examines scroll.)

NARRATOR: Basically, it was the same weapon carried by Colt's gang—*The Law and the Prophets*—but it was somehow different. It seemed a little kinder, a little more gentle. Still, I could see it was just as deadly as any two-edged sword ever made.

(PILATE hands scroll back to JUDAS, who puts it into his holster.)

MARSHAL PILATE: You boys all seem to be carrying the same weapons...

COLT CAIAPHAS: They're NOT the same. They're different.

PETER: Yeah! Ours are the ORIGINAL.

JOHN: They don't have your MODIFICATIONS.

COLT CAIAPHAS: Blasphemers!

PETER: Are not!

ANNAS: Are too!

THOMAS: I doubt it!

(All combatants look as if they're ready to draw their scrolls. PILATE and CHICHESTER step in between them. CHICHESTER faces CAIAPHAS and PILATE faces the DISCIPLES.)

MARSHAL PILATE: *(Walks toward DISCIPLES.)* Where are you boys staying?

JUDAS: Over at the boarding house. We've rented the upper room for a quiet Passover meal.

NARRATOR: These boys needed to be separated for a while so I told Chichester...

MARSHAL PILATE: Why don't we separate these boys for a while? You take Colt and his boys over to their meeting hall. I'll escort these out-of-towners back to the boarding house.

CHICHESTER: You've got it, Marshal Pilate. C'mon Colt! You and your tough guys move it. And don't try any tricks. I've got my eye on your every move!

(PILATE motions the DISCIPLES toward the back of the stage. They move back a few steps. CHICHESTER takes one step back and motions with his scroll toward Stage Right. CAIAPHAS, ANNAS and TOUGH GUYS slowly walk across the stage, hands close to their scrolls. They keep looking back over their shoulders at the DISCIPLES as CHICHESTER escorts them offstage, Stage Right.)

MARSHAL PILATE: Let's go, boys. *(Motions to Stage Left and DISCIPLES exit, Stage Left, followed by PILATE. TOWNSPEOPLE begin moving again, exiting from stage in both directions. Lights snap to black as STAGEHANDS remove Scene Two and set up Scene Three.)*

SCENE THREE: MISS COYOTE'S BOARDING HOUSE

(BOARDING HOUSE RESIDENTS are seated at tables, having lunch. MISS COYOTE is seated on stool behind registration desk, writing in ledger. THOMAS, JUDAS, PETER and JOHN enter, Stage Left, followed by PILATE.)

NARRATOR: Now, Miss Coyote ran the best boarding house east or west of the Jordan. Food was first-rate, linen was always clean and the service was friendly. Whenever there was a big to-do in Chrysler City, her place filled up first.

MARSHAL PILATE *(removing hat)***:** Howdy, Miss Coyote.

MISS COYOTE: Howdy, Marshal. Howdy, boys.

THOMAS, JUDAS, JOHN and PETER: Howdy. *(They do not remove their hats.)*

MARSHAL PILATE: (*Notices they have not removed their hats.*) What's the matter with you? Take off them hats in the lady's house. Where are your manners? Where were you born, in a stable?

THOMAS: I doubt it!

PETER: But our leader was.

(*They all remove their hats.*)

MARSHAL PILATE: A wise guy, huh? You fellows go up to your rooms and cool off. I don't want to see you out on the street again until you're ready to act like decent folks.

(*THOMAS, JUDAS, PETER and JOHN walk across the stage and exit, Stage Right. PILATE looks at dining room.*)

MARSHAL PILATE: Looks like you're pretty full this week.

MISS COYOTE: Well, Passover week is always busy. All these out-of-town folks coming in to celebrate here. But I'm never too busy to find YOU a table, Marshal.

MARSHAL PILATE (*embarrassed*)**:** Aw, shucks, Miss Coyote. I wasn't dropping no hints...

MISS COYOTE: Well, you know you're welcome anytime.

(*BOARDING HOUSE RESIDENT ONE gets up from table and moves over to PILATE.*)

BOARDING HOUSE RESIDENT ONE: We saw some trouble out in the street, Marshal.

MARSHAL PILATE: Nothing serious. It's all over now.

BOARDING HOUSE RESIDENT ONE: Nobody will be hurt, will they?

MARSHAL PILATE: No. Nobody's gonna get hurt.

BOARDING HOUSE RESIDENT ONE: Good. Because I came in for a nice, peaceful Passover.

MARSHAL PILATE: And that's the way I aim to keep it—peaceful.

BOARDING HOUSE RESIDENT ONE: Good. I'm glad to hear it. (*Exits, Stage Left.*)

MISS COYOTE: Is Colt Caiaphas causing you problems again, Pontius?

MARSHAL PILATE: Nothing I can't handle, Miss Coyote. You know he's always trying to show me up; trying to have me called back to the capitol. But I'm one step ahead of his backwater tricks.

MISS COYOTE: I wish you weren't always so sure of yourself. You might find yourself backed up into a corner one day. (*MISS COYOTE continues talking to PILATE.*)

(*MAGGIE DALENE enters, Stage Right, and crosses to them.*)

MAGGIE DALENE: Excuse me, Marshal.

MARSHAL PILATE: Howdy, Ma'am.

MISS COYOTE: Allow me to introduce you. Marshal Pilate, this is Maggie Dalene. She's visiting from Galilee.

MARSHAL PILATE: From Galilee? You with them Galilean boys who were out in the street?

MAGGIE DALENE: Kind of. They're friends of mine.

MARSHAL PILATE: I hope you're not accusing me of being too rough with them.

MAGGIE DALENE: Oh, no. I understand you're in a tough position. I just want to thank you for keeping them safe.

MARSHAL PILATE: The pleasure was all mine, Ma'am.

(CHICHESTER enters, Stage Left.)

CHICHESTER *(excitedly)***:** Marshal! Marshal!

(CHICHESTER sees MAGGIE DALENE and stops.)

CHICHESTER: Beggin' your pardon, Ma'am.

(PILATE looks at CHICHESTER and sees he's still wearing his hat.)

MARSHAL PILATE: Chichester! You're inside and there's ladies present! Remove your hat. Where were you born, in a stable?

CHICHESTER *(removing hat)***:** No, sir.

MAGGIE DALENE: But I know someone who was.

MARSHAL PILATE: *(To MAGGIE DALENE.)* You're the second person's said that today. Is that some kind of Galilean joke?

MAGGIE DALENE: No. A very good friend of mine was born in a stable. His name is Jesus.

MARSHAL PILATE: I've heard THAT name before.

CHICHESTER: That's the fellow that come riding in here on a donkey. Caused all that uproar. Folks shouting, waving branches. You remember?

MARSHAL PILATE: Right. I knew He had some funny kind of name. *(To MAGGIE DALENE.)* You mixed up with Him?

MAGGIE DALENE: Marshal, if you knew Him, you would know He's the most wonderful man this world has ever known. He's kind, gentle...

(TOWNSPERSON TWO enters running, Stage Left.)

TOWNSPERSON TWO: *(Interrupts.)* Marshal! Marshal! Come a runnin'. There's trouble down at the church.

MARSHAL PILATE: Hold on! Hold on! What's the trouble?

TOWNSPERSON TWO: Well, you know that Colt and his gang have had some kind of racket going on over there for years.

MARSHAL PILATE: Sure. He tells people they have to have special money to make an offering at the church. Then he rents out booths to money changers so they can change all the money people bring into HIS special money. I've always suspected that it was crooked...

CHICHESTER: But nobody ever complains. So we can't do a thing about it!

TOWNSPERSON TWO: Well, somebody just made a complaint. He got a horsewhip and chased off all those money changers. He turned over all their tables and scattered their money all over the place. Scared their horses away, too.

CHICHESTER *(chuckling)***:** Golly! I sure wish I could have seen that!

MARSHAL PILATE: Well, we'll see the aftermath. Any idea who did it?

TOWNSPERSON TWO: Some guy visiting from Galilee. With a funny kind of name.

MAGGIE DALENE: Jesus?

TOWNSPERSON TWO: That's it! That's His name!

MARSHAL PILATE: *(Looks at MAGGIE DALENE.)* Kind and gentle?

MAGGIE DALENE: Well, He DOES have some rather strong convictions.

CHICHESTER: Well, He's probably gonna have ANOTHER conviction now—of a different kind!

(CAIAPHAS, ANNAS and TOUGH GUYS enter, Stage Left.)

COLT CAIAPHAS: *(To PILATE.)* You've heard! You've heard what He did!

MARSHAL PILATE: I've heard. I'm on my way.

ANNAS: He should be strung up.

CHICHESTER: You be careful what you say. That kind of talk ain't legal.

MARSHAL PILATE: I'm kind of sorry to have to arrest Him. I think you got what was coming to you.

COLT CAIAPHAS: You don't need to DO anything. You don't need to arrest Him.

MARSHAL PILATE: What? You don't want to swear out a complaint?

COLT CAIAPHAS: No. We'll handle this OURSELVES.

MARSHAL PILATE: You just watch yourself, Colt. You may be a big man, but if I hear that this fellow...

CHICHESTER: Jesus.

MARSHAL PILATE: ...Jesus has been harmed, you're in trouble deep. I don't have to tell you—no killings are going to happen in MY town.

COLT CAIAPHAS: We'll see about that. We'll see about that, Marshal. *(Exits with ANNAS and TOUGH GUYS, Stage Left. TOWNSPERSON TWO follows.)*

CHICHESTER: Well, they took that better than I thought they would.

MARSHAL PILATE: Don't believe it. They're up to something.

MAGGIE DALENE: If you'll excuse me, gentlemen, I think I'll take a walk. If I'm allowed, Marshal?

MARSHAL PILATE: Feel free. Just don't cause any trouble. And if you see that friend of yours, give Him a warning. Friendly like, not official. Colt Caiaphas is a dangerous enemy. He better be watching His back.

MAGGIE DALENE *(shocked)***:** But, Marshal! I thought you didn't ALLOW killings in your town!

MARSHAL PILATE: I don't. But if one HAPPENS, all I can do is punish the killer. That won't help your friend if He's already DEAD.

(MAGGIE DALENE exits, Stage Left.)

MISS COYOTE: *(Taps PILATE on shoulder.)* Now that the excitement's over, how about I pour you two some coffee?

CHICHESTER: Well, you don't have to ask me twice. You make just about the best coffee in the world, I figure. *(To PILATE.)* How come her coffee's so much better than what we have at the office?

MARSHAL PILATE: Maybe because MISS COYOTE makes the coffee HERE and YOU make it at the OFFICE. *(PILATE and MISS COYOTE laugh.)*

(CHICHESTER looks angry, then realizes it's funny and laughs. PILATE and CHICHESTER sit down at vacant table while MISS COYOTE gets coffee pot. She pours them coffee and then proceeds around dining room, filling cups of other diners. JUDAS enters, Stage Right, slips across stage and exits, Stage Left. Lights dim slightly and the following exchange is heard offstage.)

JUDAS: Caiaphas!

COLT CAIAPHAS: What do YOU want, Galilean?

ANNAS: Blasphemer!

JUDAS: That's just it. You don't know it, but I'm your friend. You want to get Jesus, right?

COLT CAIAPHAS: So?

JUDAS: So, you can't TOUCH Him. He's too popular. If you try anything, this whole town will riot. And you know what Marshal Pilate would do to you if you started a riot.

COLT CAIAPHAS: I know. So what?

JUDAS: So, you'll have to take Jesus at night. And I know where He'll be. I can point Him out to you—for a PRICE.

COLT CAIAPHAS: We'll give you thirty silver dollars.

ANNAS: Not a penny more.

JUDAS: Done. *(Slips back onstage, Stage Left, crosses the stage behind PILATE and CHICHESTER and exits, Stage Right. Lights are raised again.)*

MARSHAL PILATE: Now, what was so all-fired important that you came running into Miss Coyote's place yelling at the top of your lungs?

CHICHESTER: I just wanted to tell you that I think ol' Colt still has some plans up his sleeve. But I guess he told you that himself, didn't he?

(MISS COYOTE finishes pouring coffee, joins PILATE and CHICHESTER.)

MARSHAL PILATE: That old fox is always scheming. But I'm always ready for him.

MISS COYOTE: Don't be too sure, Pontius. I've been having some terrible dreams. If he brings that fellow Jesus to you, don't have anything to do with it. He scares me. I'm afraid for you, Pontius.

MARSHAL PILATE: *(To MISS COYOTE.)* Don't be. *(To CHICHESTER.)* Let's go, Chichester. We've got our rounds.

CHICHESTER: Coming, Marshal.

(PILATE and CHICHESTER rise and walk toward exit, Stage Left. Just before they exit, they put on their hats. MISS COYOTE looks after them, worried. Lights fade. Everyone on stage exits. STAGEHANDS take down Scene Three and set up Scene Four.)

SCENE FOUR: THE EASTER CORRAL

(Lights rise but remain dim. JESUS and all DISCIPLES except for JUDAS are inside corral. JUDAS enters, Stage Right, and looks into corral. He crosses to Stage Left. CAIAPHAS, ANNAS and TOUGH GUYS enter, Stage Left. They whisper with JUDAS. JUDAS sneaks back across stage and enters corral. He approaches JESUS and shakes JESUS' hand.)

JUDAS *(loudly)***:** Howdy there, Jesus. How're you doing?

(CAIAPHAS, ANNAS and TOUGH GUYS all run across stage to corral. General melee takes place. One TOUGH GUY screams and falls to his knees, holding his ear.)

JESUS: Put away your weapons! If I asked, My Father would send the angel cavalry to rescue Me. But if that happened, how could Scripture be fulfilled? *(JESUS touches TOUGH GUY's ear. TOUGH GUY stands, healed.) (DISCIPLES run off, Stage Right. CAIAPHAS, ANNAS and TOUGH GUYS take JESUS away, Stage Left. JUDAS follows. As they exit, Stage Left, PETER and JOHN enter, Stage Right, and slowly follow at a distance. MAGGIE DALENE enters, Stage Right, crying, "No! No! It can't happen!" She runs off, Stage Left.)*

(PILATE and CHICHESTER enter, Stage Right. TOWNSPEOPLE and BOARDING HOUSE RESIDENTS enter from both sides of stage. All talk together and TOWNSPEOPLE and RESIDENTS exit, Stage Left. MISS COYOTE enters, Stage Right. She runs to PILATE who tries to reassure her. PILATE, CHICHESTER and MISS COYOTE exit, Stage Left. Lights fade to black. STAGEHANDS take down Scene Four and set up Scene Five.)

SCENE FIVE: MARSHAL PILATE'S OFFICE

(PILATE is seated at desk, doing paperwork. Their hats are hanging on hat rack. CHICHESTER takes wanted poster of Barabbas from trash, smooths it out and hangs it on wall.)

NARRATOR: Well, that's pretty much the story. Colt Caiaphas finally outfoxed me. I knew they brought Jesus in on a trumped-up charge. I wanted to let Him go, but they found a legal technicality. If I had let Him go, Caiaphas would have told the capitol that I had supported an attempt to overthrow the government. Of course, it wasn't true, but those government idiots will believe any wild rumor that passes across their desks. So, I had Jesus executed. I tried to wash my hands of the whole affair, but I knew they would be stained forever.

(PILATE sighs loudly.)

CHICHESTER: You still thinking about that Jesus fellow, Marshal? Shucks, that was almost a week ago.

MARSHAL PILATE: It doesn't matter. A week, a year, a lifetime. I'll always know I'm guilty of murder.

CHICHESTER: Well, look at the bright side. You and ol' Judge Herod used to hate each other. Now, just because you both fixed that Jesus fellow, you're the best of friends.

MARSHAL PILATE: Small consolation.

(MAGGIE DALENE enters, Stage Right. She is smiling. PILATE and CHICHESTER both rise as she enters.)

MAGGIE DALENE: Hello, Marshal. Deputy.

MARSHAL PILATE: Howdy, Ma'am. I didn't think I'd see you again.

CHICHESTER: 'Specially smilin' like that.

(CHICHESTER holds out chair to MAGGIE DALENE. MAGGIE DALENE sits. PILATE sits on chair and CHICHESTER sits on edge of desk.)

MAGGIE DALENE: Two days ago, I would have agreed with you. But not now!

MARSHAL PILATE: So why the smile? Your friend is still dead.

MAGGIE DALENE: No! He isn't! He's alive!

CHICHESTER: *(Shakes head, no.)* Now, Ma'am. I know you want to believe...

MARSHAL PILATE: I'm afraid Chichester's right.

MAGGIE DALENE: *(Stands, excited.)* I tell you, He's alive!

MARSHAL PILATE: No, Ma'am. That's just a rumor started because His BODY'S missing.

MAGGIE DALENE: No. You're both wrong. He's alive. I've SEEN Him!

(DISCIPLES enter, Stage Right. They all see MAGGIE DALENE and remove their hats.)

PETER: She's right, Marshal Pilate. We've ALL seen Him.

CHICHESTER *(surprised)***:** Are you fellows still here?

MARSHAL PILATE: I would have expected that Caiaphas had made this town too hot for you.

JOHN: He did, for three days. We were all in hiding.

PETER: But Jesus is ALIVE. We've SEEN Him. Now we understand many of the things He said before.

MARSHAL PILATE: So, you believe He's alive, too?

THOMAS: I don't doubt it!

(MISS COYOTE enters, Stage Right.)

MISS COYOTE: I don't doubt it, either! That's why they're all staying at my place.

(PILATE and CHICHESTER stand. PILATE moves his chair from behind desk and invites MISS COYOTE to sit. She does. PILATE and CHICHESTER sit on corners of desk.)

MARSHAL PILATE: You've seen Him, too?

MISS COYOTE: No, but I've heard His friends. And I believe them.

MARSHAL PILATE: *(Looks upward.)* The whole world's going crazy.

(CAIAPHAS, ANNAS and TOUGH GUYS enter, Stage Right. DISCIPLES move to Stage Left.)

COLT CAIAPHAS *(pointing)***:** There they are. Grave robbers! Arrest them.

MARSHAL PILATE: I'm going to need a lot more than YOUR word to arrest ANYBODY for ANYTHING. Besides, they say the reason there's no BODY is because Jesus is ALIVE.

COLT CAIAPHAS: They're liars!

ANNAS: He's dead!

PETER and JOHN: He's alive!

THOMAS: I don't doubt it.

(TOWNSPEOPLE and BOARDING HOUSE RESIDENTS enter, Stage Right.)

TOWNSPERSON ONE: What's going on?

TOWNSPERSON TWO: We heard an argument.

BOARDING HOUSE RESIDENT ONE: I thought this was a peaceful town.

(TOWNSPEOPLE and RESIDENTS move to Center Stage, between TOUGH GUYS and the DISCIPLES. MAGGIE DALENE moves to the DISCIPLES' side of the stage.)

PETER: He's alive!

(TOWNSPEOPLE and RESIDENTS turn their heads, as if at a tennis match, to look at DISCIPLES.)

COLT CAIAPHAS: He's dead!

(TOWNSPEOPLE and RESIDENTS turn their heads, as at a tennis match, to look at TOUGH GUYS.)

JOHN: He's alive!

(TOWNSPEOPLE and RESIDENTS turn their heads to look at DISCIPLES.)

ANNAS: He's dead!

(TOWNSPEOPLE and RESIDENTS turn their heads to look at TOUGH GUYS.)

THOMAS: He's alive!

(TOWNSPEOPLE and RESIDENTS turn their heads to look at DISCIPLES. Argument continues, each side saying, "Dead!" or "Alive!" and TOWNSPEOPLE and RESIDENTS moving their heads as if at a tennis match. JESUS enters from rear of Stage Left, and stands in middle of DISCIPLES. CAIAPHAS, ANNAS and TOUGH GUYS look out at audience, fold their arms and say, "Dead!" TOWNSPEOPLE, RESIDENTS, PILATE and CHICHESTER shrug their shoulders to say, "I don't know." DISCIPLES, MAGGIE DALENE and MISS COYOTE drop to their knees and point to JESUS.)

DISCIPLES, MAGGIE DALENE and MISS COYOTE: HE'S ALIVE!

(Lights snap to black.)

HOLIDAY ASSORTMENT

WOMEN IN LOVE

(APPROXIMATE TIME: 30 MINUTES)

SYNOPSIS

Three Old Testament couples provide a slightly wacky commentary on love for Valentine's Day.

STAGE SETTINGS

SCENE ONE: SAMSON AND DELILAH
- Couch or cot, Center Stage, to the front
- Drapes, Stage Left
- Chair and table beside couch

SCENE TWO: JEZEBEL AND AHAB
- Two thrones, Center Stage
- Table to right of Jezebel's throne
- Wall hangings, drapes, etc., to suggest a throne room

SCENE THREE: ABIGAIL AND NABAL
- Chair, front of Stage Right
- Table and two chairs, front of Stage Left

THE PLAYERS

DELILAH'S MAID (All ages)
PHILISTINE LORD TWO (Grade 3 or older)
SAMSON (Grade 5 or older)
AHAB'S SERVANT ONE (All ages)
AHAB'S SERVANT THREE (All ages)
ADVISOR TWO (Grade 3 or older)
AHAB (Grade 5 or older)
MESSENGER (Grade 3 or older)
SERVANT GIRL ONE (All ages)
SERVANT GIRL THREE (All ages)

PHILISTINE LORD ONE (Grade 3 or older)
PHILISTINE LORD THREE (Grade 3 or older)
DELILAH (Grade 5 or older)
AHAB'S SERVANT TWO (All ages)
ADVISOR ONE (Grade 3 or older)
ADVISOR THREE (Grade 3 or older)
JEZEBEL (Grade 5 or older)
ABIGAIL (Grade 5 or older)
SERVANT GIRL TWO (Grade 3 or older)
NABAL (Grade 5 or older)

NONSPEAKING SERVANTS, SOLDIERS and PHILISTINE LORDS (All ages)
NARRATOR (Grade 5 or older)
STAGEHANDS (All ages)

SUGGESTED PROPS
- Long wig for Samson
- Two small baskets, each containing grapes, extra grapes for refills
- Scissors
- Bag of money

- Crowns for Ahab and Jezebel
- Weapons for Soldiers
- Large fan
- Scrolls or books for Advisors
- Large handkerchief
- Dust rags, brooms, etc., for Servants
- Musical instruments
- Loaf of bread
- Slices of buttered bread on a plate
- Jewels for Jezebel
- Sealing ring for Ahab
- Paper and pen
- Candle, matches for sealing letters
- Cloth, needles, etc., for Abigail's sewing
- Cap for messenger
- Notebook and pencil for Nabal
- Sandwich rolls to represent loaves of bread (about two dozen)
- Two glasses of water
- Dish of gelatin dessert (such as Jell-O) cut into cubes, spoon
- Pair of chopsticks
- Apple
- Bible-times costumes

DIRECTOR TIPS

1. Narrator is offstage but should be in position to see all the action.
2. Narrator's part can be read.
3. In Scene One, the first two baskets of grapes should contain only one small clump each. The third basket should have two small clumps and the final basket needs to hold enough grapes for both Samson and Delilah.
4. In Scene One, there can be more than three Philistine Lords in the hair-cutting scene.
5. Great care must be taken with the scissors to ensure no one is accidentally hurt. Select the Philistine Lords carefully.
6. When dragging Samson off, he should weakly struggle to show he has lost his strength.
7. In Scene Two, music to soothe Ahab need not be tuneful. Musical instruments could be rhythm band instruments.
8. Jezebel should be played to the maximum. She is the most important person in the world and she knows it.
9. Students must be careful with the use of a lit candle or someone could be hurt. Choose Servant Two carefully.
10. In Scene Three, Abigail gradually becomes more frantic as the scene progresses.
11. Abigail's movements about the stage should always be in a large circle—beginning at the table, moving to rear of Stage Left, across to rear of Stage Right and back to the table.

Women in Love

(Stage area is dark.)

NARRATOR: Ah, Valentine's Day! The day when a young man's fancy lightly turns to thoughts of love. And who better exemplifies love than people we meet in the pages of the Bible—each one showing more concern for the other than for him- or herself.

SCENE ONE: SAMSON AND DELILAH

(Lights rise on DELILAH's apartment. DELILAH is pacing back and forth. She stops, Center Stage.)

DELILAH: Where is he? He said he'd be here by ten o'clock and it's already one minute to. If he's late, I'll kill him! *(Stops and thinks.)* Come to think of it, if he was early, I'd kill him.

(SAMSON enters, Stage Right. He is wearing a long wig.)

SAMSON: Delilah, sweetie! Miss me?

DELILAH: *(To audience.)* It's Samson. He's here.

(SAMSON walks to Center Stage. As he approaches, he stops from time to time to pose as a bodybuilder. DELILAH faces him.)

DELILAH: I counted each minute you were gone.

SAMSON: How many minutes was I gone?

DELILAH *(obviously stumped)***:** Oh... Uh... Lots and lots.

SAMSON: *(Sees grapes.)* Oh, good! You bought some more grapes.

(SAMSON takes a small clump of grapes, lies down on couch and eats. PHILISTINE LORD ONE enters from behind draperies, Stage Left, just barely onstage.)

PHILISTINE LORD ONE: *(Stage whisper.)* Psst!

SAMSON: Did you say something?

DELILAH: You need more grapes, Dear. Maid!

(DELILAH'S MAID enters, Stage Right, with another basket of grapes that she places on the table. MAID picks up empty basket.)

DELILAH'S MAID: More grapes, Ma'am.

(DELILAH'S MAID curtsies and exits, Stage Right. DELILAH hands SAMSON a small clump of grapes and then goes over to PHILISTINE LORD ONE.)

PHILISTINE LORD ONE: *(Stage whisper.)* Is he asleep yet?

DELILAH: *(Stage whisper.)* Not yet.

(DELILAH motions PHILISTINE LORD ONE offstage. LORD ONE exits and DELILAH returns to SAMSON.)

DELILAH: Did you miss me?

SAMSON: Huh? Were you gone?

(DELILAH sits on chair.)

DELILAH: Do you remember, way back when? I asked you, "What's the secret of your great strength?" Remember what you told me? "Bind me with seven green vines twisted together." Remember?

SAMSON: That sure was a good joke, wasn't it? I broke those vines like straw stretched over a fire. *(Looks around.)* Speaking of vines...

DELILAH: Maid!

(DELILAH'S MAID enters, Stage Right, with another basket of grapes that she places on the table. MAID picks up empty basket.)

DELILAH'S MAID: More grapes, Ma'am.

(DELILAH'S MAID curtsies and exits, Stage Right. SAMSON looks hungrily at grapes. DELILAH gives him another small clump. PHILISTINE LORD TWO enters from behind draperies, Stage Left, and stops just onstage.)

PHILISTINE LORD TWO: *(Stage whispers.)* Psst!

SAMSON: What's that?

DELILAH: Eat your grapes, Dear. I'll be right back.

(DELILAH goes over to PHILISTINE LORD TWO.)

PHILISTINE LORD TWO: *(Stage whisper.)* Is he asleep yet?

DELILAH: *(Stage whisper.)* Not yet.

(DELILAH motions PHILISTINE LORD TWO offstage. LORD TWO exits and DELILAH returns to SAMSON.)

DELILAH: Did you miss me?

SAMSON: Huh? Were you gone?

(DELILAH sits on chair.)

DELILAH: Do you remember? I asked you again, "What's the secret of your great strength?" And you told me, "If I was tied up with brand-new ropes, I'd be helpless." Remember?

SAMSON: That was another good joke. I broke those ropes like they were thread.

DELILAH *(annoyed)***:** And they were perfectly good ropes.

(PHILISTINE LORD THREE enters from behind draperies, Stage Left, and stops just onstage.)

PHILISTINE LORD THREE: *(Stage whispers.)* Psst!

(SAMSON begins to turn to look toward the noise. DELILAH quickly picks up small clump of grapes and holds them over SAMSON's nose. SAMSON's attention is diverted to the grapes. DELILAH goes over to PHILISTINE LORD THREE.)

PHILISTINE LORD THREE: (*Stage whisper.*) Is he asleep yet?

DELILAH: (*Stage whisper.*) Not yet.

(*DELILAH motions PHILISTINE LORD THREE offstage. LORD THREE exits and DELILAH returns to SAMSON.*)

DELILAH: Did you miss me?

SAMSON: Huh? Were you gone?

(*DELILAH sits on chair.*)

DELILAH: Ah, Samson! Do you remember when I asked you again, "What's the secret of your great strength?" You told me, "If the seven locks of my hair were woven together, I would be just like any other man." Remember?

SAMSON: I sure am good with jokes.

(*PHILISTINE LORDS ONE, TWO and THREE enter from behind draperies, Stage Left, and stop just onstage.*)

PHILISTINE LORDS ONE, TWO and THREE: (*Stage whisper.*) Psst!

(*DELILAH looks at the PHILISTINE LORDS and motions them offstage. They exit.*)

SAMSON: Did you say something?

DELILAH: Grapes? You need more grapes. Maid!

(*DELILAH'S MAID enters, Stage Right, with another basket of grapes that she places on the table. MAID picks up empty basket.*)

DELILAH'S MAID: More grapes, Ma'am.

(*DELILAH'S MAID curtsies and exits, Stage Right. DELILAH offers SAMSON another small bunch of grapes.*)

DELILAH: Last time you were here, you told me that if your hair was cut, you would be just as weak as anyone else. Was that a joke, too?

SAMSON: Of course not. Because you told me if it was, I'd never see another grape again. And I sure love grapes!

DELILAH: After all those grapes, you need some rest. Go to sleep now. I have... I have a beauty parlor appointment to keep.

(*SAMSON sleeps. DELILAH goes over to draperies.*)

DELILAH: (*Stage whisper.*) Psst.

(*PHILISTINE LORDS enter from behind draperies, Stage Left, and stop just onstage.*)

DELILAH: He's asleep.

(*PHILISTINE LORDS remove scissors from their belts. They approach SAMSON while opening and closing scissors. They surround SAMSON so that SAMSON's head is hidden from the view of the audience. DELILAH moves to back of couch to see what's happening. They raise the scissors in the air, noisily opening and closing the scissors, then quickly lower the scissors and pretend to cut SAMSON's hair. PHILISTINE LORD ONE raises wig in triumph.*)

PHILISTINE LORDS ONE, TWO and THREE (*loudly*): Aha!

DELILAH (loudly): Samson! Wake up! The Philistines have you surrounded.

(SAMSON wakes up and slowly sits up on couch. He stretches and rubs his eyes.)

SAMSON: Boy, was I ever sound asleep. I think I'll go home.

PHILISTINE LORD TWO: Allow us to help you up.

(PHILISTINE LORDS TWO and THREE each take SAMSON by an arm. SAMSON sees them and struggles weakly. PHILISTINE LORD ONE shakes wig in front of SAMSON's face. PHILISTINE LORDS all laugh as SAMSON is dragged off, Stage Right. PHILISTINE LORD ONE hands bag of money to DELILAH and follows. DELILAH watches them go, then sits on couch. She lifts money bag and shakes it.)

DELILAH: Eleven hundred pieces of silver from each of them. Just as promised. (Takes grape from basket, lies down and eats it.)

DELILAH: (To audience.) Don't you just love strong men?

(Lights snap to black. DELILAH exits. Lights can then be raised slightly to allow STAGEHANDS to break down Scene One and set up Scene Two.)

NARRATOR: Hmm! Maybe Samson and Delilah weren't the best examples to choose. But never mind. There are LOTS of other men and women who truly demonstrate love's unselfish qualities.

SCENE TWO: AHAB AND JEZEBEL

(SERVANT THREE enters, Stage Left, gently waving large fan to cool AHAB, who follows. SOLDIERS, ADVISORS and SERVANTS follow AHAB. AHAB is scowling. SERVANT THREE stops by AHAB's throne, the throne on the left, and continues to gently wave fan. SOLDIERS position themselves behind thrones. ADVISORS position themselves to left of thrones. SERVANTS remain in background pretending to dust, sweep, etc. AHAB looks disapprovingly at throne and motions to SERVANT TWO. SERVANT TWO takes out handkerchief and dusts off throne haphazardly. AHAB sits.)

AHAB (whining sadly): Poor me! Poor, poor me! (Leans his chin sadly on his hand and looks at audience in pitiful manner.)

ADVISOR TWO: (To ADVISOR THREE.) King Ahab needs cheering up.

ADVISOR THREE: He needs music. Servants! Music!

(All SERVANTS except for SERVANTS ONE and THREE move to Stage Right and pick up musical instruments. SERVANT ONE acts as conductor and leads the music. SERVANTS begin playing noisily. ADVISORS look expectantly at AHAB, who continues to look at audience in same pitiful manner.)

ADVISOR ONE: It isn't working. King Ahab remains sad.

(ADVISOR ONE looks at SERVANT ONE and gives him the "kill" sign by rapidly moving index finger across his throat. SERVANT ONE signals the SERVANTS to stop playing, and music ceases. SERVANTS lay down instruments and return to their duties.)

AHAB: (Sighs deeply.) I'm STILL sad.

(JEZEBEL enters, Stage Right, and stops just onstage. ADVISOR ONE sees her.)

ADVISOR ONE (*announcing grandly*): Queen Jezebel!

(*All activity stops. Everyone except for AHAB, SOLDIERS and SERVANT THREE bow to her. SERVANT THREE stops fanning AHAB, runs over to JEZEBEL and begins fanning her. JEZEBEL walks grandly to throne followed by SERVANT THREE. JEZEBEL stops and looks disapprovingly at throne. SERVANT TWO runs to throne and quickly dusts it off in same manner as he dusted AHAB's throne. JEZEBEL stops SERVANT TWO from leaving and points to throne. SERVANT TWO carefully polishes entire throne. JEZEBEL nods her approval, dismisses SERVANT TWO with a wave of her hand. SERVANT TWO goes back to other duties. JEZEBEL sits down.*)

JEZEBEL: (*Looks at AHAB. Speaks to ADVISORS.*) The king is sad.

AHAB (*sadly agreeing*): I am.

JEZEBEL: (*To ADVISORS.*) Cheer him up. I don't like to see sad faces.

ADVISOR TWO: Music didn't cheer him up.

ADVISOR THREE: Maybe food will.

ADVISOR ONE: Bring the king some bread!

JEZEBEL: And make sure the queen's bread is buttered!

(*SERVANTS ONE and TWO exit, Stage Right. SERVANT ONE returns with a loaf of bread in a basket that is offered to AHAB. AHAB shakes his head. SERVANT TWO returns with a slice of buttered bread on a plate that is offered to JEZEBEL. JEZEBEL accepts. SERVANT ONE takes basket of bread offstage, Stage Right, then enters again and returns to duties. SERVANT TWO returns to duties.*)

JEZEBEL: (*To ADVISORS.*) The king is still sad. I told you I don't like sad faces around me. Do something!

ADVISOR TWO: Music didn't cheer him up.

ADVISOR THREE: Food didn't cheer him up.

ADVISOR ONE: What else can we do?

JEZEBEL: (*To AHAB.*) Perhaps we could behead some advisors. That always cheers ME up. (*ADVISORS look frightened. JEZEBEL looks expectantly at AHAB. AHAB shakes his head. ADVISORS look relieved.*)

JEZEBEL: (*To AHAB.*) Why is the king so sad? Why won't he eat?

AHAB: Naboth!

JEZEBEL: What a strange oath! You Israelites say such strange things.

ADVISOR ONE: You misunderstand, milady.

ADVISOR THREE: Naboth is not an oath.

ADVISOR TWO: Naboth is a man.

JEZEBEL: Really? A mere man makes the king sad? Why?

AHAB: He won't sell me his vineyard. It's right next door. It would make a wonderful herb garden.

(*JEZEBEL is amazed that the king would purchase something and not just take it.*)

JEZEBEL: He won't SELL his vineyard?

AHAB: I offered him a fair price. I offered him a better vineyard.

JEZEBEL: He won't SELL his vineyard?

ADVISOR ONE: Technically, under the law, he doesn't have to sell.

ADVISOR THREE: Even the king cannot force him to sell.

JEZEBEL: You Israelites have such funny customs and laws. Remember when you first married me, Darling?

(AHAB nods his head.)

JEZEBEL: You Israelites insisted on worshiping one god. Well, we soon changed that, didn't we?

(AHAB nods his head.)

JEZEBEL: One god can't do everything, I told you. You need to worship many gods. And the name you called your one god. "Jehovah" you called Him. What a silly name for a god. The chief god should be named Baal. So we changed worship in Israel, didn't we?

(AHAB nods his head.)

JEZEBEL: And then, when that silly man Elijah was making trouble, didn't I have him run out of town?

(AHAB nods his head.)

JEZEBEL: See how I always give you good advice?

(AHAB nods his head.)

JEZEBEL: So, I'll fix this for you. Give me your ring.

(AHAB takes off ring and gives it to JEZEBEL.)

JEZEBEL: Paper and pen!

(SERVANT TWO exits, Stage Right, and returns with paper and pen that he places on JEZEBEL's table. SERVANT TWO removes the bread plate and takes it offstage, Stage Right. He then returns to his duties.)

JEZEBEL: Let's see. *(Thinks, then writes while speaking.)* "Dear Chief of Police: Kill Naboth! Signed, King..." How do you spell Ahab, darling?

AHAB: A-H-A-B.

JEZEBEL *(writing again)*: "Signed, King Ahab."

(JEZEBEL holds up letter and looks approvingly at it. AHAB begins to perk up a bit. JEZEBEL takes another piece of paper, thinks, then writes while speaking.)

JEZEBEL: "Dear Mayor of Samaria: Kill Naboth! Signed, King Ahab."

(JEZEBEL holds up letter and looks approvingly at it. AHAB perks up a bit more. JEZEBEL takes another piece of paper, thinks, then writes while speaking.)

JEZEBEL: "Dear Chief Priest of Baal: Kill Naboth! Signed, King Ahab."

(JEZEBEL holds up letter and looks approvingly at it. AHAB smiles.)

JEZEBEL: *(To SERVANT TWO.)* Wax!

(SERVANT TWO exits, Stage Right, and returns with lit candle in holder. JEZEBEL folds all letters, SERVANT TWO drips a bit of wax on the fold and JEZEBEL seals letters with AHAB'S ring. After all letters have been sealed, SERVANT TWO blows out candle and exits with candle, Stage Right, then returns to his duties on stage.)

JEZEBEL: There! *(Returns ring to AHAB.)*

JEZEBEL: Aren't you glad I'm here to give you such good advice?

(AHAB grins broadly and nods. Lights snap to black. All actors exit. Lights can then be raised slightly to allow STAGEHANDS to break down Scene Two and set up Scene Three.)

NARRATOR: Okay! Okay! So we made a little mistake choosing Ahab and Jezebel. Maybe they weren't exactly unselfish. Come on! Be good sports. Give us one more chance to find a couple who respond to each other with perfect love and intelligence.

SCENE THREE: NABAL AND ABIGAIL

(ABIGAIL enters, Stage Right, and moves to chair at front of Stage Right. She is carrying a piece of cloth on which she is sewing. She sits and begins to sew. As she sews, a loud commotion and cries are heard offstage, Stage Left. ABIGAIL looks up as three SERVANT GIRLS push on MESSENGER, Stage Left. They move toward ABIGAIL. MESSENGER is holding a cap in his hands that he is twisting with consternation. ABIGAIL looks up at the SERVANTS and MESSENGER.)

ABIGAIL: Yes? What is it?

SERVANT GIRL ONE: *(Nudges MESSENGER.)* Go on! Tell her!

ABIGAIL: Tell me? Tell me what?

MESSENGER: You're busy. It's not important. I've gotta run.

(MESSENGER tries to leave but the SERVANT GIRLS restrain him.)

SERVANT GIRL TWO: Tell her what you told us!

ABIGAIL: What is it?

MESSENGER: It's the master.

(ABIGAIL drops her sewing in alarm and jumps from her chair.)

ABIGAIL: Nabal! My husband! Has he been hurt?

MESSENGER: Not yet.

(ABIGAIL is becoming annoyed at the MESSENGER's hesitancy to answer. ABIGAIL grabs MESSENGER by the lapels.)

ABIGAIL: What do you mean, "Not yet"? Are you a prophet who can tell what will happen in the future?

SERVANT GIRL THREE: Tell her!

MESSENGER *(pleading)***:** Please, Mistress…

(ABIGAIL releases MESSENGER.)

MESSENGER: It's like this. We were all busy shearing the sheep…

SERVANT GIRL ONE: Skip that! Get to the good part.

MESSENGER: When some men came down from the hills...

ABIGAIL *(alarmed)*: Robbers? Thieves? Have they taken Nabal hostage? Are they threatening to kill him if we don't pay a ransom?

MESSENGER: No, Ma'am. We knew them. They were some of David's soldiers.

ABIGAIL: *(Sighs with relief.)* Well, that's all right. David is a friend.

MESSENGER: Was...

ABIGAIL: Was?

MESSENGER: WAS a friend. All through the year, we grazed the flocks in the hills where David and his men were hiding from Saul.

ABIGAIL: Did David and his men steal sheep from the flock? Is that why you say he WAS a friend? Why wasn't I told about this before?

MESSENGER: No, ma'am. No harm came to any of us from David. In fact, no harm came to us all year from anything. David and his men protected us. We never lost so much as one lamb all year.

ABIGAIL: Then what happened to change David from a friend?

MESSENGER: Well, his men came down from the hills while we were preparing for the big feast we have every year at shearing time.

ABIGAIL: I see. And they demanded to be given something for themselves! The nerve of them! That's almost the same as stealing!

MESSENGER: No, Ma'am.

ABIGAIL: It is so!

MESSENGER: No, I mean... That's not what happened. David's men were very polite.

ABIGAIL: I'm becoming more and more confused. David seems to be a friend.

MESSENGER: But when they reminded the master about how they had protected all his flocks and his servants, the master...

(MESSENGER stops talking and looks down at the cap he continues to twist.)

ABIGAIL: The master?

(SERVANT GIRL ONE nudges MESSENGER.)

MESSENGER: The master...

ABIGAIL: *(Trying to prompt MESSENGER.)* The master?

(SERVANT GIRL TWO nudges MESSENGER.)

MESSENGER: The master...

ABIGAIL: The master?

(SERVANT GIRL THREE nudges MESSENGER.)

MESSENGER: The master...

ABIGAIL: The master?

MESSENGER: (*Speaking quickly, as if hoping speed will improve the message.*) The master was rude and said that David and his men were nothing better than common criminals and runaway slaves; and if he was Saul, he would have them horsewhipped or tarred and feathered or drawn and quartered or something equally bad; and who did they think they were coming in like they owned the place; and what had David ever done for him anyway; and if he bumped into David on the street he wouldn't know him from Adam; and they better go somewhere else to peddle their papers. (*Takes deep breath and speaks more slowly.*) Or something like that.

(*ABIGAIL sinks into her chair, touching her cheeks with her fingertips in alarm.*)

ABIGAIL: Oh, my! I suppose David's angry.

SERVANT GIRL ONE: Why must the master be so foolish?

ABIGAIL: (*Scolds SERVANT GIRL ONE.*) You must not speak ill of the master. (*Aside to audience.*) But his name does mean "fool" and sometimes I think he tries to live up to it. (*To SERVANT GIRLS and MESSENGER.*) We must try to repair the damage. We'll send David a gift of our best food. I need a complete inventory immediately. How much bread do we have on hand? Wine? Corn? Raisins? Figs?

NABAL: (*Yelling from offstage, Stage Left.*) I'm home!

ABIGAIL: (*To SERVANT GIRLS and MESSENGER.*) Go! Count everything and report to me.

(*SERVANT GIRLS curtsy, MESSENGER bows and they quickly exit. SERVANT GIRL THREE exits, Stage Right; the others, Stage Left. As they are leaving, NABAL swaggers on, Stage Left, and is spun around by the GIRLS and MESSENGER as they exit. NABAL places fists on hips and watches as they exit. He yells after them.*)

NABAL: Watch where you're going! You could do someone an injury!

ABIGAIL: (*Aside, to audience.*) He practically begs David to kill him and now he's worried about servants bumping him. (*To NABAL.*) Hello, Darling.

(*NABAL continues to swagger forward to table at front of Stage Left. He flops into chair behind table. ABIGAIL rises and moves to table to sit in other chair.*)

ABIGAIL: How was your day, Darling?

NABAL: Just wonderful! I'm probably the best farmer in Caramel.

ABIGAIL: Carmel, darling. We live in Carmel. Caramel is a candy.

NABAL: Whatever! I'm the best farmer who ever lived anywhere and ate anything.

ABIGAIL: Of course you are, Darling.

NABAL: Do you know how good I am? I'm so good, I didn't even lose one lamb this year. And I did it all by myself! How many farmers can say that?

ABIGAIL: (*Aside to audience.*) None, unless his name is Nabal.

NABAL: Not one lamb. Cable would have been proud of me.

ABIGAIL: Who?

NABAL: Cable. My famous ancestor.

ABIGAIL: Caleb! His name was Caleb, Darling.

NABAL: Is that right? I must remember that.

(NABAL takes out notebook and pencil and writes. As he writes, he speaks.)

NABAL: Remember to refer to famous ancestor as Mr. Darling.

(ABIGAIL rolls her eyes and shakes her head.)

ABIGAIL: Did anything interesting happen today?

NABAL: Nothing important. I just told off some lazy, good-for-nothing desserts.

ABIGAIL: Desserts?

NABAL: Yeah! Guys that ran away from the king.

ABIGAIL: Deserters, Dear. Was that wise, Darling?

NABAL: Hey! I only do the smart thing. Why, if you take my name and spell it backwards, you know what you get?

ABIGAIL *(confused)***:** What?

NABAL: You get Laban. So you see my point.

(ABIGAIL smiles and nods at NABAL. She turns to audience, shakes her head and emphatically mouths the word "NO!")

ABIGAIL: But what if these deserters become angry?

NABAL: What are they gonna do? Start a fight? Let 'em. I'm ready for them. I'll fight them all. *(Jumps to his feet and shadowboxes.)*

ABIGAIL: *(Rises and goes to NABAL.)* But, Darling. That wouldn't be a fair fight. David has six hundred men, all of them trained soldiers. You're a farmer.

(NABAL stops shadowboxing to fold his arms, placing his chin in his hand and thinking about what ABIGAIL has said.)

NABAL: You're right. It wouldn't be fair. But David will just have to take his chances. *(Resumes shadowboxing.)*

(SERVANT GIRL THREE enters, Stage Right, and SERVANT GIRL TWO enters, Stage Left. Both motion to ABIGAIL. ABIGAIL moves to rear of stage between the two.)

SERVANT GIRL THREE: *(Stage whispers.)* We have three hundred loaves of bread.

SERVANT GIRL TWO: *(Stage whispers.)* We have one hundred fifty clusters of raisins.

ABIGAIL: *(Stage whispers to SERVANT GIRL THREE.)* Get two hundred loaves and take them outside. *(Stage whispers to SERVANT GIRL TWO.)* And one hundred clusters of raisins. *(Turning her head to speak to both at the same time.)* But don't let the master see you.

(SERVANT GIRLS curtsy and exit. ABIGAIL rejoins NABAL, who is still shadowboxing but running out of steam. ABIGAIL leads NABAL to table where he sits again. ABIGAIL fans him with a towel in the manner of a trainer fanning a boxer. In the background, SERVANT GIRL THREE runs onstage with a loaf of bread, tosses it to SERVANT GIRL ONE who has entered from the opposite wings and she exits, Stage Left, with bread. SERVANT GIRL THREE runs offstage, Stage Right. This continues while the scene goes on.)

NABAL: Do you know what I'm going to do?

ABIGAIL: Rarely.

NABAL: I'm going to David's camp right now and tell him what I think of him. *(Rises from chair.)*

(ABIGAIL places her hands on his shoulders and pushes NABAL back down into his chair.)

ABIGAIL: *(Shouts.)* WAIT!

(SERVANT GIRLS TWO and THREE have come onstage and stop when they hear ABIGAIL. ABIGAIL sees them and motions for them to continue, which they do.)

ABIGAIL: *(To NABAL.)* If you go to David's camp, there could be a fight.

NABAL: *(Starting to rise.)* And I'm ready.

ABIGAIL: *(Pushing NABAL back into chair.)* But you've had a hard day's work. If you go out without a proper meal, you could run out of steam. You need to eat first.

(NABAL places chin in hand to think. ABIGAIL runs back to where the SERVANT GIRLS are passing the bread from kitchen to outside, and intercepts pass. ABIGAIL stage whispers, "Sorry. I need this," and runs back to table. As NABAL has been considering her words, he moves his hands in an "on one hand/on the other hand" gesture. As one hand comes up, ABIGAIL places bread in NABAL's hand, drops into other chair and smiles at NABAL.)

ABIGAIL: Eat.

(NABAL begins to eat bread. After a bite, he begins to rise. ABIGAIL jumps up and pushes him back into chair.)

ABIGAIL: What do you want, Darling?

NABAL: Water. Bread's a little dry.

ABIGAIL: *(Turns to see SERVANT GIRL THREE entering from Stage Right. ABIGAIL yells to SERVANT GIRL THREE.)* WATER! *(To NABAL, in normal voice.)* I'll get it for you, Darling.

(Runs to rear of stage to meet SERVANT GIRL THREE who has entered, Stage Right, with glass of water. SERVANT GIRL THREE hands water to ABIGAIL who accepts it without breaking stride. SERVANT GIRL THREE darts offstage, Stage Right, to continue the bread relay while ABIGAIL runs to table, places water in front of NABAL, sinks into other chair and smiles at NABAL.)

ABIGAIL: Drink.

(NABAL drinks water and continues to eat bread. ABIGAIL places head in her hand in exhaustion. SERVANT GIRLS continue bread relay. While ABIGAIL's head is in her hand and SERVANT GIRLS are offstage, NABAL gets up and begins to move toward Stage Right. ABIGAIL looks up, sees him going and runs to intercept him. Just as ABIGAIL reaches NABAL, SERVANT GIRL THREE enters from Stage Right with bread and SERVANT GIRL TWO has entered to accept bread from SERVANT GIRL THREE. ABIGAIL whirls NABAL around so he will not see the GIRLS. SERVANT GIRLS manage to stop just short of bumping into NABAL. NABAL looks at SERVANT GIRL TWO who smiles and curtsies. NABAL turns head to look at SERVANT GIRL

THREE who hides bread behind her back, smiles and curtsies. As NABAL turns head to face ABIGAIL, SERVANT GIRL THREE tosses bread over his head to SERVANT GIRL TWO. Both SERVANT GIRLS exit.)

ABIGAIL: *(To NABAL.)* Did you want something, Darling?

NABAL: More water.

(ABIGAIL leads NABAL back to table.)

ABIGAIL: *(Sweetly.)* Why didn't you say so? *(Turns to see SERVANT GIRL THREE entering with bread. Yells.)* WATER!

(SERVANT GIRL THREE exits, Stage Right. ABIGAIL firmly pushes NABAL into his chair, takes his glass and runs to Stage Right, meeting SERVANT GIRL THREE who is entering with another glass of water. They switch glasses without breaking stride. SERVANT GIRL THREE exits, Stage Right. ABIGAIL runs to table, places water in front of NABAL, sinks into other chair and smiles at NABAL.)

ABIGAIL: Drink.

(NABAL takes drink of water.)

NABAL: As soon as I'm finished with this bread, I'm going to David's camp.

(ABIGAIL looks in alarm at small amount of bread left in NABAL's hand. NABAL pops last bit of bread into his mouth. ABIGAIL leaps from chair and races to rear of stage and intercepts another loaf of bread passed from SERVANT GIRL THREE. NABAL sits with his elbow on the table, palm upward, lost in thought. ABIGAIL races back to table, puts bread in NABAL's hand, flops into chair and smiles at NABAL. NABAL comes out of his reverie.)

NABAL: Well, I'm off to David's camp.

ABIGAIL: But, Darling, you haven't finished your bread.

(NABAL looks in surprise at bread, shrugs and begins eating. SERVANT GIRL ONE enters, Stage Left, and motions to ABIGAIL. ABIGAIL jumps up from chair and runs to her.)

SERVANT GIRL ONE: *(Stage whispers.)* The bread and raisins are on the donkeys. Anything else?

ABIGAIL: *(Stage whispers.)* Let me think. *(Thinks.)* Yes! The meat from five sheep. *(SERVANT GIRL ONE curtsies and exits, Stage Left. SERVANT GIRL THREE enters, Stage Right, and curtsies.)*

SERVANT GIRL THREE: *(Stage whispers.)* Finished!

(SERVANT GIRL THREE curtsies and exits, Stage Right. ABIGAIL sees NABAL pop the last of the bread into his mouth and prepare to rise. ABIGAIL races to table and pushes NABAL back into his chair. ABIGAIL drops into other chair and smiles at NABAL.)

ABIGAIL: Going somewhere, Darling?

NABAL: I'm finished with my supper. I'm off to David's camp.

ABIGAIL: Wait!

(NABAL looks at ABIGAIL expectantly.)

ABIGAIL: You need...

(NABAL continues looking.)

ABIGAIL: You need...

NABAL: Yes?

ABIGAIL: Dessert! You need to get your dessert. *(Aside to audience.)* But not his just desserts, which he will get if he goes to David's camp.

NABAL: What do we have?

ABIGAIL: Your favorite. Just wait here. I'll get it. *(Yells to Stage Right.)* DESSERT! *(Jumps up as SERVANT GIRL ONE enters, Stage Left. ABIGAIL stops by her.)*

SERVANT GIRL ONE: *(Stage whispers.)* We have eight full bags of corn.

ABIGAIL: *(Stage whispers.)* Five. Five on the donkeys.

(SERVANT GIRL ONE curtsies and exits, Stage Left. ABIGAIL continues her circuit to Stage Right where she meets SERVANT GIRL THREE entering with an apple. ABIGAIL grabs apple and takes one step toward NABAL.)

NABAL: If we have an apple, I could eat it on my way to David's camp.

(ABIGAIL whirls about and hands apple back to SERVANT GIRL THREE. SERVANT GIRL THREE exits, Stage Right, and ABIGAIL runs to the table, flops into chair and smiles at NABAL.)

ABIGAIL: We have something much better than that.

(ABIGAIL jumps up from chair. SERVANT GIRL ONE enters, Stage Left. ABIGAIL stops to speak with her.)

SERVANT GIRL ONE: *(Stage whispers.)* Anything else?

ABIGAIL: *(Stage whispers.)* What's the fig situation?

SERVANT GIRL ONE: *(Stage whispers.)* Four hundred cakes.

ABIGAIL: *(Stage whispers.)* Two hundred for David.

(SERVANT GIRL ONE curtsies and exits, Stage Left. ABIGAIL continues across to Stage Right where SERVANT GIRL THREE has entered carrying a bowl of gelatin dessert such as Jell-O and a spoon. ABIGAIL takes them, stops and smiles broadly at audience. ABIGAIL hands spoon back to SERVANT GIRL THREE and whispers to her. SERVANT GIRL THREE curtsies and exits. ABIGAIL runs to table and places bowl of gelatin in front of NABAL. ABIGAIL drops into chair and smiles at NABAL.)

ABIGAIL: Your favorite Jell-O. *(Places hand on chest and breathes heavily, getting back her wind.)*

(NABAL looks around for spoon, doesn't see one and begins to reach for the gelatin with his fingers.)

ABIGAIL: Not with your fingers, Darling. I'll get you a utensil. *(Jumps from chair. SERVANT GIRL ONE enters, Stage Left. ABIGAIL stops to speak to her.)*

ABIGAIL: *(Stage whispers.)* Wine. Two bottles.

(SERVANT GIRL ONE curtsies and exits, Stage Left. ABIGAIL continues across stage to meet SERVANT GIRL THREE who enters, carrying chopsticks. ABIGAIL grabs chopsticks and runs to front of stage. SERVANT GIRL THREE exits, Stage Right. ABIGAIL holds up chopsticks to show audience.)

ABIGAIL: *(To audience.)* This should slow him down a bit. *(Continues to table and sits in chair. She hands chopsticks to NABAL and smiles at him.)*

NABAL: What's this?

ABIGAIL: Only the bravest, smartest and handsomest men are allowed to use these. So I naturally thought of you.

NABAL: *(Smiling proudly.)* Naturally. *(NABAL tries unsuccessfully to eat gelatin with chopsticks. After several unsuccessful attempts, he finally gets an idea. Holding one stick in each hand, he spears a cube of gelatin with each stick and eats one cube, then the other. SERVANT GIRL ONE and MESSENGER enter, Stage Left, and motion to ABIGAIL. ABIGAIL runs to them as SERVANT GIRL THREE enters, Stage Right.)*

SERVANT GIRL ONE: *(Stage whispers.)* The donkeys are loaded.

MESSENGER: *(Stage whispers.)* Is there anything else?

ABIGAIL: *(Stage whispers.)* Saddle two for yourselves and one for me. Take the gifts to David. I'll be following you.

(SERVANT GIRL ONE curtsies and MESSENGER bows. They exit, Stage Left. ABIGAIL crosses to SERVANT GIRL THREE.)

ABIGAIL: *(Stage whispers.)* Prepare the master's bed.

(SERVANT GIRL THREE curtsies and exits, Stage Right. ABIGAIL sees NABAL is nearly finished the gelatin and runs to the table. She flops into her chair and smiles at NABAL.)

NABAL: *(Finishing gelatin.)* Ahh! Now, to David's camp.

ABIGAIL: *(Feigning surprise.)* What? On a full stomach? All that exercise could give you indigestion. *(Yawns broadly in NABAL's face.)* What you need to do is rest your supper. *(Again yawns broadly in NABAL's face.)* You should lie down for ten or fifteen minutes. *(Again yawns broadly in NABAL's face.)* But whatever you do, don't go to sleep. *(Again yawns broadly in NABAL's face. NABAL finally yawns in return.)*

NABAL: That's a good idea. I'll lie down on my bed for a few minutes. *(Yawns again.)* But I won't go to sleep.

(ABIGAIL leads NABAL to Stage Right. NABAL exits and ABIGAIL pretends to watch him lie down.)

ABIGAIL: Remember now. Don't *(Yawns.)* go *(Yawns.)* to *(Yawns.)* sleep. *(Yawns.)*

NABAL: *(From offstage, sleepily.)* I...won't. *(Begins snoring.)*

ABIGAIL: *(To audience.)* By the time he wakes up, he'll have forgotten his silly idea of fighting David. Now, if I can just convince David to have mercy on Mr. "Laban spelled backwards." *(Runs across stage, stops just before she exits. To audience.)* The things we do for love! *(Exits, Stage Left. Lights snap to black.)*

NARRATOR: OK, OK. Maybe not all couples in the Bible are terrific examples of selfless love.

(DELILAH and SAMSON enter and move to Center Stage as lights rise on Center Stage.)

Delilah may have been the apple of Samson's eye, but she had nothing but sour grapes for Samson. She'd go to any length—in Samson's case, a very short length—to get her silver. Poor Samson ended up with nothing but peach fuzz.

(JEZEBEL and AHAB enter and move to lighted area of Center Stage.)

And then there was Jezebel. She knew which side her bread was buttered on! She loved to wield her power, whether it helped her honey Ahab or not. But taking that land for Ahab's herb garden didn't add quite the right spice to their lives.

(ABIGAIL and NABAL enter and move to lighted area of Center Stage.)

As for Abigail, she made sure her sweetie-pie Nabal was well fed, right down to dessert—just so he wouldn't get his just deserts from David. Abigail was one smart cookie. She got the plum, too: After Nabal died, she became King David's wife. Hmm. All this talk about food is making me hungry! Maybe there IS something to what they say about the connection between love and food! After all, true love is a FRUIT of God's Spirit!

(Other cast members move to Center Stage for a final bow before lights snap to black. All exit under cover of darkness.)

THE MOTHER ZONE

(APPROXIMATE TIME: 15 MINUTES)

SYNOPSIS
Children tell all about their moms...in the Mother Zone.

STAGE SETTING:
■ Table holding two sheets of poster board lettered with *M* and *O*, Stage Right (see below)
■ Table holding two sheets of poster board lettered with *T* and *H*, Center Stage
■ Table holding two sheets of poster board lettered with *E* and *R*, Stage Left

THE PLAYERS
SPEAKING STUDENTS (Grades 1-6)
TEACHERS (Adults)
NONSPEAKING STUDENTS (Grades 1-6)
NARRATOR (Adult)

SUGGESTED PROPS:
■ Six sheets of poster board, each lettered with one large letter of the word "Mother" for children to decorate
■ Crayons or markers, stickers, glue and glitter for decorating letters on poster boards
■ Picture book to represent Alphabet Book
■ Cassette tape with music from "The Twilight Zone" (or similar music)

DIRECTOR'S TIPS
1. If stage is not large enough for three separate work tables, use one in Center Stage. Have the three groups enter and exit to prepare their letters. If using the same table, Teachers can bring the letters and decorating materials in with them and take them off again. (If using that option, have a work area backstage for the Students to work on the letters while not on stage.)

2. You might want to have a drop cloth or paper under the tables.

3. Narrator need not be on stage but should be able to see stage action. For Narrator's speeches, increase the reverberation in the sound system and bring up music from "The Twilight Zone" (or similar music) for comic effect.

4. Parts can be doubled up or split up among more players, depending upon the size of your group. Remember to designate the six who will each display one letter of the word "MOTHER" and tell what each letter stands for.

THE MOTHER ZONE

(TEACHERS and STUDENTS enter from both sides of stage. STUDENTS in grades one and two take the table and chairs, Stage Right; STUDENTS in grades three and four, Center Stage; STUDENTS in grades five and six, Stage Left.)

NARRATOR: It was a peaceful Sunday in May, a Sunday much like any other. Parents bustled about, getting ready for church. Nobody was prepared for the unusual events that would take place once they passed through the doors of the church. Suddenly, they had entered... *(Music up.)* The Mother Zone.

It is biblical for children to honor their parents. To those who honor their fathers and mothers, the Bible promises long life. Honoring parents is also a way to show one's wisdom. Proverbs says that a wise son makes his father glad, but a foolish child brings sadness to his mother. Yes, honoring parents is biblical and wise. But today, when people walked through the doors of the church, all thoughts of FATHERS were forgotten. For these people had entered... *(Music up.)* The MOTHER Zone.

SCENE ONE: GRADES ONE AND TWO

(STUDENTS are working on decorating the letters M and O. TEACHERS are supervising the work.)

TEACHER: What special day are we celebrating today?

ALL STUDENTS: Mother's Day!

TEACHER: That's right! And we're making something very special for all the mothers in the church today.

NARRATOR: We've all heard the song, *(singing)* "M is for the many things...dah, dah, dah." But no matter how many times it's been used before, the song always seems fresh and new somehow when you've entered... *(Music up.)* The Mother Zone.

TEACHER: Let's all think about what the letters of the word "mother" could mean. What about *M*? What could *M* stand for?

STUDENT ONE: *M* is for "mouse."

TEACHER: I don't think that's quite the right word, do you?

STUDENT ONE: Sure it is! See? *(Takes Alphabet Book and shows page to teacher.)* It's right here in this book.

TEACHER: That's true. Sometimes *M* is for "mouse." But do you think that's the right word for Mother's Day?

STUDENT ONE: Baby mice have mothers, too.

TEACHER: Yes, I guess they do. But what word would be good for OUR mothers?

STUDENT TWO: *M* is for "mad."

TEACHER: Mad? Is that the word you would use to describe our mothers?

STUDENT TWO: Well, when I drew dinosaurs on my bedroom wall, Mommy got mad.

TEACHER: Well, I suppose sometimes...

STUDENT THREE (*interrupting*): And when I spilled my tomato juice on the white rug, Mommy got mad.

TEACHER: That may be true...

STUDENT FOUR (*interrupting*): When my brother and I fight, Mommy gets mad.

TEACHER: Yes, sometimes mothers DO get mad. But is your mother angry most of the time?

STUDENTS: No.

TEACHER: No. Most of the time, she's happy! She loves you. So what would be a good word to describe your mother most of the time? Something that starts with the letter *M*.

STUDENT FIVE: Magic!

TEACHER: Magic?

STUDENT FIVE: Sure. When I fall down and hurt myself, Mommy kisses the hurt and makes it better. Even Daddy can't do that.

STUDENT SIX: And when there's thunder and lightning, Mommy hugs me, and I'm not scared any more.

STUDENT SEVEN: And she can see through walls. She always knows what I'm doing, even when she can't see me.

TEACHER: Then that's a good word to tell about your mothers. *M* can be for "magic." Now, what about the letter *O*?

STUDENT ONE: *O* is for "over."

TEACHER: Over?

STUDENT TWO: (*Points to mother.*) Because she's sitting over there.

TEACHER: Yes, she is. But that's not what I meant. What is a good word to describe your mother ALL the time, not just when she's over there?

STUDENT THREE: *O* is for "or."

TEACHER: Or?

STUDENT THREE: Because sometimes she says, "Finish your supper OR there's no dessert."

TEACHER: Well, sometimes...

STUDENT FOUR (*interrupting*): And sometimes she says, "Do your homework OR you can't watch TV."

TEACHER: That's true. Mothers do have to be sure that we do what's good for us. But do your mothers always scold you?

STUDENTS: No!

TEACHER: So what about the other times? What's a good word beginning with *O*?

STUDENT FIVE: *O* can be for "open."

TEACHER: Open?

STUDENT FIVE: When I was little and couldn't reach the door knob, Mommy always opened the door for me.

STUDENT SIX: She opens the bag inside the cereal box for me.

STUDENT SEVEN: When I need a hug, she always opens her arms to hug me.

TEACHER: Perfect. "Open" is a wonderful word to describe your mothers. We'll let the letter *O* stand for "open."

NARRATOR: From the mouths of babes come words of understanding. Even the youngest children have amazing insight when they enter... *(Music up.)* The MOTHER Zone.

(STUDENTS continue to work quietly decorating the letters M *and* O.

SCENE TWO: GRADES THREE AND FOUR

(STUDENTS are working on decorating the letters T *and* H. *TEACHERS are supervising the work.)*

TEACHER: What special day are we celebrating today?

STUDENTS: Mother's Day!

NARRATOR: No matter what the age group, whenever there's a special day, every teacher asks the same question. Everyone knows the answer and the teacher KNOWS everyone knows the answer. But something in a teacher requires the question to be asked. Teachers are always the same, even in... *(Music up.)* The MOTHER Zone.

TEACHER: We need to find just the right word for both of our letters. What could be a good word for the letter *T*?

STUDENT ONE: *T* is for "tarantula."

TEACHER: Tarantula?

STUDENT ONE: Even baby tarantulas have mothers.

TEACHER: True. But the first class used that joke with "mouse." Let's think of a better word for the letter *T*.

STUDENT TWO: Tapeworm!

TEACHER: Tapeworm?

STUDENT TWO: That's what my mom says when I'm always hungry. *(Imitates mom.)* "You must have a tapeworm."

STUDENT THREE: *T* is for "tongue." Because when Mom asks me what I want and I point at it, she says, "You've got a tongue. Use it."

STUDENT FOUR: *T* is for "towel." Mom always says, "Don't just wipe your hands on the towel. Wash them with soap and water first."

STUDENT FIVE *(imitating mom)*: "Did you hang up the towel after you finished? Don't just throw it on the floor."

TEACHER: Those all might be good answers, but there must be something even better. We want the best word for the letter *T*.

STUDENT SIX: How about talented?

TEACHER: *T* is for "talented"?

STUDENT SEVEN: Yeah! My mom has lots of talents. She can turn leftovers into a special meal.

STUDENT EIGHT: My mom can take old junky things and turn them into something beautiful.

STUDENT NINE: My mom took the car downtown and turned it into a parking lot. *(Laughs loudly at own joke.)*

STUDENT TEN: My mom works at her job all day. She works hard and still has time to cook dinner and help me with my homework.

TEACHER: I think we found the perfect word for *T. T* is for "talented." All our mothers have special talents. Those talents make them special mothers. Now, what about the letter *H*?

STUDENT ONE: Horse! Because Dad says Mom works like a horse.

TEACHER: Maybe your Dad should help more, and she wouldn't have to work so hard.

NARRATOR: "A man may work from sun to sun; but a woman's work is never done." Normally, we wouldn't suggest that men don't work hard enough. But today, we have entered... *(Music up.)* The MOTHER Zone.

STUDENT THREE: *H* is for "hers." Then, on Father's Day, *H* could be for "his."

TEACHER: Possibly. But let's try to get beyond pronouns.

STUDENT TWO: How about "hollow"? Because if she doesn't talk about tapeworms, she asks if I have a hollow leg.

STUDENT FOUR: *H* is for "hyena." Because Mom says I laugh like one.

STUDENT FIVE: Hydrogen!

ALL STUDENTS: Hydrogen?

STUDENT FIVE: I've always kind of liked hydrogen.

TEACHER: Those things are more about YOU. What word can describe your mothers?

STUDENT SIX: Hunter!

TEACHER *(surprised)***:** I didn't know your mother liked to hunt!

STUDENT SIX: She doesn't! But she hunts all the time. When I can't find the right clothes to wear for school, she helps me hunt for them.

STUDENT SEVEN: My mom hunts through cookbooks to find good recipes.

STUDENT EIGHT: My mom hunts through the cupboards to find things that nobody else can find.

STUDENT NINE: My mom hunts through my schoolwork to help me when I can't figure things out.

STUDENT TEN: Our mom hunts through the newspaper to find things on sale. She says that helps our family's money go further.

TEACHER: I think we might have found just the right word for the letter *H*.

NARRATOR: Children sometimes seem to think only of themselves. But all that changes completely once they've entered... *(Music up.)* The MOTHER Zone.

(STUDENTS continue to work quietly decorating the letters T *and* H.*)*

SCENE THREE: GRADES FIVE AND SIX

(STUDENTS are working on decorating the letters E and R. TEACHERS are supervising the work.)

TEACHER: What special day are we celebrating today?

STUDENTS: Mother's Day!

NARRATOR: Teachers can't help themselves. No matter the age of the students, they continue asking the same question. And every time they ask, they get the same answer when they're in... *(Music up.)* The MOTHER Zone.

TEACHER: Our letters are *E* and *R*. What could we have for the letter *E*?

STUDENT ONE: That's easy!

TEACHER: Why would *E* stand for "easy"?

STUDENT ONE: It wouldn't.

TEACHER: But you said it DID. I asked, "What could we have for the letter *E*?"

STUDENT ONE: And I said, "That's easy!"

TEACHER *(flustered)***:** What?

STUDENT TWO: *(To STUDENT THREE.)* What's the name of the guy on first?

STUDENT THREE: No, that's Who. What's on second.

STUDENT TWO: I don't know.

STUDENT THREE: He's on third.

TEACHER: Oh! Wait a minute. I get it! *E* isn't for "easy." But finding the right word to describe your mothers is easy.

STUDENT ONE: Right! The word is "eagle-eyed."

TEACHER: Why eagle-eyed?

STUDENT ONE: Because if I'm supposed to clean up the living room and don't dust all the furniture, she SEES it.

STUDENT TWO: And if I don't vacuum under all the furniture, she SEES it.

STUDENT THREE: If I don't pick up all of my clothes, she SEES that, too.

STUDENT FOUR: If I don't take out the garbage, she SEES it. And she TELLS me about it!

TEACHER *(thoughtfully)***:** "Eagle-eyed" might be a good word at that. Do we have any other ideas?

STUDENT FIVE: Exaggerate.

TEACHER: Exaggerate?

STUDENT FIVE *(imitates mom)***:** "I've told you a MILLION TIMES, 'Wash behind your ears!'"

STUDENT SIX *(imitates mom)*: "If I live to be a HUNDRED, I'll never understand why you did that."

STUDENT SEVEN: Mine says, "Why do you ALWAYS have to slam the door?"

TEACHER: I think I prefer "eagle-eyed" to "exaggerate." Any other ideas?

STUDENT FOUR: Elephant. Because she has a memory like one. She says, "I told you six days ago that you should start your big report. Don't blame me that it's not finished."

STUDENT FIVE: Mine says, "I warned you YESTERDAY about fighting with your brother. Go to your room—NOW!"

STUDENT SIX *(imitates mom)*: "I told you four times last week, always to go to the bathroom before we leave. You'll just have to wait."

STUDENT SEVEN: "You had a cookie at 3 o'clock. You'll spoil your supper if you have any more. And don't slam the door on your way out."

TEACHER: You have some good ideas. But if we tell the audience, "Mothers are like elephants," someone might get the wrong idea. Any others?

STUDENT EIGHT: *E* is for "expert." Because mothers have to be experts at everything.

STUDENT NINE: When we're sick, Mom knows just what to do to make us feel better. She's an expert doctor.

STUDENT TEN: My mom makes GOOD meals! She's an expert chef.

STUDENT ELEVEN: Mom knows where everything is. Even when we lose it! She's an expert at finding things.

STUDENT EIGHT: Mom drives us anywhere we need to go. She could run a taxi company! She's an expert driver.

TEACHER: It sounds like moms have to be experts in all areas.

STUDENT ONE: Expert plumber and carpenter.

STUDENT TWO: Expert chef.

STUDENT THREE: Expert chauffeur.

STUDENT FOUR: Expert navigator.

STUDENT FIVE: Expert coach.

STUDENT SIX: Expert doctor.

STUDENT SEVEN: Expert referee.

STUDENT EIGHT: Expert EVERYTHING!

TEACHER: I think we've found the right word for *E*. What about *R*?

STUDENT NINE: Rats!

TEACHER: No. We're not doing that joke again.

STUDENT NINE: What joke? I was gluing this and my hand slipped and ruined it. Rats!

TEACHER: Don't worry about it. You can use something else. What about the letter *R*?

STUDENT ONE: Rushing! Mothers are always rushing. *(Imitates mom.)* "Hurry. Get up or you'll be late."

STUDENT TWO: *(Imitates mom.)* "Hurry and get dressed. We'll be late for church."

STUDENT THREE: *(Imitates mom.)* "Hurry up and get to the bus, or you'll miss it. And don't slam the door on your way out!"

TEACHER: I guess that's another area of moms' expertise—getting us places on time. What other words beginning with *R* could describe mothers?

STUDENT FOUR: Rescuer! She's always getting me out of trouble.

STUDENT FIVE: Right! When I was little, she kept me from putting dangerous things in my mouth.

STUDENT SIX: She always reminds us about safety rules.

STUDENT SEVEN: When my friends want me to do something I don't want to do, I can always say, "Mom won't let me do that."

TEACHER: We've got lots of good ideas for that one. Any others?

STUDENT EIGHT: Retriever. She always manages to keep stuff I threw out by mistake.

STUDENT NINE: Radar. She always seems to know where we are and if we're getting near trouble.

STUDENT TEN: Ruby. Because she's like a gem.

STUDENT ELEVEN: Recording. Because she can play back anything we've ever said.

TEACHER: We've had lots of good ideas, but we seemed to have most agreement on "rescuer." Let's finish up.

NARRATOR: It is truly amazing how many different ways one person can be seen. But we shouldn't be surprised. Anything can happen in... *(Music up.)* The MOTHER Zone.

(All STUDENTS get up and move to Center Stage. Students who have been selected to hold up cards group together at the front, standing in order to spell the word "mother." Each one displays appropriate letter while saying line.)

STUDENT *M*: *M* is for "magic."

STUDENT *O*: *O* is for "open."

STUDENT *T*: *T* is for "talented."

STUDENT *H*: *H* is for "hunter."

STUDENT *E*: *E* is for "expert."

STUDENT *R*: *R* is for "rescuer."

NARRATOR: It's a place where anything can happen and often does. A place where anyone can suddenly realize the importance of his or her mother. A place where people who didn't seem to notice you suddenly see you as the most important person in the world. A place known as... *(Music up.)* The MOTHER Zone.

ALL: Happy Mother's Day!

NOAH AND SONS

(APPROXIMATE TIME: 20 MINUTES)

SYNOPSIS
In true father-son fashion, Noah and his sons take on a building project of monumental proportion.

STAGE SETTING: NOAH'S PLACE
- Center divider for stage (with a door that can open and close), to divide stage into outside (Stage Left) and inside (Stage Right)
- Patio chairs to represent outside, Stage Left, near Center Stage
- Table outdoors, Stage Left, a distance from Center Stage
- Outdoors facade (shrubbery, trees, etc.) to rear of Stage Left
- Coffee table, chairs or sofa, etc., Stage Right, to represent living room
- Household furnishings or facade to rear of Stage Right

PLAYERS
JAPHETH'S WIFE (JAY-fith) (Grade 1 or older)   **JAPHETH** (JAY-fith) (Grade 3 or older)

HAM'S WIFE (Grade 3 or older)   **HAM** (Grade 3 or older)

NOAH'S WIFE (Grade 5 or older)   **NOAH** (Grade 5 or older)

SHEM'S WIFE (Grade 5 or older)   **SHEM** (Grade 5 or older)

MALE NEIGHBOR (Grade 3 or older)   **FEMALE NEIGHBOR** (Grade 3 or older)

STAGEHANDS (All ages)   **NARRATOR** (Grade 5 or older)

NONSPEAKING MALE and FEMALE NEIGHBORS (All ages)

SUGGESTED PROPS
- Blueprints for Noah
- Coffee pot, cups, saucers, other dishes
- Two vases of flowers for coffee table
- Tape measure, pencil, paper for Shem
- Baseball cap and glove for Ham
- Two signs lettered "STAGEHANDS OF GOD"
- Shovel for Japheth
- Plate of cakes
- Other tools, tool belts
- Lumber or wood to be measured
- Box of stuffed toy animals
- Bible-times costumes
- Ark facade—made of sections that can be pieced together, with a door that can close

DIRECTOR'S TIPS
1. Narrator's part can be read. Narrator could be offstage or to one side of the stage, but should be able to see stage action.
2. Noah and the three sons should be of different heights so that their arms each will measure a different cubit.
3. When Female Neighbor moves vases of flowers, she should move very deliberately so that audience sees what she is doing. Noah's Wife should replace vases in the same manner.
4. Because there is a great deal of action in this skit where backs may be turned to the audience, be sure players face the audience when they speak.

NOAH AND SONS

SCENE ONE: OUT ON THE LAWN

(NOAH is inside house, beside door, ready to go outside. HAM, SHEM and JAPHETH are lounging in lawn chairs, sunning themselves.)

NARRATOR: Fathers and sons need to spend time together. And what could be a better way than to work together on a major building project?

(NOAH opens door and walks out to the table. He lays some blueprints down on the table and begins studying them.)

NOAH *(calling)*: Shem, Ham, Japheth! I have some exciting news!

(HAM, SHEM and JAPHETH get up and approach NOAH.)

SHEM: What is it, Dad?

NOAH: We're going to build an ark.

(HAM, SHEM and JAPHETH all say, "All right! Right on!" giving each other high fives, then stop and look at each other.)

JAPHETH: What's an ark?

NOAH *(excitedly)*: It's a boat!

SHEM: Terrific! Then we can pretend to be explorers, paddling our canoes across uncharted waters.

NOAH: *(Laughs.)* No, Son. It will be much larger than a canoe!

HAM: How big will it be, Dad?

NOAH: It will be three hundred cubits long, fifty cubits wide and thirty cubits high.

(HAM, SHEM and JAPHETH all say, "Wow! Colossal!" and high-five each other, then stop.)

JAPHETH: What's a cubit, Dad?

NOAH: *(Holds up his forearm and points.)* It's the distance from a man's fingers to his elbow.

(HAM, SHEM and JAPHETH stand elbow to elbow, trying to measure the projected size of the ark. They contort themselves, trying to measure its height and width.)

SHEM: Dad, don't you think that boat's a little bit BIG for our family? You could fit two of every kind of animal on EARTH in a boat that size!

NOAH: Exactly. That's just what we'll do!

SHEM: Wow! Think of all the color!

HAM: Think of all the noise!

JAPHETH: Think of all the... *(Stops, looks at ground, lifts shoe to look at sole and wipes shoe on the ground.)* Who's going to clean out the boat, Dad?

NOAH: Well, let's see. I'll be the captain so it won't be ME...

SHEM: I, Shem, will be the first mate because I'm the OLDEST.

HAM: I, Ham, will be busy in the galley, making SANDWICHES for the trip.

JAPHETH *(whining)***:** Why can't I make the sandwiches and YOU clean the boat?

HAM: Because on cruises, everybody wants HAM's sandwiches. On rye, hold the mayo. *(SHEM and JAPHETH groan.)*

NOAH: *(NOAH picks up a shovel and hands it to JAPHETH.)* Congratulations, son. It's your job.

SHEM: Dad? We don't live near a lake big enough to sail this boat. Why are we going to put all these animals on a boat when we can't sail it?

JAPHETH *(eagerly agreeing)***:** Good point!

NOAH: The Lord is going to make it rain for a long, long time.

(HAM, SHEM and JAPHETH all say, "Wow!" then look bewildered.)

JAPHETH: What's rain, Dad?

NARRATOR: For in those days, the earth had not seen rain but was watered by a mist that rose from the ground.

NOAH: That's water that falls in big drops from the sky.

(HAM, SHEM and JAPHETH all laugh, thinking he's joking. When they see he's serious, they stop.)

HAM: Water's going to FALL—from the SKY?

NOAH: And the fountains of the deep will be broken open.

SHEM: Fountains? How much water are we talking here? A bucketful? Two?

NOAH: Enough water to cover all the mountains of the earth.

HAM: Oh. So THAT'S why the boat has to be big enough to hold all the animals.

SHEM: Isn't this kind of...well, BIG for a father-son project, Dad?

(NOAH smiles and points to blueprints.)

NOAH: We can DO it, boys! I have the plans right here.

JAPHETH: Wait! I have an idea! Let's build a smaller boat, just big enough for the family. Then, after the flood, God can create NEW animals!

NOAH: *(Shakes his head, no.)* No, son. We'll do it God's way.

JAPHETH: *(Picks up shovel.)* I was AFRAID of that. *(Sighs heavily, then joins NOAH and HAM and SHEM in studying plans.)*

NARRATOR: The producers of this play wish to bring you this important disclaimer. "Although this is a Father's Day play, government regulations prohibit discrimination on the basis of gender. Therefore, in accord with ruling #495838675, we include this fictionalized account of the women in this story."

SCENE TWO: INSIDE THE HOUSE

(NOAH'S WIFE and SONS' WIVES enter interior scene from Stage Right. They carry cups, saucers, coffee pot, etc., that they place and arrange on coffee table.)

NOAH'S WIFE *(calling loudly)*: Noah! Noah! Where are you?

(NOAH does not answer. He and SONS are outside at table, engrossed in ark plans.)

NOAH'S WIFE: Noah! ANSWER me when I call you! Where are you?

(SONS' WIVES begin looking behind and under chairs, under the coffee table, etc. SHEM'S WIFE goes to door and looks out.)

SHEM'S WIFE: He's outside. With the boys.

NOAH'S WIFE: That man! Always underfoot unless you want him.

(NOAH'S WIFE goes to door and pokes her head out. HAM'S WIFE and JAPHETH'S WIFE also approach door and stand beside SHEM'S WIFE.)

NOAH'S WIFE: Noah!

(NOAH looks up from plans.)

NOAH: Yes, Dear?

NOAH'S WIFE: We have company coming. Come in and wash up!

NOAH: In a minute, Dear.

NOAH'S WIFE: You always say, "In a minute." But you don't mean it! Last Friday I called you for supper. At what time?

HAM'S WIFE: Six o'clock.

NOAH'S WIFE: And what did you say to me?

JAPHETH'S WIFE: "In a minute."

NOAH'S WIFE: And what time did you come IN?

SHEM'S WIFE: Nine o'clock.

NOAH'S WIFE: NOAH! Come in before you get yourself all dirty.

NOAH: *(Still looks at plans.)* In a minute. *(Continues to study ark plans with HAM, SHEM and JAPHETH.)*

(NOAH's WIFE throws up her hands in despair, closes door and goes back to coffee table saying, "In a minute. In a minute. In a minute." SONS' WIVES follow, repeating, "In a minute. In a minute. In a minute." WIVES finish setting coffee table while neighbors enter, Stage Left.)

MALE NEIGHBOR: *(To NOAH.)* Howdy, neighbor. What are you doing?

NOAH: Looking at plans. *(To FEMALE NEIGHBOR.)* Go on in. She's expecting you.

(MALE NEIGHBORS go to table to look at plans while FEMALE NEIGHBORS go to door. FEMALE NEIGHBOR knocks on door and opens it.)

FEMALE NEIGHBOR: *(Speaks in a singsong voice.)* Yoo-hoo! We're here!

NOAH'S WIFE: Come in. Leave the door open. The boys will be coming in soon—I HOPE.

JAPHETH'S WIFE: In a minute.

(WIVES laugh while FEMALE NEIGHBORS look at each other, puzzled. FEMALE NEIGHBORS enter house and approach coffee table.)

SHEM'S WIFE: Never mind. It's just a private joke.

NOAH'S WIFE *(indicating chairs)*: Sit. Please sit.

(FEMALE NEIGHBORS are seated.)

HAM'S WIFE: Will you have coffee?

(FEMALE NEIGHBORS all nod, yes.)

NOAH'S WIFE: *(To HAM'S WIFE.)* You pour the coffee, dear. *(To SHEM'S WIFE and JAPHETH'S WIFE.)* You two, help me get the other things from the kitchen.

(NOAH'S WIFE, SHEM'S WIFE and JAPHETH'S WIFE exit, Stage Right. HAM'S WIFE pours coffee. FEMALE NEIGHBOR looks disapprovingly at table. Switches vases with each other. She looks at the table and nods her approval.)

HAM'S WIFE *(looking toward door)*: What can be KEEPING those men?

(NOAH, SONS and MALE NEIGHBORS have been looking at plans. Suddenly, MALE NEIGHBORS all point at NOAH and begin laughing loudly.)

FEMALE NEIGHBOR: They seem to be having a good time.

(NOAH'S WIFE, SHEM'S WIFE and JAPHETH'S WIFE enter, Stage Right, carrying sandwiches, cakes, etc. They place the food on the coffee table. NOAH'S WIFE sees the vases have been switched and switches them back.)

NOAH'S WIFE: *(To SHEM'S WIFE.)* Get those men in here, will you, dear?

(SHEM'S WIFE goes to door and pokes her head out.)

SHEM'S WIFE: Mother says, "Come in right now!" No more "just a minute's"! *(Goes back to coffee table, gets her coffee and sits down.)* *(MEN come in, MALE NEIGHBORS still laughing. NOAH'S WIFE watches them as FEMALE NEIGHBOR takes the opportunity to switch the vases.)*

MALE NEIGHBOR: *(Chuckles.)* What a guy! After six hundred years, he still comes up with a new joke! What a guy!

(NOAH, HAM, SHEM, JAPHETH and NEIGHBORS all are seated.)

NOAH'S WIFE: *(To JAPHETH'S WIFE.)* Offer the gentlemen something, dear.

(NOAH'S WIFE hands JAPHETH'S WIFE a plate of cake. As she does, she notices the vases. As JAPHETH'S WIFE passes the cake to the men, NOAH'S WIFE glares at FEMALE NEIGHBOR and rearranges the vases once more.)

NOAH'S WIFE: *(To NOAH.)* And what was the joke, Dear?

NOAH: It wasn't a joke. *(Takes a bite of cake.)*

SHEM *(with a mouthful of cake)*: He was just saying...

SHEM'S WIFE *(shaking her finger at SHEM)*: Not with your mouth full!

HAM *(with a mouthful of cake)*: He only...

HAM'S WIFE *(shaking her finger at HAM)*: Where are your MANNERS?

(JAPHETH'S WIFE glares at JAPHETH who also has a mouthful of cake.)

JAPHETH'S WIFE: *(Shakes finger in his face.)* Don't even THINK about it!

FEMALE NEIGHBOR: Tell us the joke, Noah. Oh! Look there, Noah! Did you spill some cake?

> *(NOAH did not spill any cake but NOAH's WIFE looks at him carefully and suspiciously. As she does, FEMALE NEIGHBOR switches the vases one more time.)*

FEMALE NEIGHBOR: No. I guess you didn't. But tell us the joke.

NOAH: I was not joking. It will happen!

MALE NEIGHBOR: He told us that it was going to RAIN!

> *(MALE NEIGHBORS all laugh again. All females look at each other in bewilderment.)*

FEMALE NEIGHBOR: What's rain?

> *(MALE NEIGHBORS look at each other and begin laughing again.)*

MALE NEIGHBOR *(choking with laughter)***:** That's water! Falling from the SKY! *(Laughs loudly.)*

> *(All NEIGHBORS laugh loudly. NOAH'S WIFE sees the vases have been switched again and glares at FEMALE NEIGHBOR. All NEIGHBORS finish their coffee.)*

FEMALE NEIGHBOR: *(To NOAH'S WIFE.)* We hate to eat and run...

NOAH'S WIFE: *(Very deliberately switches vases' positions again, as she speaks to FEMALE NEIGHBOR.)* Please—DO.

> *(NEIGHBORS put their coffee cups on the table and leave. As they do, they laugh and talk about "water falling from the sky." NEIGHBORS go through door and exit, Stage Left.)*

NOAH'S WIFE *(angrily, still holding onto vases)***:** If that woman comes in here again...I'll...I'll...I'll throw a bucket of WATER on her!

NOAH: I don't think you'll have to do that, dear. She'll get enough when the time comes. Come on, boys. Let's get things cleared up and get to bed. Tomorrow, we begin the ULTIMATE father-son building project!

> *(NOAH, SONS and WIVES all take something from the coffee table and exit, Stage Right.)*

SCENE THREE: OUT ON THE LAWN

> *(NOAH, HAM, SHEM and JAPHETH enter, Stage Right. They go through the door of the house and to the outside set and begin assembling lumber, tools, etc. Sometimes one exits, Stage Left, and returns with something else for building the ark.)*

NARRATOR: So Noah and sons began building the ark, measuring very carefully...

> *(NOAH, HAM, SHEM and JAPHETH begin work. They carefully mark out cubits by placing their forearms on pieces of wood and making marks by their outstretched fingers. HAM and JAPHETH each take a piece of wood and compare the two.)*

HAM *(angrily)***:** It's your fault!

JAPHETH *(also angrily)***:** It is not! I measured perfectly.

NOAH: What's going on?

HAM: These pieces don't fit together! And I measured two cubits EXACTLY.

JAPHETH: You COULDN'T have! Because I measured two cubits exactly.

NOAH: Well, if you both measured accurately, the pieces should fit.

SHEM: *(Stands back, looking thoughtfully.)* I see the problem. Hold out your arms, you two. *(HAM and JAPHETH extend their arms, bent at the elbow, and SHEM compares the sizes.)* See, two different-sized cubits. We need to have a standard measurement.

NOAH: Have you got a solution, son?

(SHEM takes tape measure from his pocket.)

SHEM: Sure. Let's measure everybody's arms.

(NOAH, HAM and JAPHETH line up and hold out their arms, bent at the elbow. SHEM measures each arm with tape measure and writes the number on a piece of paper.)

Now, we'll take an average. *(Does the arithmetic on the paper.)* OK, let's make one cubit equal to eighteen inches. Then, we'll all be using the same size.

NARRATOR: So Noah and his sons continued their work, building the ark. The work took years. But finally...

(NOAH and SONS continue building. From time to time, two will exit, Stage Left, and return with a part of the ark facade and set it up. Finally, they finish.)

HAM: We're finished! The ark is done. Bring on the animals.

JAPHETH: Wait! There's a problem.

SHEM: I don't see a problem.

JAPHETH: Sure there is. Look at all the cracks between the boards!

HAM: We did that on purpose. That way, if any water gets in, it can flow out.

NOAH: No, no! Japheth is right. The Lord has told me we must cover the ark with pitch to make it watertight.

NARRATOR: We interrupt this story to bring you this important disclaimer. "It has been determined that prolonged exposure to the fumes of heated pitch can be hazardous to your health. Do not use this product without first wearing all necessary protective equipment." We now return to our story.

(NOAH, HAM, SHEM and JAPHETH pretend to use brushes to brush pitch onto the ark.)

HAM: You know what, Dad?

NOAH: What, Son?

HAM: I kind of like this pitching business. In fact, I've decided on a career after the flood. I'm going to become a big-league pitcher. I've even figured out what I'm going to wear. Hang on a minute and I'll show it to you! *(Runs into the house and exits, Stage Right. Returns with baseball cap and glove.)*

NOAH: What strange manner of dress is this?

HAM: *(Holds out glove.)* See? You get a big glove to hold a lot of pitch. Then, you take this hat with the built-in trowel to smooth the pitch on. *(Demonstrates scooping up pitch from glove with brim of cap and spreading it on the ark.)*

SHEM: And I'm going to become a master carpenter. Maybe I could even have my own TV show—"This Old Ark"!

JAPHETH: And I've decided on a career, too.

NOAH: What will it be, son?

JAPHETH: I'm going into bulk fertilizer sales. I'll have enough start-up inventory to last me for years!

NOAH: Great, boys! I'm glad all of you have chosen careers. You see? This father-son building project did wonders for our male bonding!

NARRATOR: So Noah and sons continued their work until, at last, the ark was completed and ready for the animals.

(NOAH, HAM, SHEM and JAPHETH continue working and finally stop, stepping back to survey their work. Satisfied that their work is complete, they all shake hands with each other.)

NOAH: Now, for the animals.

SHEM: *(To NOAH.)* Dad, wasn't BUILDING the ark together enough? I think we've DONE the male bonding thing now.

(NOAH glares at SHEM.)

SHEM: Oh, OK. Animals, too. Which ones first?

HAM: The lambs?

JAPHETH: The bunnies?

NOAH: No. I think we'll start with the most FEROCIOUS animals first!

(JAPHETH exits, Stage Left, to where a box of toy animals is just offstage. HAM positions himself toward the Stage Left wings and SHEM a little closer to the ark than HAM. NOAH stands by the door of the ark. JAPHETH yells, "Hut!" and throws an animal to HAM who in turn, yells, "Hut!" and throws it to SHEM. He yells, "Hut!" and throws it to NOAH, who yells, "Hike!" and throws it into the ark. They continue until all animals are in the ark.)

JAPHETH: *(Enters dusting off his hands, Stage Left.)* That's it!

SHEM: All aboard!

HAM: Coffee and sandwiches will be served as soon as we've left the dock.

NOAH: *(Puts arms around SONS.)* Splendid work, boys. You've made your old dad proud! *(To audience.)* Is this the best father-son project you've ever seen, or what?

(SHEM, HAM and JAPHETH smile at NOAH and hug him. Then NOAH and SONS enter house and exit, Stage Right. They return, each escorting his WIFE, and usher WIVES onto ark and enter ark themselves. NEIGHBORS enter, Stage Left, and stare at NOAH as he enters the ark. NOAH, SONS and WIVES all look out the door at NEIGHBORS.)

NOAH: *(Waves.)* Bon Voyage!

NARRATOR: And the hand of God closed the door of the ark. Or, in our case, the stagehands of God.

(Two STAGEHANDS wearing signs reading "Stagehand of God" enter and close the door of the ark. As the ark door closes, NEIGHBORS all laugh. Lights begin to dim and NEIGHBORS stop laughing and start to look around them, worried. Thunder is heard in the distance. Lights dim to black.)

REALLY THANKFUL?

(APPROXIMATE TIME: 10-15 MINUTES)

SYNOPSIS
Pete learns some new ways of expressing thankfulness when he asks his church friends for their help.

STAGE SETTINGS
SCENE ONE: WILLIAM AND MARY'S HOUSE
Sofa and coffee table, etc. to suggest a living room, Center Stage

SCENE TWO: ON THE STREET
Building facades, street lamps, fire hydrants, etc. to represent street

SCENE THREE: BETTY AND MICHAEL'S HOUSE
Kitchen table and chairs, Center Stage

SCENE FOUR: ON THE STREET
Same as Scene Two

THE PLAYERS
WILLIAM (Grade 3 or older)   **PAT** (Grade 3 or older)
JENNY (Grade 3 or older)   **BETTY** (Grade 3 or older)
MICHAEL (Grade 3 or older)   **MARY** (Grade 3 or older)
PETE (Grade 5 or older)   **HENRY** (Grade 5 or older)
JOE (Grade 5 or older)   **STAGEHANDS** (All ages)
NARRATOR (Grade 5 or older)

SUGGESTED PROPS:
■ Briefcase and papers for Henry   ■ Coffee pot and cups for Betty and Michael
■ Newspapers and magazines, flyers, etc. ■ Canisters, toaster, other kitchen items
■ Clipboard and pen for Pat   ■ Clipboard and pen for Pete
■ Golf magazines for coffee table   ■ Glass on its side on floor for William's putting practice
■ Golf bags, balls, clubs, shoes, etc. in living room for William and Mary

DIRECTOR'S TIPS
1. While this skit is about showing thankfulness, it may also be used as a recruiting skit. Each scene of the skit might be played out individually on successive Sundays, if desired.
2. Betty and Michael do not have to be husband and wife. If you want another female role, they could be roommates (Betty and Michelle).
3. Insert appropriate local mall and store names for Betty and Michael's ads.
4. Street scenes can be played without any props.
5. Narrator's part can be read.
6. If you cannot pull a curtain, change scenes in front of the audience. Pete could walk and study his church list while scenery is changed.
7. Narrator should stand where he or she can see stage action.

REALLY THANKFUL?

NARRATOR: There is a fictitious community, let's call it *(give name of your town)* where people are pious. Never would they forget to say their morning prayers. It's a matter of routine. If we listen carefully, we can hear them...

(Voices of MARY, WILLIAM, HENRY, JENNY, BETTY, MICHAEL, JOE and PAT are all heard from offstage.)

MARY: Thank You, Lord, for the beauty of nature...

WILLIAM: Yes. Thank You, God.

HENRY: Thank You, Lord, for Your generous bounty...

JENNY: Yes. Thank You, God.

BETTY: Thank You, Lord, for all the good things in our great land...

MICHAEL: Yes. Thank You, God.

JOE: Thank You, Lord, for good friends...

PAT: Yes. Thank You, God.

ALL: Let me always be Your servant, amen.

NARRATOR: In a community like this, where people seem to be so very thankful, volunteers for the church are always easy to find...

SCENE ONE: WILLIAM AND MARY'S HOUSE

(Knock on door is heard offstage.)

MARY: *(From offstage, Stage Right.)* It's open! Come on in!

(PETE enters, Stage Left. He carries a clipboard with pen.)

PETE: Mary? William?

MARY: Be right with you!

(MARY enters, Stage Right, carrying golf clubs in bag.)

MARY: Hi, Pete. You haven't seen a pair of golf shoes around, have you?

PETE: No. I haven't. Mary, I wanted to ask if you...

WILLIAM *(speaking as he enters, Stage Right)***:** Hi, Pete. *(To MARY.)* We'll be late, Mary.

MARY: I know! Back door. Be right back. *(Exits, Stage Right.)*

(William picks up putter and practices putting.)

PETE: William...

(WILLIAM shushes PETE by placing finger to lips, then concentrates on his putting again. MARY enters, Stage Right.)

MARY: Got them. In the bag now. *(Pats golf bag.)* You were saying, Pete?

PETE: I was hoping you and William might...

MARY: You haven't seen a seven iron lying around, have you?

PETE: No.

WILLIAM (*still putting*)**:** We'll be late, Mary.

MARY: Kitchen. I was practicing my stance over coffee. Be right back. (*MARY exits, Stage Right, and returns with seven iron.*)

MARY: Sorry, Pete, but since William and I took up golf, things have been utter chaos around here. We're in a bit of a hurry, but what did you want?

PETE: Well, the church needs greeters—people to welcome others as they come in. I was hoping I could count on William and yourself to help out from time to time.

MARY: Well, of COURSE you can!

WILLIAM: Just not in September and October.

MARY: We'll be golfing every weekend. November will be our Phoenix golf holiday, so that's out.

WILLIAM: December, we'll be preparing for Christmas.

MARY: That's right. (*Brightly.*) Do you know what our Christmas theme is going to be this year?

PETE: Golf?

MARY: How clever of you! You guessed. Well, we'll be busy all December finding just the right decorations, so December's out. January and February...

WILLIAM: Winter golf lessons.

MARY: Right. We'll be practicing at the dome every weekend. How about the second Sunday in March? We'll be free then.

PETE: (*Looks down at his clipboard.*) I was hoping for a more regular commitment. Maybe one Sunday per month?

WILLIAM: Impossible.

MARY: Be reasonable, Pete! We'd like to help, but...every MONTH?

PETE: It would sure help. And isn't worshiping God important?

MARY: Well, of COURSE it is. But you don't have to go to church to WORSHIP. You can worship ANYWHERE. Out on the golf course, communing with nature...

PETE: You CAN worship God on the golf course. But DO you?

WILLIAM: (*Looks at watch.*) We'll be late.

MARY: (*Looks at watch.*) Oops! Look at the time. Close the door on your way out, will you? We've just GOT to scoot, Pete! Bye, bye! (*Exits, Stage Left, running. WILLIAM follows, walking, carrying golf clubs in bag.*)

(*PETE crosses names off list and exits, Stage Left.*)

(*Curtain closes. STAGEHANDS break down set and set up Scene Two and Scene Three.*)

SCENE TWO: ON THE STREET

(PETE enters, Stage Left, studying church list on clipboard. HENRY and JENNY enter, Stage Right, consulting papers and talking. PETE, HENRY and JENNY collide midstage.)

HENRY: Why don't you watch...! Oh. Hi, Pete!

JENNY: Hi, Pete.

PETE: Hi, Henry. Hello, Jenny! Sorry to bump into you, but...

HENRY: Think nothing of it, old buddy, old pal.

PETE: I'm glad I bumped into you. I was wondering...

JENNY: *(Taps watch impatiently. To HENRY.)* Henry!

HENRY: *(Starts to move past PETE.)* Love to stop and talk, but we're in a hurry.

PETE: What's the rush?

HENRY: We have to get these papers filed before noon.

PETE: They're important?

JENNY: They sure are!

HENRY: You know the old Starker place?

PETE: The mansion on the lake? Everybody knows it.

JENNY *(excitedly)***:** Soon, it will be OURS!

PETE: Congratulations. I didn't even know it was for sale!

HENRY: It isn't. But I'm holding the mortgage. And old lady Starker is six months behind in her payments! Once we get these papers filed, it's all ours.

PETE *(questioning the morality)***:** Is that RIGHT?

JENNY: It sure is!

HENRY: As soon as I get these papers filed.

PETE: No, I mean, is that the right thing to do? Shouldn't you be trying to HELP her instead of kicking her out of her home?

JENNY *(amazed)***:** HELP her? She doesn't pay; she doesn't stay!

HENRY: You sound like some kind of bleeding heart. This is business. But if I don't get these papers filed, she could stop us from taking possession.

JENNY: Do you know what we heard?

PETE: What?

HENRY: Her church took up a special collection and gave it to her yesterday. If she gets to me with the money before noon and these papers aren't filed, she keeps the house.

PETE: Then the problem's solved! You get your money; she keeps her house.

HENRY: Are you CRAZY? I don't want the money. The only reason I bought the mortgage was so I could foreclose and get the house for a fraction of its value!

JENNY: *(Looks off.)* It will be all OURS.

HENRY: Look, Pete. Was there something you wanted to ask us? Make it snappy! We're busy, busy, busy.

PETE *(crossing names off list)***:** No. It wasn't important.

(PETE exits, Stage Right. HENRY and JENNY exit, Stage Left. STAGEHANDS break down Scene Two and set up Scene Three.)

SCENE THREE: BETTY AND MICHAEL'S HOUSE

(BETTY and MICHAEL are at table, reading newspapers. Knock is heard.)

BETTY: Come in!

(PETE enters, Stage Right.)

PETE: Hi, Betty. Michael. Hope I didn't catch you at a bad time.

MICHAEL: Nope. Just checking out the specials. Would you like some coffee?

PETE: No, thanks. The reason I'm here...

BETTY: *(To MICHAEL.)* *(Name of local grocery store)* has a GREAT special on coffee! *(Circles ad.)* We'll have to get a few pounds. Stock up while the price is right.

MICHAEL: Good idea. I'm sorry, Pete. What were you saying?

PETE: The church needs greeters—people to welcome others as they come in. I was hoping...

BETTY: We'd LOVE to! That's just the thing our church needs. Friendliness. Of course, we won't be available until the new year.

PETE: Are you taking an extended holiday?

MICHAEL: Of course not. We couldn't afford that. But look at all these SALES!

BETTY: They'll be going on from now until the New Year.

PETE: Sales?

BETTY: Look! *(Points out ad to PETE.)* *(Name of local mall)* is having its pre-Halloween Christmas spectacular! We CAN'T miss that one!

MICHAEL *(looking at another ad)***:** Hey! Look at these hardware specials.

PETE: How can SALES interfere with church? Couldn't you shop on another day?

BETTY: Don't be silly. Every day they bring out new merchandise. And if you don't show up right when the doors open, someone else will get the really good stuff.

PETE: But...

MICHAEL *(looking at another ad)***:** *(Name of local tire store)* has a special on tires. We'll have to get down there right away!

PETE: But...

BETTY: *(Holds up various ads as she speaks.)* And next week, *(name of local mall)* is having a special event. Then, *(name of store or mall)*. And *(name of local store)* and *(name of local store)* and *(name of local store)*. I could just go on and on!

PETE: I'm sure you could. But when will you worship God?

BETTY: If we didn't take advantage of these specials, we would be wasting money. We're worshiping God by being good stewards of the little He's ENTRUSTED to us!

MICHAEL: It was nice talking to you, but we have to go. *(Name of local store)* is having a door-crasher special. We can just make it if we leave now. *(BETTY and MICHAEL hurry to exit, Stage Right.)*

(PETE crosses more names off list, then slowly exits, Stage Right. STAGEHANDS take down Scene Three and set up Scene Four.)

SCENE FOUR: ON THE STREET

(PETE enters, Stage Right, consulting list. JOE and PAT enter, Stage Left. Pat carries a clipboard and pen.)

JOE: Pete! Just the guy we're looking for!

PAT: Sign here! *(Holds out pen and clipboard to PETE.)*

PETE: What's this?

JOE: It's a petition. We need your support.

PAT: *(Taps clipboard with pen.)* Sign here and print your name here.

PETE: What's it for?

JOE: Just what it says. "We, the undersigned, hereby demand that services on Super Bowl Sunday begin at 10:00 A.M. sharp and continue for no longer than forty-five minutes."

PAT: *(Taps clipboard with pen.)* Sign here and print your name here.

PETE: What?

JOE: Oh, I know what you're thinking. The Super Bowl doesn't happen until January, so why start now? Well, we need all the time we can get. The pastor is so UNREASONABLE about these things!

PAT: *(Taps clipboard with pen.)* Sign here and print your name here.

PETE: No. I'm wondering why...

JOE: But I figure we can negotiate if we have enough signatures. You want us to help out, Pete? No problem. But we have a few concerns of our own.

PAT: *(Taps clipboard with pen.)* Sign here and print your name here.

PETE: No. I'm wondering why it's so important to have a short service.

JOE: Look! We're just as religious as anyone. We want to get to church, but we're tired of missing the opening kickoff!

PAT: *(Taps clipboard with pen.)* Sign here and print your name here.

JOE: Besides, we're having the party at our house this year. What would our friends think if we weren't at our own PARTY on time?

PETE: I don't know. I never thought about it.

JOE: Well, you SHOULD think about these things. Goodwill toward men and all that.

PAT: *(Taps clipboard with pen.)* So, sign here and print your name here.

PETE: I can't sign this.

JOE *(offended)*: OK. But don't come around looking for favors from US.

(JOE and PAT exit, Stage Right. PETE crosses names off list and exits, Stage Left.)

NARRATOR: And so the day ends in our fictitious community. Being good Christian people, they all say their prayers before retiring for the night...

(Voices from offstage.)

MARY: Thank You, Lord, for the beauty of nature...

WILLIAM: Yes. Thank You, God.

HENRY: Thank You, Lord, for Your generous bounty...

JENNY: Yes. Thank You, God.

BETTY: Thank You, Lord, for all the good things in our great land...

MICHAEL: Yes. Thank You, God.

JOE: Thank You, Lord, for good friends...

PAT: Yes. Thank You, God.

ALL: Let me ALWAYS be Your SERVANT, amen!

Thank Heavens!

(APPROXIMATE TIME: 15 MINUTES)

SYNOPSIS

Shirley Holmes and Dr. Whatnot locate missing gratitude—even that of the great detective herself—in time for Thanksgiving.

STAGE SETTING: SHIRLEY HOLMES'S APARTMENT

■ Coffee table, two overstuffed chairs facing each other on a rug, Center Stage

■ Bookcases untidily heaped with books, papers and folders, Stage Right

■ Dining table decorated with a Thanksgiving centerpiece, Stage Left

THE PLAYERS

LOAFER (one of the Baker Street Dozen) (Grade 3 or older)

SWEETIE PIE (one of the Baker Street Dozen) (Grade 3 or older)

MRS. HUDSON RIVER (Grade 5 or older)

INSPECTOR LEE STRIDE (Grade 3 or older)

MS. SHIRLEY HOLMES (Grade 5 or older)

DR. WHATNOT (Grade 5 or older)

MRS. BEA FUDDLED (Grade 5 or older)

STAGEHANDS (All ages)

NONSPEAKING MEMBERS OF THE BAKER STREET DOZEN (All ages)

NONSPEAKING CRIMINALS, POLICEMEN (All ages)

NARRATOR (Grade 5 or older)

SUGGESTED PROPS

■ Bell to ring offstage for doorbell

■ Mustache, suit with price tag attached to sleeve, and hat for Dr. Whatnot

■ Pamphlet labeled "GOVERNMENT GRANT FINDER" in breast pocket of Dr. Whatnot's suit

■ Small notebook and pen for Dr. Whatnot

■ Baseball caps, ragged clothes for Baker Street Dozen

■ Teapot, teacups and tray

■ Pennies (at least 14)

■ Police uniforms (optional—hats only)

■ Trench coat for Inspector Lee Stride

■ Handcuffs

- Large cross necklace, large Bible, handkerchief, pamphlet marked "TRAIN SCHEDULE," large ring, expensive-looking clothing for Mrs. Bea Fuddled
- Fancy apron, gray wig and long dress for Mrs. Hudson River
- Plates, cups, etc. for setting supper table

DIRECTOR'S TIPS

1. Ms. Shirley Holmes acts bored and superior but lightens up after Mrs. Bea Fuddled's visit.

2. Dr. Whatnot is very excitable; he jumps out of his chair often and uses his hands a great deal when he talks.

3. Mrs. Hudson River is constantly trying to tidy up around her lodger.

4. Everyone should appear to be amazed by Holmes's brilliant deductions.

5. Narrator's part can be read. Consider using an adult for this role. Narrator should be positioned to see stage action.

6. The Baker Street Dozen consists of Loafer, Sweetie Pie and eleven other children—a baker's dozen. They are direct but not disrespectful. They are warm and loving toward Mrs. Hudson River.

THANK HEAVENS!

(HOLMES is seated on chair to the left of the coffee table. The table is littered with numerous empty teacups, newspapers, etc. The stage area near the bookcase is also littered with papers, books and folders scattered around on the floor. HOLMES is slouched in the chair, her hands pressed fingertip to fingertip in front of her mouth. She is obviously deep in thought.)

NARRATOR: It was late in November, as I recall. My friend Ms. Shirley Holmes had invited me to join her for dinner. Ms. Holmes is the great-great-great-granddaughter of the noted detective, Mr. Sherlock Holmes. She had followed in the illustrious footsteps of her celebrated ancestor to become the most brilliant private detective in the world. Her work in untangling the knotted yarns of lies and deception while cutting through numerous tissues of deceit made headlines throughout the world.

(HOLMES takes a deep breath and expels it in a noisy sigh.)

I had lost touch with my friend, somewhat. Her recent cases had been of great international importance and held in the strictest confidence. Hence, I had not been able to report them to the public as I had most of her past triumphs. However, I was by no means idle. My newest study in veterinary psychiatry was keeping me fully occupied. I had received a large grant to consider cud-chewing behavior in cattle. My goal was to find out what deep-rooted neuroses could account for this obsession with chewing. Unfortunately, my ruminations on ruminants had bogged down. So I was very thankful to receive an invitation from my friend asking me to call on her at Baker Street.

(Bell rings offstage, Stage Left. The following exchange happens offstage.)

MRS. HUDSON RIVER: Dr. Whatnot! How good to see you again!

DR. WHATNOT: It's good to see you, too, Mrs. Hudson River. Is Holmes in?

MRS. HUDSON RIVER: *(Speaks as she enters.)* Of course she is. She's been moping about all week long. Don't know WHAT'S wrong with her.

(HUDSON RIVER and WHATNOT enter, Stage Left.)

MRS. HUDSON RIVER: Ms. Holmes! Look who's... *(Stops speaking as she sees the mess. Clucks her tongue and starts to pick up papers from floor as she speaks.)* Really, Ms. Holmes! Such a mess! You'll make your guest feel unwelcome—and on such a special day, too!

(WHATNOT continues to the front of the stage and approaches HOLMES. HOLMES ignores HUDSON RIVER, rises to shake hands with WHATNOT.)

DR. WHATNOT: Holmes! How good to see you again! *(Shakes HOLMES's hand.)*

(HOLMES motions WHATNOT to the other chair. They both sit. WHATNOT looks around.) So, my dear young friend. How are you? By the look of the place, it seems that you've been experimenting with explosives again!

MS. SHIRLEY HOLMES: Nonsense. It just has that lived-in look. *(Sighs.)* And frankly, I'm too bored to pick up.

DR. WHATNOT *(scolding)*: You really should be more considerate. Poor Mrs. Hudson River has plenty to do without cleaning up after you!

MRS. HUDSON RIVER: *(Comes forward, wiping her hands on her apron.)* Think nothing of it, Doctor. I'm just thankful I have my health so I can keep up with it all. *(Looks at table and shakes her head. Exits, Stage Left.)*

MS. SHIRLEY HOLMES: Well, Whatnot, enough about CLEANING. Tell me about your latest escapades, and I'll tell you about mine. Except for the fact that you recently received another research grant and have bought a new suit, I can deduce nothing.

DR. WHATNOT *(amazed)*: How do you do it, Holmes? It's as if you've been spying on me all the time!

MS. SHIRLEY HOLMES *(grandly)*: Your suit does not have the sheen of one that has been worn a great deal. And your eyes have that puffiness about them that only comes when they have been used for hours of reading. You see, my dear Whatnot, like most people you see but you do not OBSERVE what is right in FRONT of you. To be a great detective, one must observe with the mind, not just see with the eyes.

DR. WHATNOT: *(Takes out notebook to copy her words.)* Excellent! Let me get that down. I'm so very thankful for the chance to write about you again, Holmes. What an INTELLECT!

(HUDSON RIVER enters, Stage Left, carrying tea tray.)

MRS. HUDSON RIVER: *(Speaks as she shoves papers aside to set down tray.)* Well, I OBSERVE that there is one detective who needs to CLEAN what's right in front of her! I hope you recover from this mood you're in, Miss. So terrible not to be happy and grateful on such a day as this. *(To WHATNOT.)* Perhaps you can help her, Doctor. I'll be getting the dinner ready if you need me. *(Starts to exit, Stage Left.)* I'm just thankful I have my health and a little set aside to see me through my old age.

MS. SHIRLEY HOLMES: If only we all felt that way.

DR. WHATNOT: I'm sure everyone who has his or her health and a little set aside feels that way. Gratitude is certainly an important quality to possess. Now, what is this about the great detective in a bad mood? Moping?

MS. SHIRLEY HOLMES: It's just that for a person of my INTELLECT, ordinary life is BORING. There is NOTHING to do unless some ARCH FIEND commits a crime worthy of my great ability! *(Sighs.)* Without a puzzle to unravel from the world of crime, there's just NOTHING to do. And frankly, Whatnot, they don't make criminals like they used to! They've become a rather dull lot. I'm hoping one of the Baker Street Dozen can turn up a crime for me.

(HUDSON RIVER enters, Stage Left, speaking as she enters. She is followed by SWEETIE PIE. They approach HOLMES.)

MRS. HUDSON RIVER: Here's one of your little friends from the Baker Street Dozen, Ms. Holmes.

(HOLMES dismisses HUDSON RIVER with a wave of her hand. WHATNOT is quick to soothe HUDSON RIVER.)

DR. WHATNOT *(loudly and distinctly)***:** Thank you, Mrs. Hudson River.

MRS. HUDSON RIVER: *(Curtseys.)* You're very welcome, I'm sure, Doctor. *(HUDSON RIVER exits, Stage Left.)* I'm just thankful I have my health, a little set aside to see me through my old age and and that the house is paid off and needs no major repairs.

MS. SHIRLEY HOLMES: *(To SWEETIE PIE.)* Hello, Sweetie Pie. Tell me, have you heard ANYTHING on the streets about new crimes? Has every criminal taken a VACATION? I am SO bored!

SWEETIE PIE: I haven't heard about any crimes, Ms. Holmes. Maybe it's the time of year. Maybe even criminals might think about what they're thankful for—it changes people, gratitude does. Not even a turkey's been stolen, from what I hear.

MS. SHIRLEY HOLMES: *(Rises and paces up and down.)* Gratitude? Sweetie Pie, what do YOU know about gratitude? You haven't even got a home!

SWEETIE PIE: But I have my friends—the other kids in the Baker Street Dozen. And I get pennies from you. And Mrs. Hudson River—well, she's good to all of us.

MS. SHIRLEY HOLMES *(surprised)***:** What do you mean? *(Stops pacing.)*

SWEETIE PIE: *(Looks down, embarrassed.)* Well, she doesn't like us to talk about it, but she lets us stay in the kitchen when it's cold. And she feeds us, too.

MS. SHIRLEY HOLMES: *(Sighs.)* That's all well and good. But it doesn't make ME feel any better! Sweetie Pie, call the gang together and see if you can find me SOME kind of crime to solve! *(Gives SWEETIE PIE a penny.)*

SWEETIE PIE: Oh, thank you, Ms. Holmes! *(Runs off, Stage Left.)*

MRS. HUDSON RIVER: *(Enters, Stage Left.)* A bunch of policemen and other gentlemen to see you, Ms. Holmes.

(INSPECTOR LEE STRIDE, POLICEMEN and CRIMINALS enter, Stage Left. CRIMINALS are handcuffed to POLICEMEN. HUDSON RIVER exits, Stage Left.)

INSPECTOR LEE STRIDE: We're on our way down to the Yard. We've caught these three, thanks to you, Ms. Holmes. Totally solved the great mineral deposit robbery from the museum. We just stopped to express our genuine thanks in person.

MS. SHIRLEY HOLMES: *(Surveys the group.)* Oh, Lee Stride, you've done it again.

INSPECTOR LEE STRIDE *(flattered)***:** Well, THANK you, Miss Holmes.

MS. SHIRLEY HOLMES: *(Slaps forehead.)* No, no, no! I gave you THREE descriptions for ONE criminal. Instead, you've caught three separate people! You'll have to release those two. They've done nothing.

INSPECTOR LEE STRIDE: Nothing? Are you SURE? They ALL had rocks in their pockets.

MS. SHIRLEY HOLMES: Thank heaven not all have rocks in their heads. The only mineral thief is... *(Points.)* ...that one.

DR. WHATNOT: Wait a minute. I recognize him. He's the geologist who was cataloging the mineral collection!

MS. SHIRLEY HOLMES: The PHONY geologist.

DR. WHATNOT: Phony? He certainly fooled me. I read his series of articles on sedimentary rock formations in the *Times*. I thought his article on granite was particularly good.

MS. SHIRLEY HOLMES: And that's what tipped his hand. *(Slowly and distinctly.)* Granite is not SEDIMENTARY, my dear Whatnot.

INSPECTOR LEE STRIDE: *(To POLICEMEN.)* Release those two.

(POLICEMEN release innocent CRIMINALS, who drop to their knees in front of HOLMES saying, "Thank you! Thank you!")

MS. SHIRLEY HOLMES: *(Looks down at CRIMINALS.)* Grateful criminals! Just like Sweetie Pie said. Listen, you two. If you're so grateful, do me a favor. Get out there and concoct a crime that I can sink my teeth into!

(CRIMINALS look surprised, then smile broadly, nodding. They exit, Stage Right, arms around each other, plotting.)

INSPECTOR LEE STRIDE: Well, we've got to get this one down to the Yard. Thank you again, Ms. Holmes!

(LEE STRIDE, POLICEMEN and guilty CRIMINAL exit, Stage Left.)

DR. WHATNOT: Well, thank heavens that you're here to stop innocent people from being locked up.

(HOLMES dismisses her accomplishment as nothing with a wave of her hand. HUDSON RIVER enters, Stage Left, speaking as she enters.)

MRS. HUDSON RIVER: A lady to see you, Ms. Holmes.

(WHATNOT, ever the gentleman, rises as BEA FUDDLED enters, Stage Left. She is sobbing and dabbing at her eyes with a handkerchief. In the same hand with which she holds the handkerchief, she carries a pamphlet clearly marked "TRAIN SCHEDULE." She wears a large cross around her neck and carries a large Bible in her other hand. On the ring finger of her left hand, she wears a large ring. As she crosses to WHATNOT and HOLMES, she almost faints. WHATNOT rushes to her aid and escorts her to chair. She is seated and places Bible in her lap. WHATNOT picks up his teacup and moves to stand behind HOLMES.)

MS. SHIRLEY HOLMES: *(Very matter-of-factly to BEA FUDDLED.)* Tell me what you want.

DR. WHATNOT *(shocked at HOLMES's manner)***:** Holmes! How can you be so callous? Can't you see how upset the lady is? *(To HUDSON RIVER.)* Some tea for the lady, if you please, Mrs. Hudson River.

MRS. HUDSON RIVER: Of course, Dr. Whatnot.

DR. WHATNOT: Thank you, Mrs. Hudson River.

(HUDSON RIVER exits, Stage Left.)

MS. SHIRLEY HOLMES: Now then, what seems to be troubling you? Other than the fact that you arrived by train and are married to a man of substance, I know next to nothing about you.

(WHATNOT looks at HOLMES in amazement that she could deduce these facts.)

DR. WHATNOT: How on earth can you...?

MS. SHIRLEY HOLMES: Remember what I said, Whatnot. Learn to observe. Not just see.

MRS. BEA FUDDLED: I'm Bea Fuddled.

DR. WHATNOT: Think nothing of it. Holmes's powers of deduction mystify many.

MRS. BEA FUDDLED: No. That's my name. Beatrice Fuddled. But my friends call me Bea.

DR. WHATNOT (understanding)**:** Ahh.

(BEA FUDDLED begins to cry again, dabbing at her eyes with handkerchief. HUDSON RIVER enters, Stage Left, carrying another teacup. She speaks as she enters and approaches the table.)

MRS. HUDSON RIVER: (To herself.) I don't ask much. Just a little thanks. But that's all right. I'm just thankful that I have my health, a little set aside to see me through my old age, that the house is paid off and needs no major repairs and that I only have ONE boarder like Ms. Holmes. (Pours tea and gives cup to BEA FUDDLED. Exits, Stage Left, still muttering to herself as she exits.)

MS. SHIRLEY HOLMES: (To BEA FUDDLED.) Now then, what seems to be your trouble?

MRS. BEA FUDDLED: Oh, Ms. Holmes. Something of great worth has been stolen!

(BEA FUDDLED places teacup on table and begins crying again. She dabs at her eyes with handkerchief. WHATNOT moves closer to hear, placing his cup on table.)

MS. SHIRLEY HOLMES: Now then, what is missing?

MRS. BEA FUDDLED: My sense of gratitude. (Bursts into a loud cry.)

MS. SHIRLEY HOLMES: (To BEA FUDDLED.) Tell me, when did you notice it was missing?

MRS. BEA FUDDLED: I'm not sure. I know I had it last winter, but now I can't find it ANYWHERE.

MS. SHIRLEY HOLMES: I have good news for you. I don't think it was stolen.

MRS. BEA FUDDLED: It wasn't? Then where is it?

MS. SHIRLEY HOLMES: You've simply misplaced it. You've stopped using it and now you can't find it.

MRS. BEA FUDDLED: I don't understand.

MS. SHIRLEY HOLMES: Simply think of the things you have to be grateful for. You are a married lady. Were you married recently?

MRS. BEA FUDDLED: Yes. September of the year of the baseball strike and hockey lockout.

MS. SHIRLEY HOLMES: And is your husband a sports fan?

MRS. BEA FUDDLED: Yes. He particularly enjoys hockey and baseball.

MS. SHIRLEY HOLMES: And before he married you, did he often ignore you because he watched so much sports on TV?

MRS. BEA FUDDLED *(sobbing)***:** Yes.

MS. SHIRLEY HOLMES: But what about after he married you?

MRS. BEA FUDDLED: Why, he's watched very little since our wedding!

MS. SHIRLEY HOLMES: There you have it. After you married him, you replaced his affection for sports. That's something to be grateful for.

MRS. BEA FUDDLED *(beginning to see the light)***:** You're right.

MS. SHIRLEY HOLMES: Now, think again. Sometimes when you come home after a hard day, you really don't want to cook supper, do you?

MRS. BEA FUDDLED *(not understanding)***:** No.

MS. SHIRLEY HOLMES: But you can always go to the freezer and take out a frozen dinner in one of those four-sided packages, can't you?

MRS. BEA FUDDLED *(beginning to understand)***:** Yes! Yes, I can!

MS. SHIRLEY HOLMES: Well, there you have it. With hardly any effort, you can have three SQUARE meals a day.

MRS. BEA FUDDLED *(very excited)***:** Yes! Yes! You're right!

MS. SHIRLEY HOLMES: But what surprises me most is that you, a Christian...

DR. WHATNOT *(interrupting)***:** Oh really, Holmes! This is too much. Nothing this lady has said could possibly have given you the slightest clue to her beliefs. And yet you calmly announce that she is a CHRISTIAN?

MS. SHIRLEY HOLMES: Observe, Whatnot. Not see.

MRS. BEA FUDDLED: I'm as baffled as you, Doctor. But she's right. I AM a Christian.

MS. SHIRLEY HOLMES: *(Rises and paces.)* You, of all people, have MUCH to be grateful for.

MRS. BEA FUDDLED: I have?

MS. SHIRLEY HOLMES: Certainly. You know the truth about God. You know His love. You know the great sacrifice He made for your salvation. *(Turns away from BEA FUDDLED and WHATNOT.)* So MUCH to be grateful for! *(Stops pacing.)* Hmm. Much, indeed!

MRS. BEA FUDDLED: *(Jumps up.)* I have! I truly have! *(Grabs HOLMES's hand.)* Thank you for showing me, Ms. Holmes!

MS. SHIRLEY HOLMES: *(Snaps out of her reverie as BEA FUDDLED grabs her hand.)* Oh! Yes! You see, Mrs. Fuddled, you have FOUND your sense of gratitude. It was only underused—and misplaced. *(Looks sheepishly at WHATNOT.)* It can happen to anyone.

DR. WHATNOT: *(To HOLMES.)* Well, as long as you've found it again, that's what matters!

MRS. BEA FUDDLED: *(To WHATNOT, thinking he is speaking to her.)* You're right, Dr. Whatnot, I HAVE found it. And just in time, too! Thank you, Ms. Holmes! Thank you, thank you, thank you.

(HOLMES dismisses her effort as nothing special with a wave of her hand. BEA FUDDLED turns and shakes hands with WHATNOT.)